Brian Mears became director of Chelsea FC in 1958 and was appointed chairman in 1969. During his time in charge, the club went from strength to strength, winning the FA Cup in 1970 and the European Cup-Winners' Cup in 1971. He also oversaw the building of the new East Stand, which is the focal point of the Chelsea stadium.

Ian Macleay has supported Chelsea since, as a boy, he saw Jimmy Greaves play for the team. Together with Brian Mears, he was the co-author of the acclaimed *Chelsea: Football Under the Blue Flag*. He lives in south London and is working on a novel.

A HITCH-HIKER'S GUIDE TO THE GALAXY OF CHELSEA

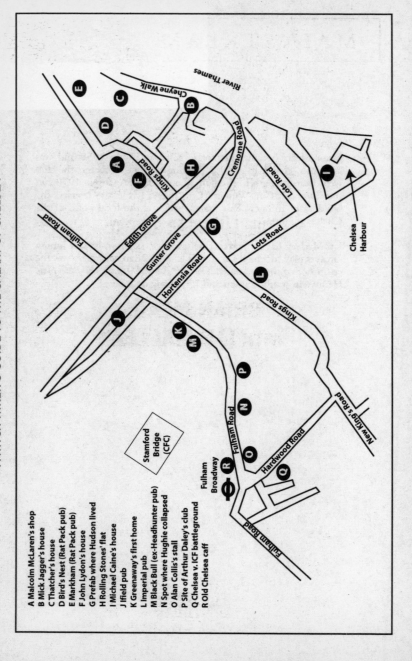

A Malcolm McLaren's shop
B Mick Jagger's house
C Thatcher's house
D Bird's Nest (Rat Pack pub)
E Markham (Rat Pack pub)
F John Lydon's house
G Prefab where Hudson lived
H Rolling Stones' flat
I Michael Caine's house
J Ifield pub
K Greenaway's first home
L Imperial pub
M Black Bull (ex-Headhunter pub)
N Spot where Hughie collapsed
O Alan Collis's stall
P Site of Arthur Daley's club
Q Chelsea v. ICF battleground
R Old Chelsea caff

MAINSTREAM / SPORT

CHELSEA

THE 100-YEAR HISTORY

BRIAN MEARS
WITH IAN MACLEAY

MAINSTREAM
PUBLISHING
EDINBURGH AND LONDON

To the memory of the late June Mears
– the First Lady of Chelsea

This edition, 2005

First published in Great Britain in 2004 by
MAINSTREAM PUBLISHING COMPANY (EDINBURGH) LTD
7 Albany Street
Edinburgh EH1 3UG

ISBN 1 84596 024 6

A catalogue record for this book is available from the British Library

Typeset in Garamond and Meta Book
Printed and bound in Great Britain by
Cox & Wyman Ltd

ACKNOWLEDGEMENTS

This book would not have been possible without the assistance and influence of the following:

Terry Venables, the stuff of legends.

Pat Nevin, who gave me encouragement right from the 'Cockney Rebel' days.

Matthew Harding, whose name will be sung as long as Chelsea fans converge.

Special thanks to Mainstream – Bill Campbell, who kept the faith; brilliant editing by Deborah Warner, Graeme Blaikie and Paul Murphy; a sumptuous cover design by Emily Bland.

My twin brother Ken Macleay, who helped in so many ways. The first game we saw together at the Bridge was in 1961 and I am pleased to say we are still attending matches together.

Thank you to my lawyer, top Chelsea boy and friend Peter Harris, for his expert advice and loyalty. Also for the specialist libel advice given by Burkey.

To true blue Steven J. Hill of Hodders, who made it possible for me to see so many games.

Specialist Chelsea knowledge and input by the Layden brothers Mark and Paul.

John Ingledew, the best photographer in the land; Frank Pierce, who helped with the collation of photographs; and Step Back in Time in Brighton for allowing us to reproduce some pictures.

Thanks to my wife, Marie, for the assistance on the map.

I could fill up the Shed with Chelsea acquaintances who have helped over the years but my thanks especially to David Ayling, the bravest Chelsea fan I ever stood with, who helped with the creation of the book; Mick Crossan, who kept a light burning in even the darkest hours; actor Kevin O'Donahoe with the '80s and '90s data, and Nicky Zblicky and Ronnie Reyes for earlier memories and insights; and Patrick Hagglund, whose Internet research proved invaluable.

Sadly, Mick Greenaway, who helped conceive the project, passed away before he could see the glory days return but I like to think he is still zigger zaggering someplace.

Also, in memory of the late Sheila Conteh.

Lastly, thanks to my family.

Ian Macleay

If there are any better football writers around, I have yet to meet them. Ian's tireless research into the history of our great club is peerless. No author could have asked for more.

Brian Mears

CONTENTS

PART: TWO DALLAS

THE APPRENTICE

I was commentating on the UEFA Champions League semi-final between Liverpool and Chelsea in May 2005. My mind drifted back to when I captained Chelsea against Liverpool at Anfield in January 1966; the time of Bill Shankly's young lions. Chelsea won a famous victory: perhaps the greatest in the short, but brilliant, career of the 'Diamonds' side. In comparison, José Mourinho has taken Chelsea to new heights with his fantastic Double of Premiership and Carling Cup victories in the 2004–05 season.

What made it even more historic was the fact that it was achieved in Chelsea's centenary season. Brian Mears' family were there from the start, and I am pleased to be celebrating these marvellous events with him.

In the foreword to the original hardback version of this book – released in the spring of 2004 – I wrote that, following Roman Abramovich's blindingly ambitious purchase of the club, it was inevitable that Chelsea would succeed. The speed at which this has happened has staggered the world.

José's side reminds me a lot of the Diamonds: young, superbly fit, full of running and tactically astute. The world has spun a few times, since I joined the club in the late '50s as a young apprentice. Brian's father was chairman, and the future looked almost as bright as it does today. For a variety of reasons, chronicled in this book, we have had to wait until the 21st century for the full potential of this massive club to be realised.

I feel this is just the start of a new dawn for Chelsea.

Terry Venables
Summer 2005

THE GAMBLER

The managers change, the owners change, but Chelsea never
does.

Claudio Ranieri, April 2004

Roman Abramovich, the youngest richest man in the world, bought
Chelsea in the summer of 2003. Whether he saw it as an investment or as
a hobby depends on your point of view. In a few months, it became a
corporate monster with plans to go global. Abramovich was hailed by
Chelsea fans as the best thing to come out of Russia since Anna
Kournikova.

Abramovich was a gambler. He gambled with huge stakes and scooped
a prize of unimaginable wealth. Then he gambled again, buying a team he
had never seen and investing in a culture he knew nothing about.

It is an old football cliché that one man does not make a team. This
book sets out to disprove that theory because some of the players that
inhabit its pages made Chelsea Football Club, from the aggression of
Hughie Gallacher and the goals scored by Jimmy Greaves to the fluency
of Gianfranco Zola. What is certain, though, is that one man can make a
club. My grandfather did and a century on, another man is remaking it.

Roman Abramovich's story reads like the definitive edition of 'Lifestyles
of the Rich and Famous'. He was rich and Chelsea were famous. (Ever
heard the song 'We are the FAMOUS CFC'?) Chelsea made Abramovich
famous. Abramovich made Chelsea rich.

All great stories are love stories. We all love Chelsea, that's what it's all
about. The same thing happened to the billionaire when he bought it. It

was to change his life irrevocably because he became a fan and fell in love with the drama of it all. You can be chairman of the biggest corporation in the world but you don't get 40,000 people chanting your name in the boardroom.

Of all the hundreds of pictures taken of the young Russian, the one that hit home most was snapped on a warm autumn evening in Rome. It was the night before Chelsea beat Lazio 0–4 on their march to Euro glory under the Blue flag. A young man in designer denims sat and watched Chelsea footballers train in readiness for their big match. A palette of different skin colours, the cream of the world's finest talent that had cost almost £150m worth of his roubles to assemble.

The young man was transfixed, watching the skill and technique of his stellar squad. Chelsea had been chasing the brass ring for a century, now the alchemy of Abramovich was turning it into a Cartier. His knuckles were whitening as he squeezed so hard. The Moscow State Circus had hit town and the Chelsea lion was roaring. Defiance.

The young man was by then a believer, falling in love with his team. It is the worst kind of love. Obsessive, possessive, claustrophobic. A Conservative prime minister once described it as a condition for which there is no known cure. Abramovich suffers from it, too. But why a team that were giants just once, as recently as 1955? Chelsea, who resemble a soufflé – fast rising, attractive to look at but just as quick to collapse. How did all this come about? Karl Marx lived in London but he didn't follow the Blues. How did a man who could simply buy anything in the world fixate on a team that were about to financially implode? What is it about a particular west London football club that demands such loyalty, emotion and all-consuming passion? Sometimes watching them is the most joyful experience in the world, other times it is like taking a bath in a tub of cold baked beans. The club is Chelsea and the Mears family invented it.

Allow me to explain . . .

PART ONE

DYNASTY

Truth is stranger than fiction, but it is because fiction is obliged to stick to possibilities; truth is not.

Mark Twain (an ex-resident of Chelsea)

ONE

ABSOLUTE BEGINNERS

This is Chelsea Football Club. Everyone is under pressure.
Eidur Gudjohnsen, Chelsea striker

As far back as I could remember, I wanted to be a Chelsea fan. Going to the ground with my family. Stamford Bridge, the theatre of dreams, a theme park for the richest young man in the world. Where Becks met Posh, where Zola sprayed his goal dust. Home to some of the biggest names that ever kicked a ball: Jimmy Greaves, Ruud Gullit, Peter Osgood, Glenn Hoddle and Terry Venables. If they don't mean much to you, try Verón and Drogba, Lampard and Cole. My family built it. Elitism is an ugly thing but it is an ugly world and I am going to pull rank and show you the pips on my sleeve. Chelsea are the greatest football club in the world. With the resources now at their disposal, they will become the mightiest.

It was the great German poet Heine who said that London defies the imagination and breaks the heart. For London, read Chelsea.

Why the name Chelsea? Where did it come from? Nobody quite knows how Chelsea obtained its moniker. Historians think it derived from the Anglo-Saxon word *chelsel-ea* meaning gravel bank. Chelsea lies on gravel. During my time at the club, I was to hear a lot of Anglo-Saxon words.

'Why do they play in blue?' is a frequently asked question. It was chosen after the racing colours of the club's president, the Rt Hon. Lord Cadogan. Chelsea originally played in light blue but later switched to royal blue. Today, the next largest London estate after the Duke of Westminster's belongs to the Eighth Earl Cadogan, who can walk from Sloane Square to Harrods on his own land. The Earl is seriously caked and could dine out with Abramovich without worrying about the bill. The estate, worth about £1.28 billion, includes Cheyne Walk and the newly developed Duke of York Square on the Kings Road. All of this land came into the family through marriage in the eighteenth century. Joseph Mears was head of the dynasty. Born in 1842 and married in 1863, Joseph was described as a builder. He had two sons, Theophilus (born 1871) and Henry Augustus (born 1873)

H.A. Mears, aka Gus, my great-grandfather, conceived the idea of giving London its very own super-stadium where prestigious games such as cup finals and internationals could be played. His brother, J.T. Mears, shared the dream. They saw it as a money-making exercise, as they did everything. At the time, in 1896, Mears did not see it as a means of running his own club. Chelsea was still pretty much a village and all the major games in the country were played at Crystal Palace, some 12 miles from London and even less accessible in those days. Hansom cabs were the mode of transport for the rich; trains and trams for the working class. Mears had his eyes on the site – a vast tract of land near Walham Green which had previously been a market garden. It was then the headquarters of the London Athletic Club, who had taken over the land in 1876.

Gus Mears tried to buy the lease but he had to wait till Mr Stunt, the previous owner, died in 1902. He had to wait a further two years because a clause in the lease gave the London Athletic Club tenure of the ground for two further years following the death of Stunt. Right from the start, the ownership of Stamford Bridge was shrouded in stunts of all description: mysteries, complications, litigation and controversy. Always was, always will be.

Eventually, on 29 September 1904, the fabulous Mears boys took possession of Stamford Bridge. They were to retain it in our family for almost 80 years. The whole deal was put together in record time, amazing for the period. At first, Gus was keen to sell the land to Great Western Railways who were anxious to turn the site into a coal-dumping yard. It would have been an instant profit but his money man and adviser, a guy called Fred Parker, told him he had seen the future and its name was football. Parker, no relation to the torn-jeaned midfielder Scott, convinced Gus that he should try to create his own team. Parker was like Matthew Harding – a fan with a business plan.

Gus loved football but asked himself if it had a long-term future. Would people still be interested in it in 100 years' time? (The professional game had been established in 1884 after rebel clubs had mutinied against the Football Association which had ruled that players should only be paid their expenses.)

Still unconvinced, Gus offered Fulham the ground to rent but was rebuffed. Parker then took Mears to Glasgow to meet the architect Archibald Leitch. Leitch was a genius who had already built Ibrox, Celtic Park and Hampden. Mears was captivated by his ideas and vision and immediately set to work building a super-stadium in London. One journalist of the day wrote: 'Chelsea will stagger humanity.' Perhaps they still will.

The ground was built in a bowl shape with one stand to the east; it was as symbolic as the Twin Towers at the time, a continual reminder of the huge gamble the Mears family had taken in creating the club. The dressing-rooms were placed so that the teams always emerged from the stand. Its capacity was 5,000, but the stadium could allegedly hold 95,000. The only time that it was seriously tested was against Moscow Dynamo in 1945.

With the construction of the ground going ahead, Mears applied to join the Southern League but was refused. It seemed an extraordinary decision. In desperation, he turned to the Football League. There were only two clubs south of Birmingham in the League – Bristol City and a team called Woolwich Arsenal.

His next task was to buy a team. Almost a century later, Roman Abramovich faced the same problem. Gus had no agents to advise him but he bought shrewdly. John Tait Robertson was signed as player–manager from Glasgow Rangers. John won 16 caps for Scotland and was an excellent signing. Mears then went on to raid three players from Birmingham, then known as Small Heath, including an unknown called Jimmy Windridge, who went on to play for England. His fee was £190, a tidy sum for those days.

The biggest signing in almost every sense was goalkeeper Willie 'Fatty' Foulke for the sum of £50 from Sheffield United. Willie stood 6ft 3in. and weighed 22 stone. He was an England international and as famous in his day as David Seaman is in the twenty-first century.

Willie was included in the persuasive promotional dossier that was presented to the annual meeting of the Football League, held at the Tavistock Hotel in Covent Garden in May 1905. Chelsea made their claim on the basis of:

- Financial stability – Chelsea had £3,000 in the bank.
- A super-stadium – the Ashburton Grove of its day was under construction.
- A strong team – which was in the process of being put together at that time, with Willie Foulke as its star name. It was said that Chelsea put their new signings in the shop window to dress it up for the Football League. Willie filled it up.

Chelsea were admitted to the Second Division of the Football League; their first match was away to Stockport.

WILLIE VEGAS

Chelsea lost the match 1–0. Willie Foulke captained the London side, which was composed of:

		Foulke			
	McEwen		Mackie		
	Key		McRoberts		Miller
Moran	Tait Robertson	Copeland	Windridge	Kirwan	

Ron Harris's name is not on the sheet and I was not born. The first League home match was a 5–1 victory over Hull. Jimmy Windridge scored a hat-trick – well, the new fans expected as much from a player who had commanded such a high fee.

Willie played 35 matches for Chelsea in total. He didn't move down to London but stayed in his beloved Sheffield and continued to train with United. He kept seventeen clean sheets which included nine in a row. In all, he let in only 37 goals. The most famous incident in which he featured was when he played against Burslem Port Vale in the November of that year. The match was refereed by a J.T. Howcroft of Bolton. Willie had history with him. J.T. had run the line in the 1902 FA Cup final when Sheffield had lost to Spurs after a replay and Willie had been unhappy with the refereeing.

During the Burslem match, with Chelsea trailing 0–1, Burslem's winger Dick Carter, miles offside, ran through on Willie's goal. The giant Chelsea captain picked him up and literally threw him into the back of the net. Howcroft blew for a penalty but Willie protested bitterly and refused to go into goal. Chaos broke out. Eventually, player–manager Tait Robertson ordered him back to his post threatening to have him taken off the field. Willie stood on his goal line, glaring at the world; he made no attempt to save the kick. Chelsea ended up losing 3–2.

After the match, Foulke menaced the ref as the teams walked off the pitch. His teammates calmed him down but, back in the dressing-room, he finally snapped and stormed back to the ref's room. The problem was that Willie hadn't any clothes on at the time. J.T. Howcroft had to barricade himself in the room as the naked keeper tried to remove the door from its hinges. The situation was defused by FA secretary Fred Wall, who a few months previously had rubber-stamped Chelsea's visa into the big time. Wall must have wondered what he had unleashed onto the world when he saw the 'Incredible Bulk'; you wouldn't have liked him when he was angry.

Willie was angry a lot, especially with refs, whom he hated, opposing forwards, whom he tried to bully and even his own teammates, whom he would castigate for any slipshod displays on the pitch. He was a very modern keeper in that he commanded the penalty box and spent the whole game talking to his defence. His tremendous shoulders gave him the power to punch the hogskin ball as far as the halfway line when he came careering off his line to clear a corner. Nobody could hinder his progress at such times.

Foulke became a dandy during his period at Chelsea. He shopped near the town hall by Fulham Broadway and the shop girls made a fuss of the man who wore a staggering 24-inch collar. Willie was constantly buying spare collars because he sweated so much. In winter, he sported a Paisley silk scarf with a gold pin. His fur-collared coats were specially made for him on the nearby Kings Road.

At Sheffield, he was on £5 a week, a fortune for a time when a typical house cost £60. He would have been offered sizeably more to move to Chelsea. Now, where have we heard that one before?

Needless to say, Willie loved his grub. Dr Atkins would have had some problems with him. He was a mere 13 stone when he joined Sheffield but had ballooned up to 22 stone by the time he left to join Chelsea. The reason was his tiny wife, who was a brilliant Nigella Lawson-type in the kitchen and very much the boss at home. She obviously knew that the way to a man's heart was through his stomach. She must have been well loved-up on Willie.

Willie boy just liked the simple food – sausages, pies, potatoes and chips. None of that organic rubbish. His tastes mirrored those of the fans who followed Chelsea to grounds like Gainsborough Trinity, wherever that was, who would bring stone jars of real ale with sandwiches an inch thick in little wicker baskets.

On one occasion when Chelsea played Gainsborough Trinity, Willie tried to link up with his colleagues. One of the manager's main duties in those days was to take care of the team's travel arrangements, making sure they sat in the right seats, etc. Willie was running late and had mislaid his ticket. The ticket collector refused to believe that the 22-stone man was Chelsea's goalkeeper, so an irate Willie picked up the railwayman, put him under his arm and set off to look for Robertson and the rest of the team.

He loved reading; the top-selling books of the time were the great Sherlock Holmes stories by Sir Arthur Conan Doyle. Willie's favourite was *The Hound of the Baskervilles*, which had been published around the time he joined Chelsea. He would read it on the long rail commutes to London. The novel typified London at the turn of the century: hansom cabs, cockneys, gas lamps and fog. When the team fly into Europe on their Championship sojourns today, there's not a book in sight, just DVD players and iPods.

Willie immersed himself in the culture of London; he revelled in the atmosphere and attention, just like José does today. His favourite pub was the Star and Garter in Sloane Square. It was actually part of the Peter Jones drapery store. Jones died in 1905, a few months after the club was formed, but like Stamford Bridge, his establishment lives on. Opposite could be found the Royal Court Theatre, opened in 1888. During Willie's spell at the club, one of George Bernard Shaw's works could usually be found playing.

Chelsea's first assault on the FA Cup ended with a 1–7 home defeat to Palace. It is still on the record books as their biggest FA Cup loss. Foulke did not play. Chelsea had put out a reserve side because of an important League game the same day against Burnley. (I have heard of fixture congestion but that is ridiculous!) As a result of that game, the FA brought in a new rule making it compulsory to play full-strength sides in the Cup. It must have worked because 65 years later Chelsea won their first (and best) FA Cup final.

The absolute beginners finished a very creditable third in 1906 with 53 points. Manchester United were one of the sides that finished above them. We spent the rest of the last century trying to catch them.

The consummately professional Foulke left the Bridge at the end of the season to join Bradford. His job was done – he had raised the profile of Chelsea and consolidated their place in the League.

Legend has it that Willie fell on hard times and ended up on Blackpool beach in a sideshow in one of those Beat the Goalie competitions. I am grateful to a wonderful fellow called John Garett for dispelling this urban myth. John is the curator for the Hall of Fame at Sheffield United and gave me a wonderful insight into the life of the big goalie. He reassured me that Willie died a prosperous man, with a thriving pub and other business interests, in 1916, an early victim of the terrible Spanish flu epidemic which killed more people in 1918 than died in combat during the First World War.

Interest in Willie is still very high. I was invited to the BBC by a young film-maker called Tom Horne, a great Chelsea fan, who was working on restoring footage of Willie Foulke. For around 70 years, 800 rolls of early nitrate-film had been sitting in sealed barrels in the basement of a shop. It had been miraculously rediscovered and lovingly restored. The quality was amazing – Willie in his pomp, wearing tight shorts and a huge fisherman's jumper, fists clenched, operatically chewing. They should make a movie out of it; get Johnny Vegas in the lead role.

Another hero emerged the following season, 1906–07, his name being George Hilsdon. Robertson signed him from West Ham, a penny farthing ride away from the West End of London. Georgie boy was a powerful centre-forward who scored five goals on his debut in a 9–2 thrashing of Glossop – another record-breaking game that has not been beaten. Hilsdon scored 27 goals as Chelsea stormed to promotion by finishing in second place to Nottingham Forest. They were finally amongst the elite. It was a blow to the critics in the press; they had built Chelsea up but were knocking them down while the mortar in the East Stand was still wet.

In 1907, David Calderhead was appointed manager and stayed there for almost three decades, throughout which Chelsea's fortunes continued to yo-yo.

During the 1907–08 season, Chelsea finished in 13th spot in the First Division. Hilsdon scored 24 League goals to help stabilise the club as they fought to establish themselves in the big time. Hilsdon also scored six in the Cup, remarkably all in one game against Worksop. It's interesting that the highest wins in the Cup and League were both recorded in the formative years of Chelsea thanks to Hilsdon's goals.

Chelsea, after crushing Worksop in the first round, went out by a solitary goal to Manchester United in the next. The Reds also won the League that season. George won the first of his England caps as well. By that time, he had acquired the nickname 'Gatling Gun', a reference to his rapid rat-a-tat-tat shooting style. In all, he played 8 games for England and scored a remarkable 14 goals, giving him an average of 1.75, the highest international average for an England player on the stats database.

Hilsdon stayed at Chelsea for six seasons, most of them struggles to stay afloat. In 1909–10, they were relegated and he only managed two goals. The team almost bounced back at the first attempt and ended up in third spot at the end of 1910–11, Hilsdon back on the goal trail, scoring 19 times. The next season, Chelsea made no mistakes, finishing second to Derby. A last-day-of-the-season win over Bradford Park Avenue was enough to take them up and edge away from their close rivals Burnley. This was Hilsdon's last season at Chelsea and he only managed one strike in ten games. His drinking had got worse and, as we were to see so often in the history of Chelsea, it affected the striker's fitness. His wife's health was also in decline and his finances were in a mess.

Chelsea missed relegation in 1912–13 by the thinnest of margins. It is interesting to note that Arsenal were relegated that season. Hilsdon was transferred back to West Ham.

There was no shortage of strikers just before the war – Bob

Whittingham hit 30 goals in Chelsea's promotion season. Another character was a one-eyed cockney centre-forward called Bob Thompson.

THE GREAT WAR

The 1913–14 season was the last during peacetime, Chelsea finishing a respectable eighth. Vivian Woodward had joined the club from Tottenham. He was a highly respected amateur player who was also an architect by trade. He became one of the first players to join up at the beginning of the hostilities. Gentleman Woodward was like a hero from an adventure novel, with his boyish good looks and immaculate blazers.

There was one final season to be played before the League closed down because of the war. Chelsea finished nineteenth, one place and one point ahead of bottom club Tottenham. In a normal season, both teams would have been automatically relegated but they survived thanks to the war. The First Division was enlarged in peacetime and Chelsea were invited back, along with the relegated Arsenal. The north London giants have never been relegated since – unlike the Blues, who have had a few dalliances in the lower reaches.

Some compensation for their wretched League form was Chelsea's first-ever FA Cup final appearance in 1915 against Sheffield United at Old Trafford – of all places – the scene of their greatest-ever FA Cup victory in 1970. Woodward came home from the front to watch the final and Calderhead desperately wanted him to play for Chelsea. Gentleman Woodward refused to disrupt the team, wanting the lads who had taken Chelsea to their first-ever final to share in its glory. One-eyed Bob Thompson had at the time dislocated his arm and was not 100 per cent fit but Woodward insisted he play.

It was a terrible day, dark and dismal. It rained all the time, as though the heavens were crying for the tragedy that was about to hit the young men of Britain when the slaughter of that terrible war got under way. A ghostly yellow mist descended, similar to the mustard gas that was to claim so many lives in the war. (Ironically, Hilsdon was to survive the gassing but his injuries stopped him playing football again.)

Chelsea seemed unnerved by the occasion and lost 0–3. The match was watched by 49,557 supporters, many of them in the khaki uniform of the British army. Most of them were to die on the Somme within a year.

TWO

GALLACHER: HEAR MY TRAIN A'COMING

Hughie Gallacher climbed over the fence and walked down onto the cinder track. Somebody came up to him and seemed to mutter something. Gallacher shimmied around him like he used to swerve past defenders at Stamford Bridge. The train was coming now; he could hear the whistle as it hurtled down the track. The noise was deafening but the Scot was oblivious to it all.

All he could hear that day was the sound of the crowd many years before: 68,386 excited Geordie voices raising the din to a crescendo. It was a lovely, early autumn evening on Tyneside; he could see the shadows lengthen on the pitch. Newcastle were already out on the playing field, warming up in readiness for their Chelsea foes. It felt strange for him to be wearing the crisp, freshly starched royal blue shirt of the London club. He had come so far, now he was back at the scene of one of his greatest triumphs.

At the time, Gallacher was the most expensive player in the history of the game. He bounced the heavy leather ball on the tunnel floor. Soon, he would be out there again.

THE DANDY WARHOL

Perhaps Hughie Gallacher was slightly past his best when he joined Chelsea, although he was only 27. Nothing could eclipse his time at Newcastle: Vialli, Verón, Hoddle, Weah, Gullit and Crespo were long past their prime when they joined Chelsea but Gallacher was still running on 80 per cent, perhaps a little more. He had survived the pressure-cooker of St James' Park and acknowledged that he had more to do to conquer London town. Newcastle did the dirty on him when they sold him to Chelsea. They cited financial pressures, a need to cut the wage bill. Sounds familiar. Nice to know nothing changes.

Hughie was in France on international duty with Scotland when they did the deed. Hughie could not stop scoring for Scotland; it seems strange when you compare that to the sorry state of their low-calorie national side today. It was Scotland's first-ever game on foreign soil and he slammed in two stunning goals to clinch a historic win. The problem was that trouble was always lurking around the corner for the star striker. Some players look for trouble but Hughie never had to seek it. All he had to do was wake up every morning and there it was waiting for him. Gallacher broke a strict team curfew to celebrate his brace of goals. Who could resist Paris on a beautiful spring night with its myriad delights of whoring, drinking and other illicit activities? Certainly not Hughie – numbing hedonism by then almost a full-time occupation for him. His action earned him another in a long list of reprimands from the Scottish FA. No matter how bad he felt about that, it was nothing compared to the news that he was on his way south to London and the Kings Road.

Hughie was the Beckham of his day: always in the news, a fashion leader and the lip-licking idol of thousands. In his prime, he was the best-dressed footballer of them all. The proportion of his income that he spent on clothes was enough to make Beckham look like an account customer of Oxfam. The Scot was always obsessive about his suits and fastidious about his hair. There were no image rights to fight over, though, and he didn't look like the star of an aftershave advert.

His first match for Chelsea was away to the windswept Grimsby Town on 30 August 1930 – a ground where over half a century later another superb goal machine, Kerry Dixon, was to thunder in the goal that clinched the Second Division title for John Neal's ambitious side. Hughie failed to hit the net on his debut as Chelsea scrambled a narrow win with a dubious penalty. It was converted by a fellow Scot and international teammate of Hughie's from the 1928 'Wembley Wizards', full-back Tommy Law. A list of famous Chelsea players who scored on their debut in the first 100 years would fill up the rest of this chapter but some of them are Jimmy Greaves, Peter Osgood, Kerry Dixon, Tommy Langley, Alan Birchenall, Tommy Baldwin, George Graham, Paul Furlong, George Weah, Clive Walker, Jimmy Floyd Hasselbaink, Carlton Cole, Juan Verón, Scott Parker and Adrian Mutu.

HUGHIE GOES TO HOLLYWOOD

By a quirk of fate, Hughie Gallacher's second match for Chelsea sent him back to Newcastle. It was Wednesday, 3 September 1930. It broke all Geordie records – it still does and always will – 68,386, the biggest-ever crowd for a midweek League game in Newcastle. It was estimated that a further 20,000 fans were locked out of the cacophonous frenzy. Thousands more watched slices of the action from nearby treetops and rooftops, even the top of the stand. It was not so much football coming home as Hughie goes to Hollywood. It was a day out for Hughie and the Geordies together. During most of the time Gallacher had spent in Newcastle, the weather had been dark and foreboding.

Chelsea were hit badly by injuries and the expectations on the new striker were bloated, even by twenty-first-century standards. As a player, Gallacher operated on the very margins of the margins but that September day they were infinitesimal. A whole city turned up to see him, thank him and then say goodbye. It was sheer sci-fi, the '30s football equivalent of *The Matrix*. The atmosphere was hypnotic, pulsating; primal screams creating a dizzying state of mind. For that is what football was and, I am pleased to say, still is for the inhabitants of Newcastle. Hughie was the soul of the city. A hero returned. He induced the jovial hysteria of a vein trapped in a tourniquet, the like of which would never be seen again. Hughie Gallacher gave people confidence. He demonstrated what was possible. He was just a little guy but he enriched the lives of the fans. Zola did the same job, a little big man.

People talked years later with pride in their voices when they said they had seen Gallacher play. My father was one of them. It is true today of the generation who speak in awe of the rare gifts of George Best, Jimmy Greaves, Bobby Moore or Charlie Cooke – now he was something. Chelsea had more than their fair share of talent over the century and have recently recruited another batch. Allow me to tell you about them later.

WHITE HEAT

Gallacher had clung to the tail of the ego-twisting, brain-battering beast that was football and still kept his dignity. The public cared about him. At that time, most were living in the crushing poverty of the worst depression this country ever experienced. Hughie was greeted with a reception that was to be the most memorable of his life. It was almost as if he had pulled back from all of the hype that was to eventually swamp him. Now, the shimmering diamond could play for the people who had helped him make it so far. There was a special frisson that existed on that beautiful autumn afternoon. The legions who crammed into St James' Park lamented the fact that their special hero had moved on and that things would never be the same.

Gallacher was amongst friends – in those days, footballers were neither patronising nor economically distant. In later years, Gallacher's alter ego was the fantastic movie tough-guy James Cagney. The cult gangster classic *White Heat* ends with a cornered convict on top of a gas container spouting the famous line, 'Look, Ma, I'm on top of the world.' Seconds later, a massive explosion caused by a sniper's bullet obliterates Cagney. Perhaps on 3 September 1930, Hughie was on top of the world – before it all went up in his face – like the Stone Roses at Spike Island, The Beatles at Shea Stadium, Frank Sinatra at the Sands Hotel, Chelsea Football Club at Old Trafford in April 1970. The show did not matter, it was the event; just being there made you part of it.

Gallacher ran about the field – he knew every blade of grass under his feet. Chelsea's newest superstar tried a little too hard. He kept straying offside in Filippo Inzaghi fashion. He peppered the Newcastle goal with shots from too far a range (how could he possibly score against his beloved?). The home team won the dreary match 1–0 with a neat second-half back header from their winger Jackie Capes. Apart from their new acquisition, the Chelsea side played like bums.

Hughie was soon opening his Chelsea account, though. He made his home debut the following Saturday against a team called Manchester United. Chelsea thrashed them 6–2 and another huge crowd of 48,648 saw him score twice. Fellow Scot Alec Cheyne notched a hat-trick, defender Jack Townrow scored the other one – if Gallacher hadn't got there first you'd be tempted to call Alec Cheyne a genius. Hughie had found time, though, to set up two of the goals with sinuous runs and unselfish passes. The fun was just starting; this was the carnival that he always wanted to run away with. The ego had landed and the Stamford Bridge roller-coaster was revving up under its new driver.

THE TANNA BALL PLAYER

On the first day of the twenty-first century, *The Guardian* (Graeme Le Saux's favourite newspaper – like the man himself, stylish but just a touch too self-satisfied) ran a list of the best football players of the previous 100 years, chosen by its top football writers. Among the selection for the Scotland team was a man called Hughie Gallacher. A player who had committed violent, horrible, grisly suicide under the wheels of a train over 45 years earlier. A player who appeared for Chelsea so long ago it was likely that there were few alive who were lucky enough to have seen him play.

Certainly, when Chelsea beat Liverpool 2–1 at the end of the 2002–03 season to qualify for the Champions League, it was likely that only a handful of the crowd would have even heard of him. His name is revered among a select few. The band Blur, whose singer Damon Albarn is a huge Chelsea fan, included a time-warped cigarette picture card of him on their website.

There is a case to be made for Gallacher as the blueprint for the greatest football star of all time, in the same way Beckham and his wardrobe of woe transcend all levels today. He was the first 'maverick', a breed Chelsea continue to clone and indulge: meet the latest, his name is Adrian Mutu. Perhaps they go hand in hand, swathes of dark talent and bad habits. Chelsea would not have been Chelsea if they did not specialise in players who were outrageously skilful and aggressive, perched on the very brink of greatness but whose careers were undermined by overindulgence, injury and constant clashes with authority.

There is a Scottish artist called Jack Vettriano (if you don't recognise his name, you would be familiar with his work). Jack specialises in film noir-style paintings. If Hughie was still playing, Jack would be doing his posters.

Zola topped an Internet poll in 2003 to find the greatest Chelsea player ever. Osgood trailed in a poor second. Only anorak Chelsea fans would recognise the name Roy Bentley, yet we will acknowledge the huge part he played in winning the first championship for Chelsea in 1955 (get Grandpa to explain that one to you). Gallagher (*sic*), now wasn't he in the pop group of gobshite Mancs? City fans, if I recall.

But it started with Hughie. Everything in the modern game started with Hughie.

THE SMALL FACES

Hughie Kilpatrick Gallacher, a Protestant of Irish extraction, was born on 2 February 1903, two years before Chelsea Football Club was established. His birthplace of Bellshill, just outside Glasgow, was in those times a breeding ground for football talent. George Best's mentor Matt Busby (who played for Chelsea during the Second World War) and former Glasgow Rangers sharpshooter and pundit Ally McCoist were both products of that area. A bus ride in any direction would lead you into Bill Shankly country or towards the birthplace of Celtic legend Jock Stein. It was a tough industrial environment and the antidotes to the Steinbeck-style poverty and back-breaking labour were drink and football. A century later, you could say the same thing applies.

Hughie was kicking back at life from the moment he was born. He spent his youth kicking a little rubber ball around in the back streets. He perfected his control and that's what made him the greatest ball-playing centre-forward that Scotland has ever produced. It really is as simple as that: superior skill with the ball sets players apart. It is why people recall Osgood and not Bill Garner. That is why there are so many foreign players in our game today – their technique is superior. That is why Chelsea lavished fortunes on Drogba and Crespo when they already had competent strikers like Gudjohnsen and Forssell on the books.

As a child, Hughie was only interested in playing football; nothing else bothered him. Every spare second was spent either on the cobbled streets or some waste ground, kicking, heading, running, jumping and hacking. Despite his Protestant background, the young Hughie was a huge Celtic fan and his hero was his namesake Patsy (not to be confused with the lovely Ms Kensit who was Mrs Patsy Gallagher for a while). Hughie was very small and stopped growing when he reached 5ft 5in. Zola was only an inch taller. If you want a reference point for what Hughie was like, then think David Speedie. I was always a fan of the impish Speedie; he was one of the few players from the '80s that would have got a game in the great Dave Sexton Chelsea side of the early '70s. Speedie was of the same boyish stature as Gallacher. Both were incredible in the air: Speedie was a better jumper than the Champion Hurdle winner Istabraq and Gallacher could leap higher than Superman. Both had a low centre of gravity and could dive in any direction instantly. Gallacher was a much deadlier finisher than Speedie, though, in my view. David missed too many chances at the highest level for my liking. That is what stopped him from being remembered as a truly world-class player and Chelsea legend, and just as a very good player. Hughie, like Jimmy Greaves, was a clinical finisher. The easier the chance, the more coolly they converted it. They just did not miss easy chances; it simply did not happen. That is why they scored so many per season – over 30 straightforward goals and maybe half a dozen 'specials'. They would shoot from any conceivable angle, any position, any height – waist, shoulder or knee. You rarely see that today; it seems so precise and mechanical.

Life was hard on Hughie from day one. No O levels or computer courses for him. At 15, he was working in the coal mines after a stint in the munitions factories and then a spell labouring. It is unthinkable today that a player could make the transition from manual work to the Premiership. Ex-Chelsea midfielder, hod carrier and movie star Vinnie Jones was the last example.

For Hughie, the rigours of his teens were to prove the bedrock of his success in the game. Any punishment dished out to him on the pitch was very minor to the harsh realities of colliery work. Conditions were primitive: there were no proper facilities to wash or change, soap was scarce, hot water at a premium. That is what Hughie found the hardest to take – the grime and the filth. It was always freezing cold or raining, or both.

Queen of the South (Elton John's favourite team north of the border) were the first senior team to sign Hughie after spotting him playing in a Scotland Youth match. He only played nine games for Queen and scored a remarkable nineteen goals before he joined Airdrie. Things were looking up for him – he had escaped the colliery and was earning a living doing what he loved: playing football. His teenage years were not happy on a personal level, though. At the age of 17, he married a girl called Annie McIlvaney, whom he met at the pit. Annie was Catholic and the added pressure of their young age was soon to cause major problems. They call it a starter marriage these days. Tragedy struck the young couple when their first son died suddenly, only a few months old. (Exactly like the tragedy that befell another Chelsea legend, Jimmy Greaves, whose firstborn son James died.) After a year of marriage, the couple split but later reconciled for a brief period during which they had another son. However, when Hughie was only 20 their second split was irrevocable. The failure of his marriage and the loss of his son were to haunt him for the rest of his life.

Hughie actually signed his transfer papers in a funeral parlour owned by one of the Airdrie directors. Rather than act as the kiss of death for his career, it was in fact the launching pad for his trip to the stars. At the time, Airdrie were just seen as a mediocre side, no real challenge to the Rangers–Celtic axis which has an even firmer stranglehold north of the border today. They were known as the Diamonds (perhaps it was from here Tommy Docherty copped the tag for his brilliant young Chelsea side of the '60s?) because of the red marking on their Madrid white shirts. The strip looked better suited to a rugby team but soon it was to become very well known. In his first season, they brought him on slowly. Gallacher scored seven goals in eleven games as he painstakingly learnt his craft. Ranieri showed the same level of patience as he nurtured the precocious Carlton Cole during his early Chelsea career. Then Abramovich arrived and the rules changed.

In his next season, though, Airdrie stormed to second place in the League. They finished five points behind Glasgow Rangers but four up on Celtic. A similar achievement today would be Southampton finishing second to Manchester United but in front of Arsenal, Chelsea et al.

Hughie scored ten times that season in exactly twice that number of appearances. More importantly, he made the number 9 shirt his own.

Throughout the rest of his illustrious career, he wore it wherever he played.

At the end of the next season, 1923–24, Airdrie again finished second but lifted the Cup. Gallacher's goals were the cornerstone of the triumph: 39 in 44 League and Cup matches. He won the first of his 20 caps for Scotland that season when he played against Wales. The next season, Airdrie finished second to Glasgow Rangers for the third year running. A mere three points divided them and they were on the wrong end of some bizarre refereeing decisions. The Airdrie player was now undisputedly the top striker north of the border. He cracked 46 goals in 40 games despite being heavily marked wherever he played. The problem was he was racking up suspensions as well as goals now. The tackling on him became savage as well as the verbal abuse. In one particularly heated exchange, he received a five-match suspension after being sent off at Partick Thistle and continuing the brawl in the tunnel. It makes the recent Premiership flare-ups between Chelsea and Arsenal look like a bout of jostling in the ladies' room at The Ivy.

As his goal tally grew, so did his reputation which was soon to turn into legend. Hughie manifested signs of both welcoming and resisting his sudden iconic status. He viewed his meteoric rise to fame from the bottom of the mine shaft with nervous scepticism. He was the harbinger of a new attitude that was already worrying the powers that ran the game. Gallacher had this loquacious high energy and a contempt for any form of authority. The commonplace behaviour amongst some footballers today – taking advantage of groupies and trashing hotels – is a direct result of this conflict.

Hughie's international profile was rising, too. In his second game for his country, he scored twice as Scotland ran out easy 3–1 winners over Wales. His second effort, which he cherished as his greatest-ever goal, was a solo run past five defenders.

Like Beckham today, he was front-page news wherever he went, his blank persona becoming the role model for cool. Before the Scotland v. Ireland match, a reporter claimed that he should not have been playing in blue because he was in fact Irish. Hughie's mother had to produce his birth certificate to prove otherwise in an episode worthy of the superb comedy show *Father Ted*. Hughie had the last laugh, though – even Ardal O'Hanlon, who plays Father Dougal Maguire in the show, would have seen the funny side – as he scored one and made another, the Scots crushing the Irish 0–3.

Gallacher's next run out at Hampden was the biggie – England. As was proved again at Euro '96, it doesn't get any bigger than this. Hughie was up to the task, though, scoring two audacious goals to win the game as Scotland overpowered England. At 22, he was the fulcrum of his nation's football ambitions. To many, he had the image of the alienated loner, living constantly on the cutting edge. Gallacher had the skill of Verón, the tempestuous nature of Best, the showmanship of Ali and the cold detachment of Senna. Life was a trip, then you get there. Hughie took the fast train to the very top. Every major club in England fought for his signature. Chelsea had looked at him for a season. His last game for Airdrie was a 1–2 defeat against Morton, their first loss in 67 home games. Hughie had scored 116 goals for them in 137 games.

NORTHERN STAR

Eventually, he signed for Newcastle, beating off Chelsea and fellow Londoners, Arsenal. Today, Mr Abramovich would not have allowed such a thing, he would just have upped the stakes. Everton were also keen and some reports had him going to Notts County. 'Notts County!' I hear you say, but they could have been contenders. Juventus were glad to borrow their kit around the time the Bridge was emerging from the cabbage patch.

Like all the small teams trying to live with the big boys, Airdrie gradually had to sell their stars. The goal-obsessed Hughie was the biggest jewel in their crown. The official fee was never made known but £7,000 is about right. The week before, Sunderland had smashed the transfer record by paying around £500 less for a player called Bob Kelly. Can't say that I recall much about old Bob. Abravomich with his Croesus-shaming wealth would have bought him as back-up. What could you get for £7,000 now? A morning's training from Joe Cole? A deposit on a watch for Brooklyn Beckham?

Newcastle had been trailing Hughie like a celebrity stalker eyeing Jodie Marsh. The cult of the number 9 shirt was about to be born at Newcastle. Geordie historians point to the great heritage of the shirt: Jackie Milburn, Malcolm MacDonald (an old drinking buddy and fellow air miles collector of Alan Hudson), Andy Cole and Alan Shearer carried it on. Chelsea never had the number gimmick. Maybe with Zola's departure things will change. The only London side to remotely approach it was QPR with the number 10 shirt. It was handed down from Marsh (Rodney, not Jodie) to Stanley Bowles and later to Tony Currie. The American-born Roy Wegerle (who had the talent to have been a Chelsea legend) also tried to fill it for a short while.

Hughie made his debut at St James' on 12 December 1925 against Everton, both sides adrift in mid-table. (Chelsea, who finished third in the Second Division, won 1–2 at Middlesbrough.) It was a clash of the titans, though, because up front for Everton was the legendary William Ralph 'Dixie' Dean who wore the number 9 shirt for the Toffees. Dean was on his way to scoring the all-time record of sixty goals in a season. Sixty goals! Eat your heart out Henry and Greaves. He should have got a platinum boot for that one. Dixie scored a hat-trick that game. Hughie, not wanting to be outdone by the England number 9, scored twice and made the goal which put them 3–1 up at one point. Defensive frailties let Everton back into the game. It was to be a familiar story throughout his career in England and pretty apt for Chelsea. Just over 36,000 watched the game, and their first reaction to Hughie was one of amazement. They could not believe how tiny he was. The first television pictures demonstrated by our friend John Logie Baird were still a year away from being shown. Des Lynham did not even have a show. There were no videos or DVDs or expensive glossy magazines. The only glimpse the public might have had of Hughie would have been on Pathé newsreels which usually showed him scoring for Scotland. Most of the crowd had only seen his picture in the paper. Tabloids did not exist, there were no pull-out soccer supplements; they thought he was a pygmy, then he started to play . . .

Hughie never looked back. He came out with both guns blazing. I cannot stress how important it is to get off to a good start in front of your new fans. That is why Chris Sutton found it so hard at Stamford Bridge and Adrian Mutu was accepted immediately: Sutton failed to put away his chances on his debut and from there on in the inhabitants of the lower reaches of the Matthew Harding Stand were always looking for him to foul up; Mutu scored a spectacular left-footed goal on his debut against Leicester City and cemented his relationship with the Chelsea fans. In his first nine games for Newcastle, Hughie hammered in fifteen goals, including a hat-trick against Liverpool and scoring four at Bolton. It was raining goals that season. The offside law was changed in 1925 and the under-coached defences just could not cope, they were simply overwhelmed. During the 1924–25 season, the average number of goals per game was 2.44. The following year, it jumped to 3.45. Hughie led the way with his one-man Mel Gibson/Braveheart assault on the English defences. Of course, it could not last. Nothing good ever does. Around that time, Arsenal modified their defence and for the first time in the modern game a centre-half was deployed as an out-and-out defender. Prior to that, the centre-half role was one of a central midfield player – almost the role defined by Petit in his first season at Chelsea and his glory days at Highbury. Trust Arsenal to come up with a plan to make the game even more defensive.

After the offside rules had changed, Chelsea played a friendly match against Arsenal. Lines were drawn across the pitch to indicate areas where players could not be considered offside. It was highly experimental and confused not only the crowd but the whistle blower and the players. Chelsea won 1–0.

Hughie arrived too late in that goal-saturated season to win anything for Newcastle. They finished like an express train, though, and he ended up with 25 goals in 22 matches. The shrewd money was on them to lift the Cup but they were sensationally dumped out by Clapton Orient. Clapton put three men on Hughie throughout the game and kicked him and Newcastle out of the competition. Clapton Orient later metamorphosed into Leyton Orient, who in recent times abbreviated their name still further by dropping the Leyton. Almost 50 years later, Orient knocked the 'galactico'-packed Dave Sexton side out of the Cup in a shambles of a match. That defeat, followed by the Wembley League Cup loss at the hands of Stoke City, signalled the beginning of the end for the 'House of Mears'.

For Chelsea, the '20s were always up and down. In 1920–21, they finished 18th with 39 points, Jack Cock scoring 15 goals. The next season, Chelsea jumped to 9th with 46 points, with 13 goals from Jack. In 1922–23, they plummeted back to 19th and amassed 36 points, Jack Cock scoring a single goal in 11 games.

The following season, 1923–24, the Blues were relegated to the Second Division with a total of only 32 points and having scored a meagre 31 goals. Their worst results were a 4–0 loss at Bolton where the superstar of the day, David Jack, hit three, and a 0–6 drubbing at home to Notts County.

In 1924–25, Chelsea finished 5th in their first season down in the Second Division, the result of 16 wins, 15 draws and 11 losses. That season, a crowd of 40,000 attended a 0–0 draw at home to Manchester United, also banished to the wilderness.

The 1926–27 season was an all-time great for Newcastle (the same as the 1954–55 and 2004–05 seasons were for Chelsea). That was the only time the League title has been won by the Magpies. My dear friend Sir Bobby Robson made that dream a little more possible: under his stewardship, Newcastle almost became a superpower in the game again. Mondomondo.

The 1926–27 season saw Chelsea finish fourth in the Second Division. They had won twenty of their games, drawn twelve and lost ten. They assembled fifty-two points, just two behind Portsmouth, who edged out Manchester City on goal difference to win promotion.

Newcastle started that fateful season like Juan Pablo Montoya in his Williams and gained speed with each passing game. In the first match, they crushed Villa 4–0 (Gallacher scoring all four). On the eve of the season, Hughie was made captain, replacing Frank Hudspeth. By all accounts, Frank was a man so dour that he would have made Ron Harris appear like Dale Winton. At the time, the press raised a few doubts about the maturity and temperament of Gallacher to captain the side.

The tackling on Gallacher that season was as ruthless as anything he had faced at Airdrie. He was almost hacked to pieces in some games by defenders desperate to stop the Scottish fireball. It seemed, however, that nothing could stop the cocksure livewire – no matter how many times he was chopped down, he would bounce back and resume the battle. Hughie had a fast, sharp, prickly tongue which he would use to berate, needle and goad opponents. His language was the vocabulary of the pits: foul-mouthed, vulgar and crude. A torrent of abuse would find its way to any official or opponent whom he deemed not to have given him fair treatment. When I see that chef chap Ramsay on TV, I think of Hughie.

At first, the London crowds were blasé about the Battler from Bellshill. Notoriously cool, they were yet to be convinced of his burgeoning superstar status. As is the way so often in football, one game changed all that. The match was against our old friends at White Hart Lane. Spurs fans are still the hardest to please in the capital and each year they have more to moan about. In November 1926, Newcastle came to town riding high in the top three with Spurs in the pack snapping at their heels. Even in the twenty-first century, the Tottenham crowd are known for their fickle support and hyper criticism of managers and players. The man that might have given them a brighter future, George Graham, was hounded out of office because of his associations with Arsenal.

Incited by their jeering fans, the Spurs defenders went after Hughie from the start and singled him out for scything tackles, clattering charges and vicious lunges. The Scot responded as only he could by hammering in a spectacular hat-trick. In addition to that, he had a goal disallowed, smashed a shot against the woodwork and saw countless efforts just flash past the post. He could easily have finished with half a dozen goals. At one stage, the referee called both teams together after a pitched battle broke out when Hughie was hacked down yet again and another square go was sparked. The victory gave Newcastle the belief that they could win the title. In every Championship season, there is a particular game that seems to propel a side on to glory. Chelsea's amazing see-saw 4–3 win at Wolves in 1955 (when they were trailing 2–3 with two minutes left) set them up for the title and triggered their push for glory.

THE CORINTHIANS

Another extraordinary match played in London in January 1927 involving Hughie was Newcastle's fourth-round tie against The Corinthians. Gallacher v. The Corinthians must have been on a par to Mike Tyson v. Richmond Polo Club.

The view that football has working-class roots is largely erroneous. The Corinthians, a team of mainly 'old boys' from the public school domain, was formed in 1882. The idea was to give the most talented English footballers the chance to play together and prepare for matches with the national side. From these beginnings grew one of the most respected amateur clubs in the country. In 1907, the professional–amateur split in the Southern League hit them hard. From then until the First World War, they were barred from playing against big professional sides like Chelsea. The Great War decimated a generation of young men from the public schools who would normally have found their way into the Corinthian ranks. After 1919, they were allowed to compete in the FA Cup. They played on the old Cup final pitch at Crystal Palace.

The Corinthians v. Newcastle was the second-ever football match to be broadcast on the radio by the BBC. For those first games, the Beeb attempted to make it easier for the listener by printing a grid in the *Radio Times* which carved the pitch up into eight squares. While the commentator described the game, another voice would call out the square in which play was occurring. When the ball was passed back to square one, it would get transferred back to the goalkeeper and any attack would start again (this was long before the pass back was outlawed) and that is how the expression 'back to square one' evolved. It was also highly significant that the first match to be broadcast featured Arsenal – some shrewd judge must have anticipated a lot of passing back! Once again, I am tempted to mention how little things have changed.

Those sporting chaps at The Corinthians didn't really like the concept of sudden-death matches; rather like their objections to the penalty kick. They had such an aversion to them that they deemed them unsporting. It was recorded that against representative sides, like the army, and foreign teams such as Grasshoppers of Zurich, they advocated the following should take place: in the event of an opponent ever being awarded a penalty against them, the Corinthians' goalkeeper, B. Howard-Baker, would immediately vacate the goal line to give the penalty taker a clear shot.

I had not heard of such sportsmanship until I encountered those other 'Corinthians' from Elland Road, managed by Don Revie around the time of the 1970 FA Cup final. I recall a tackle by Jackie Charlton on A.A. Hudson that still makes me shudder. Mind you, the sporting spirit is still maintained at grounds like Anfield. After making a nonsense of his first penalty kick, Michael Owen was generously allowed a second attempt at it in the opening League match of the 2003–04 season against Chelsea.

B. Howard-Baker was a fine goalkeeper, by the way. Like Terry Venables, he was capped at both amateur and full England levels. He played for Chelsea for a spell and was also British high jump champion. For added cachet, he appeared in the 1912 and 1920 Olympic teams. Now, Beckham never managed that. Nor did Robert Frederick Chelsea Moore.

Anyway, The Corinthians wanted to switch the tie to the Bridge. Newcastle would not have objected, having lost no fewer than five finals at the Crystal Palace ground, but the authorities would not allow it. The toffs in the Corinthian team gave the Magpies the fright of their lives and dominated the first half. The splendidly named C.T. Ashton put them ahead from a centre by K.E. Hegan and they held the lead till 15 minutes from time. At this point, *The Times* reported:

> The professional team turned in their desperation to what boxers call the 'rough stuff' – some of it fair, some of it decidedly not. They scored an equalising goal from a free kick and then R.G.C. Jenkins retired hurt. Against ten men, Newcastle forced their advantage and ran out 3–1 victors.
>
> Once again it cannot be too strongly urged that the defence in those matches, strengthened as it was by A.H. Chadder, gave a display as good as any in the history of the Club.

Gallacher was totally dominated by the Corinthian centre-half. He was not amongst the goals but stayed clear of any fisticuffs with the public-school chaps. He moderated his language in his dealings with Chadder. There was sadly no penalty awarded in the game.

They were strange twilight years between the wars when The Corinthians could still match the big clubs. With each passing year, the game became more corporate and cynical and the gap between rich and poor grew wider.

Chadder epitomised the qualities of The Corinthians. He showed all the grace, style and panache which Chelsea tried so hard to incorporate into their mediocre side. Educated at Taunton School, Chadder went to St John's College, Oxford, and appeared in the varsity matches from 1923–25 as an inside-forward. Chelsea wanted to sign him in that role but instead he opted for a life as housemaster at Malvern College. For more than two decades he was master, in charge of football, and lived to be 91.

Chelsea's FA Cup hopes had perished in the third round at Molineux, going down 2–1 to Wolves. Newcastle looked set for the Cup after crushing Notts County 8–1 (perhaps not such a force in the game, even then). Hughie grabbed three goals but the Magpies crashed out in the next round. They made no mistake with the title, though, fighting off a challenge from Huddersfield. The Yorkshire side were the Manchester United or Arsenal of the Roaring '20s. They had won the League three years running. Hughie finished the season with 39 goals in 41 matches. None was more valuable than the only goal of the game he shot at home against Huddersfield on the Championship run-in. It was the goal that brought the title to Tyneside and finally snapped the stranglehold Huddersfield held on the English game. That was why Newcastle bought him – to score the goals that delivered the League title. That is why Abramovich invested a fortune in Drogba and Co. – to give Chelsea the firepower required to release the vice-like grip Manchester United and Arsenal had on domestic honours. The billionaire spent more on them than he invested in a tank factory in the Siberian city of Omsk. The factory had fallen on hard times after playing an important role in supplying Stalin's Red Army. Firepower of all sorts, that's what it's all about.

GATSBY

Hughie Gallacher was the Jay Gatsby of football. *The Great Gatsby*, with its eponymous anti-hero, was F. Scott Fitzgerald's most renowned book, written during the same era that Hughie was strutting his stuff. It was *the* Jazz Age novel, considered by many to be the greatest book of the twentieth century. In July 1922, Fitzgerald expressed a wish to write something new, something extraordinary, something beautiful but simple, as intricately patterned as the passing movements conjured up by Cole and Lampard to sustain their incessant attacks. Out of this desire, *The Great Gatsby* was created. Fitzgerald took nearly a year to write it and made every effort to keep away from the drink that was to finally kill him – and ultimately Gallacher.

Hughie carried a dream with him that was to prove his undoing. So did my dear friend Matthew Harding. Gallacher wanted to be the biggest star ever in the galaxy of football; perhaps for a while he was. Matthew never realised his dream of leading Chelsea, as the biggest football club in the world, into the twenty-first century. The irony is that, even in his wildest dreams, Matthew would never have dreamt of doing what Roman

Abramovich did in the course of a few weeks – underwriting a shopping spree the like of which had never been seen in the history of the game. Yet Matthew was a true fan and had been since his first game at the ground, the day he saw Barry Bridges score twice in 1962 against Newcastle of all people, or the night Alan Hudson ran the length of the pitch to score possibly the greatest goal ever seen at the Bridge. When Abramovich flew over London in a helicopter, he mistook Craven Cottage for Chelsea's ground. In a helicopter. How ironic that a helicopter took Harding away from Chelsea and another one brought in its saviour.

On the field, by the age of 25, Gallacher had nothing else to prove. After a certain stage, it is just repetition. Ask George Best. Off the field, both men's lives were playing out the same trajectory as Fitzgerald's, from romanticism to alcoholism. For Hughie, no matter what success he found as a player, the pain of his harsh upbringing, his broken marriage and his son's death left lasting fingerprints on his memory. By then, he was surfing the first wave of real fame. He was blinding himself with whisky every night in the clubs and bars that were the spooky grandeur of the underbelly of Newcastle. (When director Mike Hodges set the English gangster classic *Get Carter* in Newcastle 50 years later, he knew what he was doing.)

Also, for the ex-miner there was a huge class barrier to overcome. To the directors of Newcastle, Gallacher was regarded as a social inferior and was held in barely concealed contempt. A.H. Chadder received his Blue from Oxford in 1921. Hughie joined the Blues but was dead by the time Chadder's son Dick gained his at Oxford.

Fame was different then. Beckham speaks 'council' but transcended all that class stuff when he married Posh. The psychological changes and all they encompass were the same, though. There were no red tops, no TV crews nor media circus to deal with but the alienation of a pressurised industry was the same. Soon, Hughie was increasingly seeking refuge in booze, swimming in a sea of alcohol against the same current that was to eventually engulf Best, Greaves, Merson, Gascoigne, Hudson, Osgood, Adams and Cooke. Paul Merson wrote the following in his book *Hero and Villain*: 'I was shocked this morning to read about Gazza. He was found sobbing and shaking on Stevenage station after coming back from a bender in Dublin. "He looked ready to throw himself under a train," someone said.'

The period when the freewheeling Gallacher's career was at its zenith was known as the Roaring '20s, the Jazz Age, the Aspirin Age. (What have we today? The Heroin Age, the Prozac Age, perhaps?) The killing fields of the First World War were over and it was a period of easy money and false gaiety. High living and merrymaking were seen as reactions to the aftermath of global warfare. Jazz music filled the air, people danced the Charleston and the first flashy motorcars started appearing on the roads. Fashion was just starting to take hold of the young. Nobody dressed better than Hughie Gallacher, from the crown of his razor-barbered head to the soles of his handmade patent shoes. His time spent wallowing in the filth of the pits had taught him the golden rule of the dead cool superstar: *always* dress to kill. Hughie was a dandy by anybody's standards, the very essence of contemporary style.

My Chelsea boys of the '70s modelled the *fin-de-siècle*, Kings Road–Regency Bucks look with their long, overwashed hair and velvet suits. Prince of dandies, Beau Brummel, meets the inspiration for the Rolling Stones, Brian Jones, at a crossover point where Chelsea forward Tommy Baldwin joined the act. A good 50 years before, though, Gallacher was defining the look on his vertiginous climb to the top of Stamford Bridge: 'Look, Ma, I'm on top of the world.'

The movies were just starting to talk and the golden era of the on-screen tough guys was dawning. Humphrey Bogart, Jimmy Cagney, Edward G. Robinson and Paul Muni in Hughie's favourite 1932 gangster film *Scarface* (how he would have loved the remake with Al Pacino). Verón and Crespo must model their wardrobes on this movie. Pacino made references throughout the film to the Diaz brothers, the sworn enemies of the Tony Montana organisation. (Verón and Crespo are the sartorial equivalent of the Diaz brothers.) The actors of the day played savage first-generation gangsters but if you wanted the real thing, then John Dillinger's prison escapes and hijackings in the Midwest were just starting to make news. In 1929, just prior to Hughie signing for Chelsea, Al Capone's mob turned their tommy guns on seven of 'Bugs' Moran's gang in what was to be known as the St Valentine's Day Massacre. (I always thought that was when Palace knocked us out of the FA Cup on 14 February 1976.) The slaughter in a Chicago garage was Big Al's way of enforcing his monopoly on the city's bootlegging.

Gallacher was by then looking like he'd stepped down from the screen or the back of a Stutz Bearcat. His pupils seemed hidden and colourless, dilated so much by the late nights. More often than not he wore a beautifully cut doubled-breasted tweed suit with a pin-through collar shirt (they became fashionable again for a time amongst Venables' class of '65) and a shiny silk tie, which was always worn with a high-buttoning waistcoat. The outfit was rounded off with a hat Jimmy Cagney would have died for: a fedora with a snap brim, rather like the pork-pie headgear worn by ace Chelsea fan Suggs during his two-tone period (around the time of Eddie McCreadie's promotion side). It was the overcoat that won it for him, though. Always double-breasted, exquisitely styled, the broad lapels always hand-stitched, sometimes worn with a velvet collar or a silk handkerchief (either Paisley pattern or polka dots). Gallacher would wear a printed scarf, sometimes a cashmere one. In recent times, George Graham has worn the smartest topcoats in the game – usually Armani or Cerutti with the occasional Hugo Boss. José looks like he buys his coats from Milan as well. I don't know where Hughie got his coats from. Savile Row, probably.

Legend has it that one freezing night close to Christmas, Hughie was walking down the Kings Road in temperatures more suited to the area in Russia where Abramovich is governor. He was approached by a dosser. We are talking pre-*Big Issue* times and the only issue at stake was the cost of a warming drink. Hughie caught the clipped Glaswegian accent and did better than that. He stuffed a wad of notes in his fellow countryman's hands and gave the poor wretch the very coat off his back. Hughie had his 'beer coat' on to get home – the invisible but warm clothing worn walking home hammered at 2 a.m. on a winter's night.

Hughie had a fetish about his footwear. Those tiny plates of meat that scored five goals per match on six occasions were usually to be found in a pair of spats. Possibly our friend Beckham could revive this fashion and start a new trend. It may well improve on his hair bands, ribbons, thongs, tattoos, sarongs, gangster suits and Ronnie Harris haircuts.

In the summer months, Hughie would sport a huge white Borsalino hat that Gatsby would have been proud to wear to one of his fabulous parties. Crystal Palace manager Malcolm Alison sported similar headwear during their epic Cup run in the '70s. He wore the hat at Stamford Bridge when Palace knocked us out at that St Valentine's Day fixture. The Shed gave him a lot of stick but Big Mal had the last laugh. Terry Venables was his lieutenant, listening to and learning everything. Anthony Hopkins tried to adopt the same look for those *Silence of the Lambs* films.

When it rained, as it had been known to do in Newcastle and even London during the summer, Hughie would unfurl a huge, beautifully rolled umbrella. Gallacher was in great demand socially, especially when he came south. What he craved was acclaim. Specifically, the mixture of awe and sycophancy which greets the supremely talented. There were no film premieres with minor celebrities to attend but instead a constant round of parties and dances. Hughie loved jazz and would wander around Newcastle and, later, the lower reaches of the Kings Road soaking up the sounds and influences.

The world, as one Arthur Daley (whose very own Winchester Club was situated off Fulham Broadway in the classic series *Minder*) might say, was 'his lobster'. Around the time of the title win, Hughie met his own Arthur Daley-type character called Tot Anderson. Tot was an entrepreneur and a licensee of several of Hughie's favourite watering holes. You see, players always had their favourite bars and clubs. Adrian Mutu was spotted at a bachelor party thrown by the Bambuddha Grove nightclub in London the night after Chelsea had won in Prague in the Champions League. When Dave Sexton in the '70s wanted to track down some of his wayward stars he soon knew where to find them: the Markham and the Bird's Nest on the Kings Road were favourite pubs, while Scotch of St James' and Tramps were the most popular clubs.

Hughie soon struck up a friendship with Tot but he had an even closer one with his 17-year-old daughter named Hannah. That old devil called lurve raised its ugly head and soon Hughie was smitten. He was also smitten (about the head) by one of her brothers when it came out that Hughie was still legally married. The incident happened under Newcastle's High Level Bridge and was another thing that passed into folklore.

Amongst the mad social whirl and his alcohol-imposed vigils, Hughie still found the time to play the odd game for Newcastle. In 1927–28, the Geordies, like most defending champions, were finding it hard to retain their title.

Meanwhile, down south, Chelsea were finishing third in the Second Division, winning 23 games, drawing 8 and losing 11 with a goal tally of 75 and 45 against. They finished three points behind promoted Leeds.

FOGG ON THE TYNE

On New Year's Eve 1927, Newcastle went to Huddersfield for a vital League game. If Newcastle were to have any chance of retaining their crown, they had to grab an away win. Their away form was on a par with Chelsea's in the first year of the twenty-first century (i.e. awful). The season they won the League, Newcastle contrived to lose ten games away from home. Their home form won it for them, though. They registered nineteen home wins and averaged over three goals a game. If you lost ten away games in the Premier these days you just wouldn't be in the running for the title.

Huddersfield were still seething at losing their title to Gallacher and his pals. Hughie had already rubbed salt into their gaping wounds by scoring three times against them in a home game at Newcastle at the start of the season. The pitch resembled the scene from *Doctor Zhivago* when the Cossacks came sweeping down through the trees and across the frozen lake. Before the contest started, the referee, a Mr A.E. (Bert) Fogg, advised Hughie that because of the treacherous surface he would not tolerate any heavy challenges. This was music to the tiny Scot's ears because he had been having a running battle with the brutal Huddersfield defence since he had left Scotland. The Waffen-SS had more compassion than the Yorkshiremen. It was the cornerstone of their success; just as their near-neighbours Leeds United were to base their triumphs on their impregnable (almost) back line. The Arsenal Championship-winning side assembled by George Graham was based on a ruthless back four built around Tony Adams. It could be argued that Chelsea's failure to land championships in the latter half of the twentieth century was because they were never able to build a formidable enough defence to sustain any long-term League challenge. The acquisition of Marcel Desailly (albeit at the end of his career) and the turbo-powered Willie Gallas gave them two world-class defenders, the equal of any player in that position in the modern game.

Gallacher scored twice that day but it was not enough to stop his side going down by the odd goal in five. Huddersfield's winner came from a hotly disputed penalty scored by Hughie's Scotland buddy Alec Jackson. Jackson was destined soon after to link up with Gallacher at Chelsea when an Abramovich-style swoop took the pair to London. On paper, it was a dream pairing on a par with Verón and Crespo, but . . .

Hughie had been denied a couple of blatant penalties after being mown down in full flight by the Huddersfield rearguard. The second was even more obvious than the first and proved more than Gallacher could stand. He found it particularly galling after he had been promised protection by the referee. With the linesman frantically flagging for a foul, Hughie lost it in a large way. He flew instantly into a torrent of abuse against the referee, considered a bit strong even by Gallacher's high standard of invective. It was an obvious pun but when the ref asked Hughie for his name, the Scot demanded to know the same of Bert and then snapped, 'Fogg is your name and you have been in one all game.' (It's the way you tell 'em, Hughie.)

Worse was to follow. Hughie, in the words of Vic Reeves, 'wouldn't let it lie'. At the end of the match, he went looking for Mrs Fogg's little boy Bert. Some players say he was going to apologise but the general view was that he wanted to continue the row. The game had ended in a near riot with Hughie still pointing his finger at Fogg and swearing uncontrollably. Perhaps it was a comedy (more like a farce) but when Hughie burst into the ref's little room he was confronted with the hapless official running his post-match bath. There was no bubble bath available, just eight years after the end of the Great War. Perhaps Fogg was trying to wash the little Scot out of his hair. Whatever, he should have washed and gone. You can guess what happened next, it was always going to happen. For once, the ref was the one that had the early bath.

What would a picture of Roy Keane involved in a similar incident be worth today? Once again, Hughie was in hot water with the authorities. The shower that ran the FA wanted to clean up the game. It was a real soap opera and ended with Hughie being suspended for two months. He was given a clean break from the game. He had tried to soft soap his way out of it but the FA saw it as a load of flannel. Eventually, he chucked in the towel. Any chance Newcastle had of retaining their Championship went down the plughole. They had chucked the baby out with the bath water.

Newcastle finished up ninth in the League. Hughie was stripped of his beloved captaincy and severely reprimanded by the board. The first cracks were appearing.

THE WEMBLEY WIZARDS

The only good thing that happened to Hughie in that dramatic season was that he played in Scotland's 1–5 destruction of England at Wembley. It was the time of the Wembley Wizards and to this day their greatest triumph over their bitterest foe (think of England's win in Germany by the same score in modern times).

It was Hughie's first game at Wembley and only the second time that the two sworn enemies had clashed on the hallowed turf. Scotland had the all-time 'Small Faces' line-up: Alex James (who had grown up with Hughie in Bellshill), Alan Morton and Jimmy Dunn all only stood as high as the 5ft 5in. Hughie. Alec Jackson, who cracked in a hat-trick that afternoon, towered over the 'wee men' at a modest 5ft 10in. (In the '80s, Pat Nevin was nicknamed the 'Wee Man' by sections of the Shed. It was a homage to the superstars of the Gallacher era of which Nevin was a throwback.) The Scotland party arrived at Wembley in a downer mood. With Hughie still serving his ban, Scotland had played poorly and lost to a mediocre Irish team. For the Wembley fixture, there had been wholesale changes in the side with several star names axed. It was getting very political behind the scenes: the Scottish authorities were concerned about the growing number of domestic stars that were moving to the south. Once again, there was a great deal of controversy over the inclusion of Hughie in the starting line-up. He had not kicked a ball in anger for over two months and there was a growing lobby north of the border for the inclusion of the Celtic sharpshooter James McGory in his place. There was an increasing antipathy in Glasgow against the 'Anglos' (those footballers spending more and more of their time playing south of the border). How times change. At first, Chelsea were criticised for their pasta-associated roots, now the transfer market is global. A Scot in the Chelsea line-up would almost be considered a local hero. Being uncharitable, I couldn't think of a Scottish player that would make the team. In 1999, Chelsea under Vialli played a complete team without a British player in the line-up: seventy years earlier, the Newcastle team featured ten Scots and a Welsh bloke.

The weather suited Scotland that day. It poured with rain. This was long before global warming and all that. The game started like a volcano erupting. England smacked a shot against the post in the opening seconds. It was the only time during the game they were involved. Scotland broke away to score. The Scotland skipper Jimmy McMullan (who had prayed for rain all night) put in Alex James who instantly crossed for Jackson to head the first of his three goals. Jackson was being watched by my father and a contingent of scouts from Chelsea. The word was that the Scot was unsettled at Huddersfield and hankered after a move to London. Chelsea were favourites to sign him.

Alex James, whose brilliance overwhelmed the home defence, bombshelled in the second from 25 yards. He then proceeded to run the game. My father, witness to a football miracle, said that the only player he saw pass the ball as accurately was Terry Venables in the Docherty promotion season. My father died before Hudson emerged a few seasons later. James, on that rain-lashed afternoon, would pass the ball diagonally to the left-winger Morton, or switch the ball to the right where the plundering Jackson would then take over. James would also play it through the middle to find Hughie galloping down field. Soon, the England defenders were dizzy, stranded yards from one another and cruelly exposed in the one-to-one situation against the tanna ball players.

In the second half, with the rain still bucketing down, the Scots gave England a football lesson they never forgot, their nippy ball-playing midgets literally running rings around the immobile white-shirted defenders on the sodden pitch. Alan Morton (perhaps the most technically gifted of all the Scots) came more into the game as Hughie's ceaseless runs tore a gaping hole in the centre of the defence. England tried vainly to plug the gaps but it was like trying to stop the rain from falling. Morton engineered two more goals for the gazelle-like Jackson. Sandwiched between the shots a dazzling piece of skill by Hughie set up Alex James to smash home his second goal of the match. It was a supreme moment for the street urchins from the slums. They had simply recreated one of their boyhood pavement moves to carve out a goal for their beloved country in its greatest-ever triumph. Amazingly, Alex James won only eight caps for Scotland. Nothing was ever again to taste as sweet as England's total failure to stop the Scots running amok at Wembley. Hughie was at the hub of it all but, as always with him, it was a bittersweet moment. As he left the battlefield, covered in glory and mud, mobbed by hundreds of delirious Scots, he learnt of the sudden death of his sister-in-law. He missed out on the post-match celebrations as he rushed north to comfort his grief-stricken brother.

Hughie was to stay at Newcastle for just over two more strife-ridden seasons. He was still in majestic scoring form with an unquenchable thirst for goals. The storm clouds were gathering fast, though. During the 1928–29 season, he scored 24 goals in 33 games. However, Newcastle, after briefly scaling the heights to win the title, were falling fast. That season, they could only finish mid-table. A comparison could be made with Sexton's Chelsea team of the early '70s. After briefly exploding across the stratosphere, they crashed to earth like a burnt-out firework. Today, clubs often have Europe as camouflage with which to prop itself up if it has a less than successful domestic campaign. That season, Newcastle were in the throes of rebuilding their side and the club was in turnaround. Chelsea finished only ninth in the Second Division that year, winning 17, drawing 10 and losing 15 games. Their goals were 64 scored with 65 against.

The Northeast was known as the hotbed of talent but the real home-grown players, like Jackie Milburn and Len Shackleton, and later Chris Waddle, Peter Beardsley and Paul Gascoigne, only broke through after the Gallacher era.

Hughie's drinking was increasing, along with the tantrums, grandstanding and pyrotechnics. Stories circulated in Newcastle that he could be found in the bar before kick-off. There was a distinct change in his personality: he had become like a character in a movie by the austere Italian director Michelangelo Antonioni: alienated, at odds with his own existence, desperate to escape from the confines of the role football demanded that he play. Off the field, his pampered leisure activities and meaningless sensuality only seemed to render his whole life pointless. He became almost a creature of the night: the vampire Lestat, tunnelling through the dark.

Gallacher only seemed happy playing in the dark blue of Scotland. That international season he scored eight goals in three games – three against Wales and then five in the 7–3 jamboree against the Irish team. Another urban myth surrounding Hughie is that someone fired a gun at him in Belfast but I could find no evidence of such an event. If the marksman was as deadly as Hughie that day then it would have been all over. Gallacher is still the only Scot to be credited with five goals in an international. The only Englishman to register the same feat was the iconoclastic Malcolm

MacDonald, another Geordie legend. The game in which 'Supermac' went into the record books was one against Cyprus, the same match that fellow maverick Alan Hudson played his second and last England game.

Guess who referreed the Irish match? That respected official Mr A.E. Fogg. Hughie managed to stay away from the hot tub on that occasion!

HUGHIE GOES TO EUROPE (GAMES WITHOUT FRONTIERS)

> The difference between an alcoholic and a heavy drinker is an alcoholic believes his flaws are sincere but his virtues are fake. A heavy drinker keeps his virtues for himself and cripples others with his flaws.
>
> Phyl Kennedy, *Where Am I Now When I Need Me*

Newcastle's tour that season was as controversial and chaotic as Malcolm McLaren's Sex Pistols tour of America in 1978. The first stop was a game against Ambrosiana in Milan, a name that sounds not unlike that of the winger signed for Chelsea by Vialli, heralded as the new Ryan Giggs. I think he had a couple of games and drifted away. In a brutal match, the Geordies won 0–1 but each side had a player sent off. The Italian defenders made the Huddersfield rearguard look like The Corinthians. They always had a reputation for being hard cases. A riot broke out at the end of the match as the players clashed. Mussolini's notorious Brown Shirts moved in to restore order. Benito Mussolini (who, facially, could have passed for Vialli's grandfather) had seized control of Italy and the men in brown were his secret police. Football had become an increasingly important focus of Fascist propaganda and the government realised the game could be used in international politics. In their thinking, it diverted attention from other matters – especially the lack of opportunity for meaningful political choices. Why bother with the Hutton Report when the Scouse derby is on Sky?

The tour continued with Hughie and his chums taking an 8–1 pulverising in Slovak. (Don't ask me what they call it now.) Worse was to follow in Budapest when they lost 4–1 to a select Hungarian eleven. Hughie scored the Newcastle goal from the penalty spot. They were not as chivalrous in Budapest as those splendid Corinthians and Hughie actually had to beat the keeper, who, rather unsportingly, opted to stay in his goal. Legend has it that Hughie infuriated the locals by actually pointing to the spot in the back of the net where he was going to plant the ball. (I thought Terry Venables was the first player to ever try that trick.) They became even angrier at him late in the game when he became the second Newcastle player to be sent off. The Ambrosianians must have seemed mild in comparison – Hughie was pelted with stones, rocks, garbage and anything else they could lay their hands on. Those who could not find any objects to throw just spat at him. Charming behaviour, I am sure you will agree.

After the game, the Hungarians accused the Geordies of being drunk on the pitch. Needless to say, Hughie was branded as being the most drunk. Shock! Horror! The outrage of it all! Now Chelsea have had some heavy drinkers over the years and though I have never actually seen any drunk players on the pitch, that's not to say we did not have players who were drunks on the pitch. Though thinking about it, in the last few years of my chairmanship, as things fell apart, it may have explained a few things. George Best, I think, mentioned in one of his many books that he was drunk during a match and Dave Sexton said he could smell drink on one of our midfield players' breath, still suffering from a medieval hangover after a bad defeat one Boxing Day morning. I haven't a clue who he was talking about.

The Hungarians withheld the purse and lodged a complaint to UEFA or FIFA, or whoever was in charge in those days – perhaps it was NATO or the British Government? – and it caused an international incident (not enough to plunge Europe into war but Mussolini and his chums were already working hard on that one).

Finally, Hughie was cleared and Newcastle received their share of the gate money. (Newcastle would not have been too much out of pocket in the event of them not being paid because Hughie, being Hughie, still had the coins that were chucked at him.) Gallacher refuted the tales of drunkenness and cruelty levelled against him. He claimed that as it had been a sunny afternoon, the players had rinsed out their mouths with Johnnie Walker and water. This was before the advent of Listerine or Diet Coke. I understand the current Chelsea squad's favourite tipple is Stolichnaya vodka drowned in so much Fanta and ice that it barely qualifies as an alcopop.

The slurs continued against Hughie and he put in a transfer request that was rejected by the board. The clock was ticking for him, though. The 1929–30 season was his last for Newcastle. They missed relegation by a point and only a last-match win kept them up. Hughie had kept them afloat, scoring 34 goals in 44 games. Injuries were slowing him, though, and he had been troubled by nagging aches and pains throughout the campaign.

For Chelsea, 1929–30 was a watershed season. They won promotion back to the First Division, finishing second to Blackpool. Chelsea won 22 games, drew 11 and lost only 9, scoring 74 goals and letting in 46. Their best performance was a 4–0 Boxing Day victory at the Bridge over Blackpool. George Mills, looking a prospect as he raced through defences like a bat out of Meatloaf's hell, finished top scorer with 14 goals.

In 1930–31, Newcastle tried to arrest the slide by choosing a specialist team manager. This was unprecedented at the time and pointed the way forward. The problem was that the appointed coach, Andy Cunningham, got on as well with Hughie as Venables did with Alan Sugar. They poisonously irritated each other, and within a few tense months Hughie finally moved to London. Not, as everyone predicted, to Arsenal but to Chelsea. It was a move as unexpected and controversial as any conducted by Abramovich in that amazing summer of 2003 when he signed Panini sticker books of players for beaucoup bucks. For Hughie, it was the start of a short but, at times, beautiful friendship with the Stamford Bridge club.

THREE

BETWEEN EACH LINE OF PAIN AND GLORY

Why would one want the applause of fools?

Marcus Aurelius

The exact fee Chelsea paid for Hughie Gallacher in 1930–31 was never disclosed. Some said it was a record-shattering £12,000. Most pitched it around the £10,000 mark. At the time, the record stood at £10,890 – the fee Bolton Wanderers had received from Arsenal for the talented David Jack. Today, the media has become almost obsessive about this kind of fiscal niggle. The record books showed that the transfer of Hughie Gallacher was the second-highest in League history. Hughie was always convinced that it was more and thought he was the most expensive player of all time. Who knows? When Chelsea played Blackburn in their second home game of the 2003–04 season, their line-up included Hernan Crespo, the 29-year-old Argentinian striker who, when he joined Lazio from Parma, was the most expensive player in the world. His fellow teammate and countryman Juan Sebástian Verónwas the most expensive player in the English game when he joined Manchester United, also from Lazio.

At his peak, what would Hughie have been worth in today's game? Combine what Verón and Crespo cost Mr Abramovich and start from there. He was that good, he was that much of a star.

THE BEAUTIFUL SOUTH

The manager who purchased Hughie was David Calderhead, a fellow Scot who managed Chelsea for 26 years. An astonishing feat by modern standards – some Chelsea fans were of the view that Vialli was not given enough time; some Chelsea fans say Graham Rix should have been given more.

Calderhead, like his major signing, was also a Scottish international. A very subdued character, he carried the burden of living with a cynicism for the game which somehow managed to avoid bitterness. He had built his teams around ball players from north of the border and the whole club was categorically Caledonian. The dressing-room was full of porridge-thick brogues. All his players conveyed, by their very demeanour, a kind of proletarian deference to the management. All the players except one, who didn't give a monkey's. During his first few months at Chelsea, Hughie didn't create too many scenes or precipitate too many crises. Like Costello sang, he didn't want to go to Chelsea.

Chelsea had won promotion from the Second Division after a long spell in the doldrums. A direct comparison could be drawn between the '80s Chelsea side, with the mainstays of Dixon and the two Scots, Speedie and Nevin, that won promotion under John Neal and had been destined for great things. The club was very ambitious in the '30s and was not afraid to splash the cash even back then. Calderhead signed three other top jocks: Alec Cheyne and two Wembley Wizards, full-back Tommy Law and the godlike Alec Jackson. As with Crespo, Mutu and co., Chelsea were optimising as opposed to maximising. If things had worked out a little differently that season, perhaps Chelsea would have had an alternative history. The parallels to the present day are uncanny.

Cheyne cost £6,000 from Aberdeen. Alec, with his boyish Di Caprio looks, hyperactive style and clever dribbling, was an instant hit with the fans. Charlie Cooke, who joined the club three dozen years later, also played for Aberdeen. They were both very alike in technique: excellent passers of the ball, equipped with the sonic sleight of foot that was obligatory for Scottish attackers. They loved beating defenders and imposing their unique passing styles. Stern critics would say that they spent too much time and energy in their mazy dribbling but try to tell that to the Chelsea fans. Calderhead had the gift of attracting star players to the flagship at Stamford Bridge. He exuded a feeling of stability and confidence. Like at the present club, though, the eternal Chelsea problem was trying to blend them into a satisfactory team. The tradition of unfulfilled expectation and inconsistency started around then.

Jackson was the next into the kaleidoscope. Signed from Huddersfield for £8,500, in his last season at Leeds Road he had been plagued by an ankle injury which hindered his later career at Chelsea. Up until the ban on 'Anglos', Alec was a permanent fixture in the Scotland side. Jackson was always well turned out, complementing his polite and friendly disposition. Like so many great players, he always possessed an innate appreciation of the fact that the key element underpinning all of his game was the ability to control the ball first time. The three freewheeling Scots were to practise their rarefied craft, sublime as well as ridiculous, in front of the adoring Shed, built that year.

The Shed was to stand for over 60 years before making way for the irrational Chelsea Village site – that strange concentration of bars, fashionable restaurants, perplexingly numerous hotel rooms and luxury flats jammed together by the Fulham Road. So much power, so much space, so much expense, so little fun. The Shed reached its peak in the late '60s and early '70s when Osgood and Cooke were at theirs. It is fitting, though, that it was created around the time that Hughie Gallacher and Alec Jackson were confecting and promoting their epic talents. Feng Shui was not a concept that was well known at the time but whoever placed the Shed structure at that location must have been an expert.

Chelsea were struggling financially at that time. Stamford Bridge had not become the enterprise envisaged by Gus Mears. It had staged three Cup finals at the start of the '20s but the crowds were well down on the 120,081 that watched Aston Villa beat Sunderland 1–0 at Crystal Palace just before the outbreak of the First World War. In the 1921 final played at Stamford Bridge, Spurs actually won the Cup; a piece of trivia we shall quickly gloss over and consign to the dustbin of history. After that, Wembley staged the Cup finals, right up until the time Roberto Di Matteo scored the last-ever Cup final goal in front of the Twin Towers in 2000. Highbury took the internationals, Chelsea staging only four at Stamford Bridge. The ground was criticised for not having enough seats, having poor cover and limited access. The food was pretty vile, too. It was starting to look like a corporate bean-counter's worst nightmare: superstar players with big ideas, huge overheads and a dwindling fan base.

Hughie's first season down south was disappointing, wholly forgettable. Chelsea won only two of their first eight games. They took a bad 4–1 beating at Upton Park. As the Abramovich all-stars were to find out early in their fledgling Chelsea careers, it takes time to marry style with substance. It was to get worse. Perhaps it was the fluttering of a butterfly's wings in Java that rolled into a breeze in the South China Sea. The breeze blew across the Pacific and became a thunderstorm that was to settle over

Stamford Bridge. Arsenal, always the great rivals, came and rattled in five goals on the last Saturday of November. Record signing David Jack hit three as he bulldozed the Chelsea defence. Jack was in great form that season with Alex James setting up goal after goal. Jack had scored the first-ever goal at Wembley in a Cup final for Bolton in 1923.

The Highbury men's defence was deployed especially to snuff out the goal threat of Gallacher to admirably malevolent effect. Hughie was kicked all over the park and ended up with severe bruising of the ankles. They inflicted similar punishment on Alec Jackson.

Derby and Birmingham both recorded wins over Chelsea. The gap between success and failure can be no more than a nanometre. Chelsea continued to serve up pleasing passages of play that would have worried any team. How little has changed over the years. Mature Chelsea fans just see the past recycled. The same old act with a different cast.

After these setbacks, Chelsea crushed Sunderland with an unfazed Hughie radiating supreme confidence, mowing them down with two virtuoso goals. Tommy Law scored with a penalty, also. Grimsby went down by the same score with Hughie again wreaking havoc. His ice-cool killer instinct for goals, coupled with tremendous courage, made him such a dangerous striker. The Grimsby defenders, seething at the debacle caused by the Wee Man, started dishing out leather, the adrenalin of their acute embarrassment egging them on. Soon, Hughie was involved in petty retaliation and stood cursing the statuesque defenders. The Grimsby captain Alec 'Ginger' Hall interceded to tell the referee what (as if he needed reminding) a lively fellow Hughie was. Gallacher felt obliged to respond in kind. You can guess the rest. Inevitably, he was sent off and given a two-month suspension. Once again, the Chelsea goal machine had crashed and burnt. Hughie was rarely injured in his spectacular career but luckily the suspension coincided with him breaking a bone in his foot.

Gallacher received no wages from Chelsea during this period. There were no lucrative Sky commentary sound bites or glossy magazine columns for him as 'earners'. Had he lived in the twenty-first century, a DVD of his on-field exploits would have been a bestseller. Instead, he went back home to Scotland and schlepped around. During his spell with Chelsea, he lived in Barons Court but never really settled in his lock-down days in London. Today, the superstars are wealthy enough to inhabit addresses in leafy London squares or live it large on country estates but Hughie had to make do with a back-street flat. His reaction to the funny accents of his grey-flannel neighbours, with their iced tea and lemon drizzle cake, was one of incomprehension. Back home, he quickly forgot his London problems and absorbed himself in his roots. Most mornings, he awoke with no recollection of the previous night's roisterings. Focusing on his drinking is like talking about Toulouse-Lautrec and only mentioning his dwarfism; however, Gallacher's problem became worse as he struggled to adjust to life at Chelsea.

Without him, Chelsea gained revenge over Arsenal, knocking them out of the Cup 2–1 at the Bridge in the fourth round. Hughie's replacement, George Mills, scoring the winner with a raking left-footer. Lowly Birmingham then put Chelsea out 0–3 in a sixth-round replay at home.

Hughie returned to London in the early spring of 1931 and scored in his 3–2 comeback win against Blackburn Rovers but the season petered out as only Chelsea's can. Calderhead could call upon ten internationals but they could never play as a cohesive unit. Another 'Legion of the Lost' in royal blue shirts. Eventually, they finished 12th – far, far behind the champions, Arsenal. Not a lot changes, then. Hughie finished top scorer for Chelsea with 14 goals in 31 games (Alec Jackson came next with 11 League goals) – a good, healthy return considering how unstable the club was at that time. Gallacher's effort, skill and positional sense could never be faulted, though his attitude always hinted at rebellion and degeneracy. Living in London was very unsettling for him and he put in a transfer request which was instantly rejected. Arsenal were keen to sign him but the Chelsea board refused point-blank to sell their star player to their bitterest rivals. A reverse situation arose when Abramovich allegedly bid for Arsenal superstar Thierry Henry. Even the king's ransom on offer could not tempt them. The balance of power had suddenly shifted in the capital. When Hughie was playing for Chelsea, though, it was a vastly different story. Arsenal had established a power base as strong as that of Manchester United in the last decade of the twentieth century.

To placate Hughie, he was made captain of Chelsea (as he had been in the honeymoon period with Newcastle). The position, whilst prestigious, carried no real power or financial rewards and after a while it added to his increasing frustration. His international career had ground to a halt because the Scotland selectors were no longer picking players that were employed by English clubs. (It could be said that Zola's career and to a lesser extent Roberto Di Matteo's with Italy met a similar fate when they decamped to London.) A succession of centre-forwards were chosen but nobody could replace Hughie. The discerning reader will be aware that praise comes no higher.

THE CUP RUN

The 1931–32 season proved to be chequered, to say the least. Christmas found the Blues one place off the bottom and sinking fast. In that turbulent time, Chelsea called upon 26 players as they strove to find both form and consistency. They were potentially capable of doing so very much better. In 2002–03, Claudio Ranieri used 23 in the whole of the Premiership. Yet, 'The Tinkerman' Ranieri and his scatter-gun selections used nineteen players in just two matches, Spurs and Sparta Prague, at the start of the following season.

Both the Alecs, Cheyne and Jackson, struggled with injuries. Cheyne was a particular disappointment. His goals dried up and his general forward play was erratic. Sometimes, his game was as wild as a March hare. Jackson's attacking bent was curbed by his continuing ankle problems. He was at his most lethal when he reached the byline and crossed for the rampaging ex-Newcastle striker. The only consistent element was Hughie, who was, as always, scoring regularly and leading the line with as much aggression and panache as ever.

They took some whippings: 3–6 at home to Villa, the wonderfully named 'Pongo' Waring hitting four; Dixie Dean went one better scoring five as Everton won 2–7. Ken Bates was born on 4 December 1931. A few days later, West Bromwich scored four times without reply.

Once again, the FA Cup was the only option available to them. The first tie saw them drawn away to Tranmere Rovers. The Merseysiders shook Chelsea by taking an early lead but then Hughie scored twice to earn the Blues a scarcely deserved draw. Pictures of Hughie scoring in that match depict him in the unusual striped shirt that Chelsea wore that day.

The only other striped strip I recall Chelsea wearing was the infamous Inter Milan blue-and-black outfit worn in the 2–0 semi-final defeat to Sheffield Wednesday in April 1966. Legend has it that Chelsea's Scottish manager, Tommy Docherty, saw Inter play at Anfield in the semi-final of the European Cup a year earlier. He was awe-inspired by the European Cup holders and World Club champions, a team fashioned by the genius of Helenio Herrera. It included the legendary Luis Suarez and the amazing talent that was Sandro Mazzola. Docherty's dream was to spawn a Chelsea team that could follow in the footsteps of Inter and dominate Europe. The first step was to look like them. Perhaps the signing of Hernan Crespo for £16.8m from Inter Milan was another step.

Hughie smashed in another beauty as Chelsea rolled over Tranmere 5–3 in the replay. The next round of the Cup saw Chelsea entertain West Ham at the Bridge. Gallacher was on target again as the Blues ran out easy 3–1 winners. It was a game that was marred by crowd trouble as Chelsea fans and the East Enders started a feud that is carried on to this day. The acquisition of crowd favourites Frank Lampard, Glen Johnson and Joe Cole did nothing in recent years to alleviate a tension that is always present amongst the two sets of fans. The West Ham crowd that afternoon were as vociferous as they were in the infamous clashes in the '80s. Maybe it was the area, home of Jack the Ripper, the Elephant Man and the Kray twins. They spent most of the afternoon questioning Hughie's sexuality. Hughie silenced them in the best manner possible, scoring with a blistering shot on the turn after Alec Jackson's corner was only partially cleared. The undervalued Mark Stein scored a similar goal for Glenn Hoddle's team of 1995, silencing racial abuse from a section of the Upton Park crowd.

In the fifth round, Chelsea were drawn against Sheffield Wednesday, who were slugging it out with Arsenal for the title. Hughie missed the Cup-tie through injury but Chelsea won after a replay. Stamford Bridge had 60,004 shoehorned into the ground. In the drawn game at Hillsborough, former Wembley Wizard Tommy Law scored for Chelsea in front of another large crowd. In 1989, the same terraces were to prove a deathtrap for the fans in the Liverpool–Forest Cup semi-final. It begs the question, did things improve over the years?

The quarter-final draw pitched Chelsea against Liverpool and a return back to Merseyside. Liverpool was a notoriously unlucky ground for the Londoners, who have only had a handful of hard-won victories there in their entire history. They started their momentous 2003–04 season with a victory on Merseyside, thanks to a late winner from Jimmy Floyd Hasselbaink. The Gallacher-era Chelsea side finally gelled as a team that day in Liverpool, steamrolling the men in blood-red shirts 0–2. A gleeful Hughie slammed in the second to clinch the match in front of a stunned Kop. In goal for Liverpool was the legendary Irish international Elisha Scott. He had joined Liverpool in 1912 and was still playing for them 20 years later. Scott's duels with Gallacher were the stuff of dreams. Harold Miller, that day a midfield dynamo for the Londoners, crashed in a tremendous drive that Scott spilled and Hughie did the rest.

Near the end of the match, Liverpool threw everything but the Kop at Chelsea, in a desperate effort to stay in the Cup. There were fears that Anfield was on fire when what appeared to be a thick cloud of smoke began rising from the tightly packed Kop. There was no need to evacuate the 57,804 crowd, however, the 'smoke' turning out to be steam rising from the bodies of the supporters.

The Wee Man was smoking, though, as Chelsea roared to the semi-final. They had never won the Cup and hopes were sky high amongst the fans. Chelsea drew Newcastle, again avoiding Arsenal, who were red-hot favourites for the competition. Gallacher could not wait to clash swords with his old team but the semi-final jinx that was to haunt Chelsea throughout the twentieth century struck again. Two early goals from the Geordies gave the Blues an impossible hill to climb. Jack Allen, Hughie's replacement at number 9, side-footed a simple goal to put the Geordies ahead. Tommy Lang (not to be confused with Langley) scored a heartbreaking second with the Chelsea defence missing in action. Lang was a constant threat to Chelsea. He had survived being bitten during that Ambrosiana match on the ill-fated tour a few years earlier. Hughie refused to admit defeat, though, and just on half-time gave Chelsea heart with an opportunist strike. 'Like a trout slipping round a rock,' a reporter for *The Times* commented. The second-half was a direct contest between Hughie and Newcastle's England keeper Albert McInroy. What a duel it was! Only a string of wonder saves kept Newcastle ahead as Gallacher tried every trick in his extensive book to equalise. At one point, Hughie found himself a few yards out with the ball at his feet after a terrific scramble on the goal line. He cracked in a powerful shot but McInroy reacted instinctively and brilliantly to push the ball away. It was a miracle on the level of the loaves and the fishes. In the closing minutes, Newcastle were pinned in their own penalty area. The ball rattled around the box as Chelsea poured down on them. Wave after wave of attack ensued, like one of those Chinese Red Army human waves from the Korean War. They held out, though, and went on to win the Cup. A good goalkeeper can win you the Cup: Peter Bonetti did for Chelsea.

It was the nearest Hughie ever came to winning an FA Cup medal. It was another 40 years before Chelsea were to eventually lift the Cup itself after a replay at Old Trafford; a further 27 before they won it at Wembley. Hughie took a modicum of revenge a few weeks later, scoring three in a 4–1 victory over Newcastle. His hat-trick included two of the most clinically finished chances ever seen at the Bridge. Hughie was like Schumacher today at the Grand Prix. He knew all the angles, the edges, the odds. Despite his off-the-field antics, his football mind was like an Apple Mac. His eyes and feet were the software. McInroy had won the semi-final on Huddersfield's pitch but Hughie extracted his pound of flesh. Alec Jackson grabbed the other goal. As the Cup dream perished, so did Chelsea's season. Another fizzle-out. Chelsea finished the season without any trophies, 12th in the table, winning 16 and drawing half that figure.

PUBLIC ENEMY

> What's the point of getting sober if you're not forgiven? You might as well keep drinking.
> Michael Barrymore, Edinburgh Festival, August 2003

Soon, trouble found our hero again. Hughie was enjoying the hot summer and one balmy evening decided to take himself off to the cinema. His favourite movie, William Wellman's *Public Enemy*, was showing, his screen idol James Cagney appearing in one of his most famous roles. It is worth noting that *Enemy* was considered to be the definitive gangster movie of its time. Cagney's complete comprehension of the part shot him to worldwide fame. The bleak reality and cold nihilism of the film impressed Gallacher, who could identify with the young hoodlum. To him, it was so vivid. One of the requirements of being successful is the ability to bear envy and even plain dislike. On leaving the cinema foyer (the gruesome finish had shocked audiences and had led to calls for it to be banned), he found himself side-boxed by a gang of Fulham fans. Nowadays, in a poll of the most violent and dangerous hooligan fans, Fulham's name would not figure very high. In the '30s, though, there was a much harder element which attached itself to Chelsea's neighbours. The hooligans had an active dislike for Chelsea. Contemptuous and provocative, they chanted abuse at the little striker, cursing him like drunken stokers and pulling at his expensive clothes. Fulham Broadway was still known as Walham Green and Hughie took refuge in a café a few yards down from the Tube station. It's a Virgin record shop today. The Fulham thugs followed him into the café, spewing a barrage of venom at him. It ended up, in the words of the all-time Chelsea fan and expert on crowd control, the late Mick Greenaway, in 'an off'. Mick deserves a place in the history of Chelsea. Born yards from the ground in Billing Street, he was the fans' acknowledged figurehead in the Shed for nearly 30 years.

Punches were thrown, chairs and tables knocked over, windows smashed, food sent flying, skin and hair everywhere. The police were called. Hughie, the fist magnet, was arrested and carted off to the station sporting a shiny black eye. He had not been in a scrimmage like that since Arsenal visited the Bridge. Granted bail, he appeared before the magistrates the next day. Putting on the demeanour of a victim and tastefully dressed in his Chelsea blazer, Gallacher was not convicted. Instead, he was ordered to put ten shillings (50p, almost a euro) into the poor box.

The incident was met with John Leslie-style headlines. Pictures of Hughie, hair brilliantined and highly polished blazer buttons gleaming, made the front pages. Of course, the Chelsea star received the full treatment, being castigated for this headline-grabbing felony, portrayed as a pseudo-thug and troublemaker. Hughie was the new Jimmy Cagney. Today, the footballers are protected by a phalanx of minders. Dennis Wise allegedly had an easier ride (if you excuse the pun) when the pensioner cabbie would not give him one outside Terry Venables' club, Scribes.

Sentenced to three months in prison, he was subsequently acquitted after being given leave to appeal. In Hughie's case, though, Chelsea were furious at their most expensive player's discombobulation. Just as the disastrous European tour upset the old hierarchy and signalled the end of Hughie's career at Newcastle, the Walham Green shenanigans started the rift between him and Chelsea. His obvious boredom in London did not go unnoticed by the management. When the season restarted, he was dropped from the Newcastle away trip: denying him a return to his favourite stomping ground in the Northeast and another reunion with the adoring Toon Army. It seemed petty and Hughie seethed inwardly at the titanic injustice of it all. Chelsea were tonked 4–1.

One of the most famous quotes of the era of celebrity was Andy Warhol's prediction that 'Everyone will be famous for 15 minutes'. Celebrity would eventually cease to have any value. Gallacher had a lot more than 15 minutes but the dandy in the Chelsea blazer was the first celebrity footballer.

PLAYER POWER

The 1932–33 season was to prove to be one of the most traumatic seasons in the strife-filled history of Chelsea. If the closing years of the twentieth century belonged to the hackneyed phrase 'Girl Power' then the 1930s saw the start of player power. It was born at Stamford Bridge. How ironic! In a remarkable parallel to the Osgood–Hudson–Sexton three-headed-monster battles that destroyed the brilliant '70s Chelsea side, the Gallacher–Jackson power struggle had almost as destructive an influence on the club. Hughie and his mates basically paid for spit. Discipline in the club was poor. Amidst a blizzard of egos, delusional aspirations and agendas, money was, as it always is, the root of all evils. In the twenty-first century, football is a billion-pound industry. After the Abramovich takeover, Chelsea were all of a sudden arguably the richest club in the world. The resources available to them were seemingly limitless as their patron's fortune grew at scarcely measurable rates. In the Depression-hit 1930s, it was a looking-glass world; it offered the players illusions of hope which were only shattered when touched.

David Beckham was rumoured to be earning over £100,000 a week playing for Real Madrid, a decade after joining Manchester United as a schoolboy. It was said that he lived in a fabulous property with a huge veranda overlooking his private pool area, gazebo and landscaped gardens. It would have taken Gallacher, who earned £500 a year, centuries to earn what the England captain took home in a month. In 1932, just as Beckham had been lured by millions of euros, the top London stars had been approached by European clubs. Alec Jackson had been the first to have been tapped by the Johnny Foreigners and had threatened to quit Stamford Bridge unless Chelsea broke the maximum-wage structure. His unforgettable performance at Wembley for the Wizards made him a legend. The Chelsea crowd, always connoisseurs of the exotic, realised he was a special player. Similar in style to Steve McManaman (another player who, during his spell at Madrid, earned an absolute fortune), Jackson loved nothing more than dribbling past his defender. Like Beckham, he was something of a free-kick virtuoso. If the England midfielders knew their worth and got it, then Jackson aspired to it. He had no agent or team of lawyers to help and advise him.

Unlike the stars today, Alec's insurrection could not benefit from any Bosman ruling under which he was free to move to another club at the end of his contract. Chelsea were determined to make an example of the Scottish rebels who had the audacity to challenge the system. Like in Westerns, the pioneers always get the arrows in the back. The management were prepared to sacrifice the glittering talents of the Wizard of Wembley and any other insurrectionists who challenged them on a point of principle. Just like 40 years later, when I was ramrodding the Bridge, the board of directors were prepared to jettison similar towering talents in Osgood and Hudson rather than accede to player power. It was a slightly different kind of problem in the 1970s, of course. Osgood and his long-haired amigo had personality problems and major differences with their manager, Dave Sexton. Hudson used Sexton as a conduit for his anger and frustration. Chelsea were about to plunge into financial freefall and the revenue from selling two of the best players of their generation was another issue.

In the '30s, the Chelsea board effectively ended the career of Alec Jackson at the age of 26 – an age when, even today, a player is acknowledged to be at the peak of his powers. The flamboyant Jackson, really on his game, was driven from the highest level into non-League football. It was an outrage.

Hughie and Tommy Law were approached by the crack French side Nîmes to join them. A deal was almost cut that was as staggering for those times as the riches given to Beckham and McManaman at the Bernabeu. However, the deal crashed at the last moment and the pair stayed put. Rumours were rife, though, and not for the first time or certainly the last Chelsea were in a state of flux and ready for the wrecking ball. The Aberdeen ace Alec Cheyne and fellow Scot Andy Wilson did end up going to France – the first Chelsea Eurostars, you might say. The squabbles continued as the stars argued that they were worth more than some of the lesser mortals in the team. That never changes. In a radio interview, Jimmy Greaves warned in the early days of the Abramovich reign that after the initial euphoria had waned and the pats on the back had subsided, then the real problems would emerge amongst the huge galaxy of stars assembled at the club.

Chelsea slid towards the bottom of the League in 1932–33. Morale was very low and the whole team was disgruntled. At the end of October, Chelsea travelled up to Blackpool for a League game; winter had come unusually early and they encountered freak arctic conditions. Chelsea were thrashed 4–0 with the tangerine-shirted Jimmy Hampson scoring three. They ended up with six men on the field, the other five players retiring to the dressing-room suffering from exposure. It summed up the season and gave Chelsea a reputation of being a soft touch, a tag that dogged them for the rest of the century.

In the end, they missed relegation by two points, finishing a grim eighteenth. Bolton and Blackpool were relegated. A sudden burst of form in the closing matches kept them afloat. How typical of Chelsea Football Club to internally combust, then, at the last gasp, start performing. One of their notable victories was a 1–4 thrashing of Cup finalists Manchester City at Maine Road, which included a sublime Gallacher hat-trick. Leeds were crushed 6–0 at the Bridge, Hughie scoring with an amazing dipping volley. The evening before, the United players were taking an early evening stroll, rubbernecking the Kings Road, when they saw a scruffy little man thrown out of a pub and into the gutter. They recognised the wino as the then-current Chelsea centre-forward, the same player who destroyed them the next day.

Only Hughie kept his form and performed consistently with precious little support. (The previous season, Alec Jackson had scored 16 times and he was sorely missed in both making and taking goals.) Gallacher's goal total of 19 kept Chelsea up and made him the Blues leading scorer, celebrating 10 straight years as the top scorer of whoever he was playing for, be it Airdrie, Newcastle or Chelsea. He was a real winner he always delivered. It was easy to see why people in the game were wary of him.

THE ROYLE FAMILY

Arsenal completely dominated the '30s and were the true giants of the English game. They exerted an iron grip over the major honours. Chelsea were more a cabaret act than a football team. Hughie loved his tussles with the rampant Gooners, just as Peter Osgood enjoyed his duels with Jack Charlton and the Leeds defence of the '70s. They were a team of snarling pit-bull players and in their short time equally as dominant. The north London club invariably came out top in their '30s clashes with Chelsea but Gallacher still waged a one-man war against their armour-clad defence. England defender Eddie Hapgood was a sworn enemy; they would clash each time they met. I recall in recent years Graeme Le Saux had a long-running feud with Arsenal's Lee Dixon.

Highbury unveiled its new West Stand that season and the clash with Chelsea was chosen as the opening ceremony. It was always considered then, as it is today, a high-profile fixture. Chelsea were hammered 4–1, with David Jack calling all the shots. A crowd of 53,206, which included the future King Edward VIII, came to the Highbury garden party. Hughie, in his capacity as Chelsea captain, had to introduce the team to the monarch to be. It was viewed as a very important event, the Royal family usually only attending Wembley Cup finals. Hughie struck up an instant repartee with the then Prince of Wales, so much so he put a friendly arm around him during the introductions. This was obviously a gesture that Hughie had picked up from his post-match bonding sessions with all those friendly, helpful referees that gave him such adequate protection, not to say the habits he picked up from The Corinthians. Of course, the manhandling of a future king by a common or garden footballer was seen as a massive breach of etiquette. The social gaffe was illustrated all around the world and the legend of Hughie Gallacher grew even more. At least he hadn't gargled with Scotch and water before the match!

I was lucky in my day. I had the perfect diplomat to deal with such occasions and one of nature's gentlemen in Ronnie Harris, the Hugh Grant of football.

AND NOW I FACE THE FINAL CURTAIN

The last full season that Hughie was to play at Stamford Bridge was 1933–34. He made a total of only 28 appearances for Chelsea, his lowest since he entered English football. Blessed with superhuman stamina, his clock was overwound. He was about to confront the nasty reality of age in a footballer: waning powers and the loss of dreams. The Wee Man managed to finish top goalscorer again with 16 goals, another respectable total considering. Chelsea had a new manager by then, Leslie Knighton, who replaced Calderhead. Gallacher had an uneasy relationship with his new gaffer. It was an awkward season for the ex-manager of Birmingham. Once again, the chequebook was flourished and more imports were made from across the border. They included the Scotland goalkeeper John Jackson, who vied for the goalkeeping jersey with England keeper Vic Woodley. (Jackson was injured and lost the job to Woodley though he was number one for his country.) Chelsea have been well stocked with great goalkeepers over the years. In the '60s, for a short while, they had two England keepers on the books, Peter Bonetti and Alex Stepney.

Chelsea struggled. Leslie Knighton flirted briefly and unconvincingly with a new defensive system but it leaked goals. Hughie played infrequently; he was by this stage the wrong side of 30. His face was seamed and his hair more grizzled and a bit less plentiful than before he came south. The years of fierce challenges and ruthless bone-jarring tackles were rapidly catching up with him, the pathos of greatness slowly in decline. Gallacher was still the best goal taker there was, though. The fans knew it and loved him even more.

One freezing afternoon, a few days after Christmas, Chelsea were playing Stoke. Hughie was lying injured on the frosty Stamford Bridge pitch, the victim of another crude kicking. Stoke defenders, tiring of Gallacher's extravagant behaviour and large press coverage, had come to Stamford Bridge with the intention of 'beating him up', as Nigel Benn used to say. The other players stood around sniggering and waiting for him to get to his feet. It was a dreary game and Chelsea were holding on to a narrow lead given to them by Tommy Law. Suddenly, a cockney voice boomed out of the Shed, cutting through the stale smoke and crepuscular gloom: 'Practise, Chelsea. Practise!'

You had to be there to appreciate the irony of it, my father used to say when he told the story.

Chelsea had the briefest of Cup runs. Hughie got the only goal of the game, after extra time in a replay with West Brom in the third round. Another replay took place against Nottingham Forest in the next round and Gallacher scored twice as Chelsea cruised to a 0–3 win. Stanley Matthews ended the Cup run with a deuce as Stoke knocked the Blues out 3–1. What a career the late Stanley had – he must have been the only player to have played against Gallacher and Ron Harris! When interviewed on his 80th birthday and asked if he had any regrets, he jokingly replied that he 'retired too early'. In May 1963, Matthews helped Stoke beat Chelsea 0–1 in a vital Second Division promotion match at Stamford Bridge. He was a few months short of his 50th birthday.

Scotland recalled Hughie for the England clash at Wembley. It had been four hard, long years since he had last played for his country. During that time, nobody had been able to stake a claim to the number 9 shirt. It could also be argued that nobody has worn it with as much distinction since. Billy Dodds, who only made two substitute appearances for Chelsea, was the last player from Stamford Bridge to wear it in more recent times. Frank McAvennie, Maurice Johnston and Duncan Ferguson did their best to keep the bad-boy centre-forward image going with their antics.

In 1935, the composition of the Scotland side was wrecked by the 'Anglo' bans and the politics behind them, dictated by the cabal that ran the game then. It was obvious even then that the most talented players would be sought out by the highest paymasters. Isn't that right, Mr Abramovich?

There was to be no storybook return for Hughie, though, as Scotland went down 0–3. The Battler from Bellshill was Scotland's best player, leading the England defence a merry dance with his hard running and constant pressing.

Once again, Chelsea stayed up by a mere two points whilst Gallacher's former employees in the Northeast nosedived into the old Second Division to begin their long, long term in purgatory. The transfer rumour mill was working double shifts, as it still does about Chelsea players. Every week, Hughie was linked with a new club: Manchester United (then not the force they are today) were in for him; Everton tried to sign Hughie as a replacement for the old warhorse Dixie Dean. Both moves might have reignited his career but in the end they stalled. Agents are blamed today for most of the problems in the game but were Hughie to have had the services of über-agent Pini Zahavi then things might have turned out a great deal better for him.

A WEDDING AND A BANKRUPTCY

Hughie was becoming increasingly hemmed in by his dire financial situation, his stuttering career at Chelsea and the grandiose pressures of stardom. His marital problems added to his financial ones. We all know that one. Hughie had been trying to obtain a divorce from his first wife in order to marry his new sweetheart, Hannah. In 1926, he failed with his first court action and lost out again on appeal a year later. It was third time lucky for him in 1932 but this also went to an appeal, which he eventually won. The legal fees, as in any era, were astronomical and drained all of Hughie's meagre resources – those not already eroded by his profligate lifestyle. In the autumn of 1934, he literally ended up in Carey Street facing a bankruptcy petition. Once again, the story of his misdemeanours made headlines. It is interesting to note that the extent of his debt was just under £800, roughly the cost of a season ticket in the West Stand today. As always, when it came to walking the walk, everybody secretly was in it for what they could get. Hughie's debt was less than the 12,087 franc meal enjoyed by the Chelsea 'High Command' during a Champions League trip to Marseille before the Russian Revolution. The new owner has sushi delivered from a swanky Mayfair restaurant on match days. It would appear that there's not much change from £100 a pop for the trendy Japanese cuisine.

Hughie was desperate for cash and his only chance of obtaining a wedge was to move from Chelsea. Free to wed, he married Hannah shortly after the start of the 1934–35 season. The ceremony took place at Hammersmith Registry and, though not in the Posh and Becks league for glitz, it was a media event. It was an actual phenomenon for that era. A large crowd gathered, the press and the newsreels (the nearest thing to Sky News) covered it. What a handsome couple they made; they were the embodiment of fashion and glamour. If only Hannah had been a singer in a group or a weather girl, all their financial problems would have been solved.

Footballers' marriages have always been of great interest to the press. Within a few weeks of joining Chelsea, the problems in Adrian Mutu's marriage to Alexandra, a glamorous TV presenter, were the subject of extensive tabloid articles. Whilst on the subject of television presenters, the showboating Juan Sebastián Verón's near ruinous affair with Laura Franco, Argentina's sexiest television star, received almost as much coverage as his fall-out with Fergie. The papers also carried news of former Chelsea manager Gianluca Vialli's marriage to the splendidly named Cathryn White-Cooper at the Marquess of Northampton's drum, Castle Ashby.

Hughie wore one of his three-piece specials, a handsome tweed job with lapels that must have been a foot wide. (He was the first person at Chelsea to wear handmade shirts.) Later in the day, he went off to play for the Blues. I do not have a note if he scored in the afternoon, but I am sure he did in the evening.

Gallacher's name was forever being linked to the illegal payments scandals. There was heavy betting on the matches and wealthy businesspeople populated the fringes of the game even then; incentives were offered to players. Hughie's parlous financial state left him very open to such inducements. More allegations were made against him than even Fash had to contend with but Hughie was never convicted of anything. He would never have been party to any bribes to fix a match. Nobody in the sport was as determined or focused as the Wee Man.

The Scottish ace's argument for his increased-salary demands was that he was an entertainer and should be paid accordingly, on the same basis as his idols on the silver screen. Today, there is such a parity but for decades clubs had no conception of the huge debt they owed the players. Now they owe huge debts because of the players. The cult of Beckham in the early years of the twenty-first century is greater than that of any pop group or film star of the day. Former Chelsea midfielder Vinnie Jones, who I think would have been an acolyte of Hughie, launched a movie career on the back of his football personae. You see, as Mick Greenaway would say: 'The media create these football heroes and then, sooner or later, they get fed up with them.'

THE SWASTIKAS

Around this time, Chelsea arranged a short tour of Germany. It seemed a curious decision as a fellow called Adolf Hitler had taken control of the Fatherland and had some interesting ideas about future European competitions. His idea of a Champions League involved the Third Reich top of the group and guess who at the bottom. The grounds were covered in huge swastikas and flags. One of the pre-match rituals was a Nazi salute by both sides, given when their national anthem played. No pictures of this particularly tasteless incident were available. (There is one of the England team giving the salute in the Olympic Stadium in Berlin in 1938. Len Goulden, a future Chelsea star, scored a brilliant goal in the 3–6 slaughter.) Years later, some elements of the Chelsea crowd must have remembered this obscure piece of trivia because they would often spend long periods in matches doing *Sieg-Heil* salutes. The boot-droogs of Stamford Bridge and their Nazi salutes seem a long time ago.

By the late autumn of 1934, Gallacher was no longer guaranteed a regular first-team place at Chelsea. The cynical Leslie Knighton was persisting with Hughie's long-term understudy George Mills. At 32, bankrupt and as volatile as ever, Hughie was seen as being past his sell-by date. In seven starts he scored twice, both in away games. He shot the only goal of the match at Birmingham and a consolation in a 5–2 drubbing at Leeds, his last game in Chelsea blue. In 144 games for Chelsea, he notched 81 goals – one more than Zola and five more than Wise. That worked out at a goal every 1.78 games. His average was 0.56. (Compare that to the all-time record holder Bobby Tambling's average of 0.55 (he took 366 games to achieve this, though), or Roy Bentley with 0.41. Hasselbaink's was 0.44. Mutu scored two in his first two games.)

Derby signed him for a fee of £2,750. From this, £200 of the fee went directly to the bankruptcy court in Carey Street to help straighten out his debts, or repair his credit, as they say today. An illegal £300 gift was later alleged to have sweetened the deal. I suppose this would have been considered a 'bung' but Hughie kept shtum and nothing was proved. Derby were one of the most entertaining sides of that era. They were a cavalier attacking side who, like Scotland, believed in playing nippy, ball-playing wingers. This was food and drink to Hughie, who had seen a declining service at Stamford Bridge, particularly after the departure of Jackson. The Rams centre-forward was an England striker called Jack

Bowers. He was a prototype Alan Shearer-style goalscorer but he had sustained a serious knee injury, the surgery on which was complicated. He also needed complete rest and recuperation so Derby signed the Chelsea forward as a short-term replacement. It was to many judges in the game a tremendous gamble to take. Hughie, like those other Chelsea greats, Greaves and Osgood, proved that they were never more dangerous than when they were being written off. He remains one of the few players whose myth has not been destroyed by re-evaluation.

In November 1934, Hughie Gallacher left the jaded denizens of Stamford Bridge and made his Derby debut at the then Baseball Ground against Birmingham City. Within seven minutes, he had scored with a cracking drive against the England goalkeeper Harry Hibbs. Harry could only watch transfixed as the ball whistled over him and high into the roof of the net; he was a great adversary of Hughie and they had huge mutual respect for one another. A famous story of the day relates what happened when the pair met on the Fulham Road on the morning of a match. Hughie nodded over to Hibbs but the England keeper was already diving into the gutter to save the 'header'. That story still does the rounds in different guises, often featuring Dixie Dean in the lead role, but Hughie was the original.

Gallacher exploded at Derby, scoring heavily in a three-week burst. A goal away at Portsmouth, then a double in a 9–3 thrashing of poor old West Brom, the second of which was a spectacular half volley, savagely hit as he raced into the penalty area. The irony was that in accepting the loss of his godlike talent, he began to regain it. Belying his age and defying logic, Hughie went goal crazy in the next match, scoring all five as Blackburn were crushed 2–5 at their place. He was simply unstoppable that freezing afternoon. Hughie's speed off the mark was incredible; he seemed to be everywhere, out on the left, then on the right, in the middle, even dropping back to morph into the midfield to confuse Blackburn. The first goal was his 300th in top-class football on both sides of the border. The fifth was brilliant, as good as any he had scored in his previous haul. The new Derby striker just strolled through the ruins of the Blackburn defence to score with a full-circle spin and thunderous shot. In those weeks, he was outrageous, the best striker of the twentieth century, with no sign of the impenetrable confidence in himself crumbling.

Another great striker, Ted Drake, was at his peak for Arsenal and bagged four as Chelsea, without Hughie, caved in 2–5 at home. Knighton should have been pelted with the previous week's tomatoes for selling him.

Hughie started his career in the Midlands like a whirlwind and by the end of the season he had smashed in 24 goals in 30 games. Derby finished in the top six whilst Chelsea continued to flounder and staggered up to twelfth place. Lowly Luton knocked Chelsea out of the Cup in the third round. Hughie had the last word that season.

END OF THE LINE

Hughie gradually wound down his amazing career, the Second World War finally putting an end to the amazing trail of goals. Today, thanks to the large squad system, players like Zola can extend their dazzling careers by being used in short bursts or by clever rotation. Such a system was introduced to the English game by Ruud Gullit. It saves wear and tear and allows players to be utilised in games where they are best suited. Artful timing is the name of the game. Vialli was a past master at it. Like a faded chanteuse using her last pair of tights sparingly, the increasingly fragile talent of Gianfranco could be stopped in time and perpetuated by myth. Zola was 37 when he left Chelsea. Jimmy Greaves retired from the game at 31. There was no such luxury for Hughie. In the third and last act of his career, he still had the glamour, the smouldering aura of greatness and astounding professionalism. The ageing aristocrat became almost a gun for hire, moving from club to club like the cowboy Paladin in the classic Western show *Have Gun Will Travel*. The defenders still took liberties but now he had a world-weary indifference to it all. He cured himself of his Tourette's syndrome whilst playing. In 624 games, he scored 463 goals. He is still the third-highest scorer of *all* time. Football has changed so much I cannot see these figures being overhauled.

Hughie spent the war years working in an arms factory and driving an ambulance. He had a few more rivers to cross and played in countless exhibition games to raise funds for the war effort. I searched the archives for records of any return matches at the Bridge but could find nothing. When the war ended in 1945, he tried to get a job in the game. His reputation and huge profile, though, so widely and ferociously lauded, made it impossible to gain employment in the only thing he knew about and cared for. This was a terrible indictment of the crusty establishment that ran football. It would be nice to say things will change under the 'Russian Revolution'. Talents like Hudson and Bowles were also unable to find employment in the game. Nobody knew better than them the pitfalls of vacuous fame and success at an early age. It was like life lived in the Colosseum. They concentrated on being interesting, not interested. Who would have been better qualified in advising young players? If Hudson had spoken to Jody Morris before he started frequenting the Wellington Club maybe he would have been the next Alan Hudson, as he was strongly tipped to be. Instead, he became the old Alan Hudson.

Maybe the mavericks lacked all the qualities to be managers but as youth-team coaches or as advisers they would definitely have brought something to the table. In the last weeks of his young life, Matthew Harding spoke of harnessing the knowledge of Hudson and myself to develop a think tank for the youth system. Sadly, it never came to pass. Harding died, and Hudson was last in the papers accused of shoplifting. I look at the paucity of home-bred London talent, though, and know something needs to be done. I am saddened to witness the present generation bearing the effects of past choices.

Gallacher, like Hudson, drifted down. It is so easy to trample on the legacy of a star name. Hughie took up employment in a few blue-collar jobs. He was keen to take a pub, about the only option left to ex-pros in those days. Hannah thought that he would be better off away from the grim beer-and-vomit-sodden world of the licensee. Hughie settled down to domesticity. He no longer caroused till dawn, his temper was still quick but it was years since he had been in a fight in a bar. Gallacher wrote a column for his local paper and flashes of the old Hughie emerged in scathing attacks on Newcastle. What ex-player did not savage the modern game? We are warned never to trust the artist, only the art. Eventually, he was banned from the press-box at St James'.

On New Year's Eve 1950, tragedy struck Hughie when his wife died of heart trouble. It would be fair to say that he never recovered. Hughie seemed to age overnight. He became more tired and vulnerable. In the last few months of Hannah's life, he had become increasingly aware of the deterioration in her condition and desperately tried to stabilise his home life. Her death completely shattered him and he began the slow train ride into madness and death. Once again, the experience of loving someone brought him only pain and loneliness. After Hannah's death, Gallacher's moods were subject to severe stress. He became increasingly disillusioned and disappointed with his life. In low spirits, he became sentimental and very self-pitying. In his rare up periods, he was overzealous. The expensive suits were long gone but he still wore the flash overcoats, although they were getting threadbare and fraying. He still kept himself immaculate, though, as if dreading a return to the squalor of the pits.

Reporters who talked to his neighbours about his state of mind were greeted with a few mumbled words and then they scuttled away. It was like in the Hammer horror movies when the peasants are afraid to talk about the vampire in the castle. Hughie's life was a firestorm. Today, his name is little, very little, more than a name on ageing newspapers that have gone out of circulation. Hughie Gallacher appeared, and then disappeared, in much the same way as a sheet from one of those old papers would twist and twirl down a dark and windy street on a winter's night.

Gallacher was a rare talent, born out of oppression, out of the particular economic and social circumstances in the early years of the twentieth century. Verón's early adolescence was also tempestuous. He ran with Buenos Aires street gangs and was a joyrider. Crespo wanted to be a binman. What drove all of them was the conviction that they were the masters of their own destiny. When Hughie ran into the limits of his mastery – the inability to hold on to money, his first failed marriage and his constant clashes with authority on and off the field – he had to face the hard facts of life. Like Best, Gazza, Collymore, Hudson and Bowles, he was not really comfortable with life. Gallacher was a ghost from a past few had heard about. Yet, in reality, he was light years away, waiting for the others to catch up. Gallacher's career history states that he played and lived with a deeper autonomy than other players. Only Hudson came forth at Chelsea to confirm that autonomy. Gallacher was to discover the limits of the autonomy and make them real. The fact that he played with more ferocity and passion than the others marks him as being the most important figure of that era. Would it be premature to say I see flashes of that in Adrian Mutu?

In the first decade of the twentieth century, football made a rent in the culture of Britain and it was the Mears family who started it by buying Stamford Bridge and turning it into London's first theatre of dreams. It could be said that in the 1930s, Hughie Gallacher made a rent in football itself. The first 50 years of the twentieth century produced only one Hughie Gallacher. The next 50 years merely reproduced clones of Gallacher in Best, Hudson, Osgood, Gazza, Collymore et al.

STATION TO STATION

> I think I would more readily die for what I do not believe in than for what I hold to be true.
>
> Oscar Wilde

On the morning of Tuesday, 11 June 1957 Hughie Gallacher awoke in a place where reason faltered, tottering on the brink of psychic and psychotic thresholds. In the years since he had last kicked a ball on active service, Hughie had gone through chronic changes and had slowly become unhinged. Photographs of him in the last few months of his life are painful to look at. In his last years, Gallacher seemed like someone already living out amongst the shadows. One day he just dissolved into them. Someone commits suicide every 40 seconds.

'Early this mornin', ooh, when you knocked upon my door, And I said, "Hello, Satan, I believe it's time to go."' This line comes from the famous song 'Me and the Devil Blues', written by the enigmatic Robert Johnson, a legend of the genre, sometime in the 1930s, the same time that Hughie was causing havoc in the blue shirt for club and country. The story of Johnson is so vague, so shrouded in mystery that exact dates cannot be found. He was always depicted as a young hooligan, trapped in a tormented life of hedonism and fate. Legend has it that he sold his soul to the devil to become King of the Blues and was consequently pursued by demons intent on driving him to an early death. Colourful hocus pocus, perhaps, but a little spooky and not too far removed from the image of a maverick footballer. After all, how many young men would sell their very souls to be captain of Chelsea or King of the Blues today? The reason that players like Frank Lampard and John Terry are so popular with the inhabitants of the Matthew Harding Stand is that young men who pay their wages see them as mirror images of themselves.

That beautiful summer morning, Hughie did not go to the menial blue-collar job through which he eked out a living. Instead, he wandered about the town. Neighbours spotted him moving slowly in a stupor as if he was bone weary. He seemed distressed and deeply disturbed, taken up by the serious business of death. Only his eyes were gentle, as often is.

At noon, he was spotted climbing over the wire fence by the railway track at Belle Vue embankment. A trainspotter approached him; it was a warm day but the man was wearing a thick overcoat. It was in poor condition but looked as if it had been expensive at one time. Gallacher was wearing an expression on his face of half fretful resignation, half dreamy contentment. Hughie had one last body swerve in him which he took past the trainspotter and down onto the cinder track. In the distance, the whistle of the 12.08 Newcastle to Edinburgh express could be heard.

Later in the day, the headless body of Chelsea's and Scotland's greatest centre-forward was discovered alongside the track.

AFTERMATH

According to records, on 12 October 1935, a crowd of 82,905 crammed through the turnstiles into the Bridge to watch the mighty Arsenal strut their stuff. To this day, it remains the record crowd at Chelsea and unless Abramovich builds a new stand as high as the steel hoop of the new Wembley Stadium, it is unlikely to ever be beaten.

Arsenal took the lead but Joe Bambrick equalised for the home side. The gloriously self-aware Bambrick was the rising star in the Chelsea firmament. Signed from Linfield, the burly Irishman was already a legend over the water. In one season, he rattled in an amazing 94 goals. You read it right – 94 goals. I would have thought it deserved some form of recognition. By all accounts, he was a tremendous player. He owned an ancient sports car in Ireland, the bonnet held down by leather straps and when he was not scoring goals, he was roaring through villages terrorising the rural inhabitants.

The 1935–36 season was one of upheaval. In a few short weeks, the upper echelon of the Chelsea management team was decimated. First, my grandfather Joe, the vice-chairman of Chelsea and the creator of the club, died. His place was taken by my father, another Joe. He was to lead Chelsea for a further 30 years (longer than Ken Bates) and during that period we won the title.

Two further deaths on the Chelsea management team rocked the club to the very foundation: assistant secretary Bert Palmer, who began at Chelsea in 1907, and club secretary Claude Kirby both joined the great boardroom in the sky. Kirby was a great loss; he had a very modern and vital outlook, and great youthful energy.

Plans were drawn up to build a North Stand for the fans. The rickety structure on stilts went up the year that war broke out. It was to stand for three decades.

Chelsea just attacked throughout the season. Manager Leslie Knighton was determined to improve Chelsea's performances. After a poor start, Knighton shuffled the pack. If there was any blamestorming to be done, he did not want to end up like the previous sacked manager, Calderhead.

The undoubted star of the team was goalkeeper Vic Woodley, famous for his huge rustic caps. With the dearth of modern-day England international-level keepers, England could have used a goalkeeper of Vic's class. Signed from the Spartan League side Windsor and Eaton in the summer of 1931, the deal cost Chelsea the princely sum of £10. Like that other famous son of Windsor, Peter Osgood, it was one of the bargains of the century. Vic won 19 England caps. The legendary Dickie Spence lined up alongside Bambrick, goal machine George Mills and a new acquisition, the veteran Harry Burgess. They all hit double figures as Chelsea reached the dizzying heights of eighth in the League, their highest placing in fifteen years.

FOUR

THE RUSSIANS ARE COMING!

What's past is prologue.
William Shakespeare, *The Tempest*, Act 2, Scene 1

The match of the century with its sepia-tinted heritage could be said to be Chelsea's clash with Moscow Dynamo on 13 November 1945. Beyond official records, it was certainly the biggest crowd that ever gathered at Stamford Bridge. In excess of 100,000 exigent fans were present; about 20,000 of them gaining entry by smashing down the gates instead of paying to go through the turnstiles. For a 13-year-old Brian Mears it was his first-ever Chelsea match and all that that involves. The collection of lies, untruths and myths about the tour of the Russians hung together in such a way as to tell the absolute truth about the Dynamo team. In all of the thousands of matches featuring the Blues that I have seen since, nothing could ever approach the dynamic memory of Moscow. Like Orson Welles once said of his career: 'I started at the top and worked my way down.'

Let's wrap up the war years first. In 1937–38, Chelsea finished tenth. They started brightly, crushing Liverpool 6–1 in the first home match of the season, George Mills helping himself to three. Looking for strike power after the departure of Gallacher they had bought Joe Payne from Luton Town for £5,000. Joe had suddenly flashed into prominence with Luton, for whom he made his career debut in 1934. The Chesterfield-born Payne scored ten out of twelve League goals on 13 April 1936 during a match for Luton against Bristol Rovers. It was his first appearance at centre-forward. Even more remarkably, nine of his massive goal tally were scored consecutively – this is still a record. Are you reading, the two

Jimmies? In season 1936–37, he established another record by scoring 55 goals in the Third Division South. That was three more than the whole team managed for Chelsea that season – George Mills, we observe, scoring 22 of them for the Blues.

After a dozen games in 1937–38, Chelsea led the table from near neighbours Brentford. But Chelsea, being Chelsea, soon after fell apart at the seams and slid down to eventually finish tenth. It was a tough time for the club: Everton knocked them out of the Cup at the Bridge. Their classy side included the swashbuckling striker Tommy Lawton (more of him later) and Joe Mercer, who became one of the most famous managers of all time.

Season 1938–39 was the last League season for seven years because of the war. Chelsea finished twentieth, missing relegation by one point. Joe Payne ended up top scorer with 17 League goals. The only bright spot was a Cup run to the sixth round – it included an exciting 2–1 win over Arsenal but Grimsby eventually put the Blues out by scoring the only goal of a dreadful game at the Bridge. In typical Chelsea style, inspired by Joe Payne they thrashed them 5–1 the next week in a League game.

FROM TOMMY LAW TO TOMMY LAWTON

The imminent threat of war put an end to transfer dealings. You could say the window was shut for a long time. No club was going to risk an investment in new players with the strong likelihood that they could get blown to pieces in wartime action, with the result that Chelsea's side continued to grow old together. Tommy Law, the ex-Wembley Wizard, was still playing well into his 40s. Leslie Knighton left the club to be replaced by Billy Birrell. Knighton had been unable to bring any success to the club despite the wealth of talent he had at his disposal and was de-cruited, as they say in the Square Mile. People said he chopped and changed the side too much. Oh yeah. It felt like the world was getting ready to explode; with war imminent, it actually was. Things might never be the same again.

Stamford Bridge came through the war relatively unscathed. West London took a terrible pounding at the hands of the *Luftwaffe* and the first 'flying bomb' (a prototype guided missile) fell just down the road at Chiswick. Only two bombs actually fell on the football ground: one on the West Terrace, which now houses the Millennium Suite, and the other in front of the new North Stand which was under construction at the time (where the Matthew Harding Stand is now). They were hardly the MOAB super bombs used during the 2003 Iraqi war, though, and only superficial damage was done to the stadium. West Ham caused more damage in the

'60s when they tried to take the Shed from Mick Greenaway and his chums.

A huge balloon flew over the north end of the ground to prevent bombers from interrupting the games. That must have been where Sky got the idea for their airship from – today we would paint it Day-Glo orange and pack it with cameras.

Football still continued but was obviously downsized to a regional basis. The new league was called the Football League South and included Brentford, Portsmouth, Aldershot and Brighton. Gates were very small, understandably (3,441 packed out the Bridge on Christmas Day 1940 to see Fulham thumped 5–2), and there was little coverage in the press. Servicemen based in London guested for Chelsea in a precursor to the loan system of today. Future England manager Walter Winterbottom and Manchester United legend Matt Busby played for Chelsea during that period. Chelsea yo-yoed as always, finishing 21st (there were 34 teams in the League that year), 13th, 7th, 8th, 4th and 10th. The high spot, though, was a 2–0 victory over Millwall in the Football League South final played at Wembley in front of 90,000 supporters in April 1945, with George Wardle and John Macdonald scoring the goals for Chelsea. Charlton great Sam Bartram played in goal for Millwall, the team also including a player called Jimmy Jinks. D-Day and El Alamein were historic battles in the war but the victory against Millwall must rank as one of the most memorable. It made the Members Cup victories at Wembley pretty small beer. I begged my father to let me attend the Millwall game. He thought it would be too rough (even in those times, Millwall had a tough element in their support). The trophy commemorating this unique event was still in the trophy cabinet in my era. A priceless artefact from a bygone age.

When Chelsea played Moscow Dynamo they stood at 11th place in the Football League South. Football's treasured rattle-shaking 'golden age' was about to start.

Chelsea had played thirteen games, winning seven and drawing one. There were some bizarre scores amongst them. The structure of the League dictated that the clubs played each other home and away in consecutive matches. Chelsea entertained West Brom and after trailing 3–4 at the break (only five minutes in those days, by the way), they eventually recovered to win 7–4. The following Saturday, though, West Brom gained sweet revenge by beating Chelsea 8–1, which must have been some sort of record Chelsea away defeat in the Football League South. Only five players remained from the squad that existed before the outbreak of war, including England international goalkeeper Vic Woodley and Scotland winger Peter Buchanan. Buchanan was a favourite of mine, the missing link between Alec Jackson and Charlie Cooke, then add a twist of Pat Nevin. Chelsea had signed him from the youth academy side St Mungo in 1933. Peter found it hard to settle at first and returned home. Hughie Gallacher had spotted his potential, though, and badgered the coaching staff to persevere with the wee lad. Resigned from Wilshaw, Peter had a sensational trial match against Racing Club in Paris and never looked back from his flying start. He only won one Scotland cap, though, the war depriving him of further honours and seven years of his career.

Birrell, in an endeavour to rejuvenate the side, purchased England internationals Tommy Lawton from Everton for £11,500 and Len Goulden from West Ham in another Abramovich-style spending spree. Goulden at 33 was approaching the end of his exciting career but Tommy was only 26 and desperate to make up for lost time.

THE LIBERTINE

> Alan Moore: 'Who is Tommy Lawton?'
> Rupert Rigsby: 'Who is Tommy Lawton? Only the greatest centre-forward that ever lived. That's all. Look at them now prancing about the field like a lot of male models. All Tommy got when he scored was a brisk handshake. Not like today, score a goal and they end up covered in love bites.'
>
> *Rising Damp*

Rising Damp starred Leonard Rossiter (Rupert Rigsby) who lived next door to Stamford Bridge for a few years. Born in Liverpool, he was a lifelong Everton fan and always made the trip across the road when the Toffees came to town. Interesting that a comment like that was made in the 1970s, a time when Revie's Leeds dominated the game and centre-forwards like Joe Jordan roamed the earth. Such was the strength of the macho image exuded by Lawton to all those who saw him play, that it never left them.

When Chelsea signed him, he was the current England striker with a burning hunger to score goals. His average for England was 22 goals in 23 games, or 0.96. Tommy was settled at Everton but his wife's deteriorating health, exacerbated by the northern cold and damp, forced him to move south.

Born in Bolton on 6 October 1919 he soon showed what a prospect he was by scoring a hat-trick in an English schools international trial. On leaving school, he signed for Burnley (then in the Second Division).

Tommy made his debut as a 16-year-old amateur and in his second game scored twice against Swansea. At 17, he turned professional and celebrated with a hat-trick against Spurs, thus breaking the record for the youngest hat-trick scorer in League history. Everton swooped to buy him for £6,500, an outrageous price for the time.

Lawton once told my father an amusing story of his first visit to the ground. Boarding a tram on Lime Street in Liverpool, a conductor recognised him and said. 'Son, you're young Lawton, aren't you?' Preening himself at the new-found fame, Tommy nodded in agreement. 'You will never be as good as Dixie,' the conductor snapped.

Dixie Dean, Hughie Gallacher's old sparring partner, was coming to the end of his fabulous (it included 37 hat-tricks) career and Lawton had been bought to replace him. They played together for a spell but the all-time dream Merseyside goal partnership never really clicked. Lawton scored on his debut at Wolves but ended up on the wrong side of a 7–2 thrashing. That goal gave him the mantle of the youngest goalscorer for Everton until Wayne Rooney exploded onto the scene 65 years later. In his first two seasons at Everton, Lawton topped the nation's scoring charts. Who knows what would have happened to Dixie Dean's record of 349 League goals if the war had not intervened.

Tommy joined the army and became a PT instructor. He was just as prolific in the wartime regional leagues and guested for many teams, including several in London. Despite the constant threat of Hitler's bombers, the relative comfort of the big city and the constant sense of living on the edge hooked him. On being demobbed, he opted for the smoke and chose not to return to Merseyside. And so another Chelsea legend was born.

I saw Tommy before the Russian game, chatting with some fans, a gentleman and a legend, unassumingly masculine, grounded and polite. The Russians had watched Chelsea lose 2–3 at home to Birmingham the previous Saturday. The Cold War started in earnest a few years later, along with all that KGB, Philby, Burgess, McLean espionage stuff. People used to ask my father if the Dynamo team was a cover-up for a massive spying mission. If it was, the players were the best agents ever. They had certainly perfected their roles as footballers. Tommy made his debut for the Blues and hammered in two fine goals. The second was a vicious flick of his head as he soared above a pack of defenders. The Moscow side were mightily impressed by the big man who typified the stereotype of the bustling English centre-forward of that era. Chelsea played a long ball game in those days, in a style very reminiscent of Wimbledon in their pomp: the old Crazy Gang with the doggedness of Fash up front and little Wisey pumping in the crosses.

The physical side of the English centre-forward's game, shoulder charging and roughing up goalkeepers, was alien to the Russians. They even went so far as filming the drab Birmingham match so they could study more closely the physicality of Lawton's game. The cine camera equipment they watched it on looked like something made for showing silent movies.

Moscow Dynamo came to London in a spirit of great friendship between the two nations: the war had finished barely six months earlier and the British people were grateful to the Russians for their enormous contribution in helping the Allies win the conflict. They had lost millions of lives in smashing the German war machine and their courage and sacrifice had not gone unnoticed by the British people. Russian diplomats were regular visitors to Stamford Bridge and my father was delighted to accede to requests for match tickets from the nearby Russian Embassy. It was located in Kensington Palace Gate, just off the High Street, next to the former residence of the late Princess of Wales. I think that Burrell chap lived with her there, too. The Russians could saunter to the ground or take a Tube from High Street Kensington, the station that was to be the scene of a notorious and violent ambush in the mid-'80s involving Chelsea Headhunters and a posse of Everton fans.

The Russians from the Embassy loved their Saturday afternoon football – just as a certain Russian billionaire does some years later – and soon became Chelsea fans. (Highbury had been badly damaged by bombing in the war and they were at that time ground sharing at Tottenham – shame, I hear you say – so options were somewhat limited.)

The location of Chelsea Football Club always played a huge part in its dilettante history. It was always fashionable, genteel, classy and trendy, and the Russians were instantly attracted by it. Today, the original Chelsea Village (which we walk through on the way to the match) is a shopping precinct. The stucco-fronted houses still gleam like diamonds and even the wisteria looks manicured. When Roman Abramovich purchased Chelsea, the surrounding area must have influenced his decision to invest so heavily in the club. Huge sums are paid for the handsome houses near the ground in excellent condition, which are then gutted to create new kitchens, conservatories or basement pools. Would Roman have bought Bolton Wanders or Wolverhampton? I think not, somehow.

My father had told the family some weeks in advance that a high-ranking official from the Soviet Ministry of Sport had arranged a match between Chelsea and a crack Soviet team. Sir Stanley Rous, secretary of the FA and my father's best friend in football, had brokered the deal a few days after we had lost 1–2 to West Ham. We were sworn to secrecy because it was a political hot potato and the FA did not want to let the press get hold of the story too early. He did not want the Mears family and Chelsea FC to be blamestormed if anything went wrong.

The tour took longer to arrange than I thought but was finally set up for Tuesday, 13 November. My father was continually searching for the perfect London restaurant, and so he ended up in the Connaught Grill arranging the match with the Russian officials. Some days I can liken to the actress Isabella Rosellini – beautiful – but this was not one of them: grey, very cold, cloudy.

The reasons for the mammoth congregation of fans were many. It was seen as a historic occasion. Also, there was the added attraction of Tommy Lawton, who was a huge name in the game. The demand for tickets had been phenomenal. In my extensive catalogue of memories, I cannot recall a game like it. They had gone on sale the day before, cash only: 1/6 to stand (8p); grandstand tickets 5/6 (27p) and 10 shillings (50p) each. There were no credit or debit cards in those days and it was too late for postal applications to be considered. Fans queued for hours in the freezing cold for tickets but in the end thousands were turned away when they sold out. Billy Birrell, his sandy hair blowing in the wind, had to go down to explain and tell them to disperse. It was extraordinary how the match caught the imagination of the public. There was no television coverage and in the absence of star names, the Dynamo side was unknown. They had kept a very low profile media wise since they had landed at Croydon airport a few days before. They came with no household names. Today, the names Zidane, Rivaldo, Maldini and Roberto Carlos are as deeply imprinted in the public consciousness as those of Greaves and Charlton at the time of the '66 World Cup. The visit was of huge importance to the Russians. It was hinted that quality players, not necessarily on the books of Dynamo, had been added to the squad. In essence, it was the Russian national team. With a Cold War looming, the football team was required to epitomise the best traits of the Russian character: courage, reliability, reserve and perseverance.

It was an unbelievable match for a work-day Tuesday.

Even the Tommy-twice-a-seasons had turned up in force. People were outside the Bridge at 8 a.m., the kick-off scheduled for 2.30 p.m. The grey two-piece was the leisure uniform of choice, a badge of largely proletarian honour. It may have been out of Burton, it may have been demob, it might have been both. The only people wearing suits when Chelsea play today are those looking to arrest Headhunters. My father, wearing a new black suit and a starched shirt, arrived at the ground about 10 a.m. The

Chelsea chairman had to meet some representatives from the Soviet Government about 11 a.m. Their English was as good as our Russian and an interpreter was required. They seemed very pleasant and spent a great deal of time bowing and smiling. I could not help but notice that their hair and eyebrows were neatly trimmed. One of them wore what appeared to be ostrich shoes.

The streets were already packed, the gates were set to open at one o'clock, but the police requested that they open earlier to reduce the congestion outside. People were standing on walls selling sweets, peanuts and toffee apples (which were just excellent). My father had the sense to park his gas guzzler away from the crowd – there was no way we could have proceeded through it. The supporters were very peaceful though, smiling and chatting. The ten-shilling tickets were changing hands for four times that amount and the touts were doing a brisk trade. The peddlers selling rosettes and badges on the Luftwaffe bombsites were enjoying a boost in trade, lamenting the fact that they could not get any more Moscow Dynamo colours. They were probably the antecedents of the modern street traders who sell the Chelski T-shirts and those ghastly baseball caps displaying a Hammer and Sickle over the Chelsea badge. There was a high contingent of Russians there, some carrying large red flags. One stood out – an enormous, faded Soviet battle flag. I expected the Russians to be covered in snow or something, wearing heavy boots and fur hats. I did not see any strange military uniforms but some of their fans were wearing sailor suits. The programmes were doing a roaring trade. I could see the official blue version but there was a pirate version all in red. (On Christmas Day 1948, Chelsea, for their home game against Portsmouth, started a revolution in programmes by introducing a 16-page magazine for sixpence (2p) to replace what had been a mere pamphlet at half the price.)

The bulk of the fans were coming out of Fulham Broadway station and making their way slowly down the Fulham Road. Some shop windows were in danger of cracking under the weight of the bodies pressed against them. Policemen on horseback struggled to contain the crowd. Such was the crush, they literally could not move in the human sea. The fans were making a political statement: despite the years of heavy bombing, London, the wounded city, would not be cowed. Football and life must go on. By 1.30 p.m., many fans were attempting to get back the way they had come, the one thing more difficult than pushing on as part of the crowd.

Eventually, just after two o'clock, the police ordered the gates to be shut. Estimates of how many people were still outside the ground vary; some say 20,000, others nearer 25,000. I just could not say. With the gates locked, the real panic set in. Houses overlooking the ground were stormed by mobs. They charged inside and then clambered onto the roof to view events. The homeowners were pushed aside and it was not until police reinforcements were called that order was restored and the home-invaders were repulsed.

About 15,000 ticketless fans gained entry by various means. A large mob at the Shed end (where else?) of the ground battered down a gate with a fence that they had ripped down from one of the gardens. The fence had spikes on it and looked like a device from some King Arthur movie where the knights are storming the castle. An unmanned staff entrance at the north end of the ground was kicked down and another part of the citadel was breached. At the back end of the East Stand, a huge group of fans gained entry by crossing the electrified District Line side and scaling the wall. It was a miracle nobody was killed by the Tube trains packed with fans en route to Fulham Broadway. The Tube ran better in those days, too.

Many ticket holders never reached their allotted stand seats; others got to them in time but were pushed out of them by the hard-bitten mob.

Another breach of the Chelsea fortress was via the Oswald Stoll Foundation for Disabled Soldiers (which is the building next to the Blue Spice Indian Restaurant, a few yards from the new exit at Fulham Broadway station). The gates of the Foundation were stormed and the fans ran through the grounds, across the railway tracks and through a hole in the wire at the back of the North Stand. This was a well-known route into the Bridge – Malcolm MacDonald confessed to using it in a recent radio interview. Supermac was a Chelsea fan of long standing and would use that method to watch the thoroughbred Venables team in the early '60s. One of the most famous Headhunters, who was sentenced to many years imprisonment by the Thatcher regime for football-related offences, admitted to me once that it was a familiar route into the Bridge for many young Chelsea fans eager to watch Geoff Hurst's team two decades later.

It was estimated that 75,000 fans were inside the Bridge before the invaders. The only way they could get any space was to go up onto the roof of the stands or onto the pitch by crossing over the dog track and going towards the touchlines. It was a surprise to me that a fan never took a throw-in during the match. The playing pitch looked a picture when I first saw it. Later on in the day, there were tens of thousands of fans almost standing on it. It was covered in orange peel and litter. Most of the fans around the pitch were not there of their own volition, they were forced there by the sheer weight of the crowd. Fuelling the nostalgia of the Moscow game was the statistical purity that numerically it was the biggest game ever played at Stamford Bridge. Two people actually fell through the stand roofs, which were partially made of glass. Neither was badly hurt but some fans were cut by the glass. Barriers snapped on the West Terrace with the Chelsea supporters stretched tighter than a Salvation Army tambourine; some fans sustained fractured limbs. It was a miracle that nobody was killed. The difference was nobody panicked. Most of the fans had been fighting a war only a few months before so a large crowd held no particular terror for them. They had been used to standing still for long periods, plus I doubt if they had been hooched-up in the pub before the game.

Pictures of the match cannot convey the atmosphere. The crowd were very quiet, no chanting or singing. It was an event. The Russians had a unique grip on the London fans' psyche. My father bought me an ice cream, but I would have preferred a hot drink. I asked him if it was always like this. 'Shut up and eat your ice cream,' was his reply.

RUSSIAN RHYTHM (APOLOGIES TO SIR MICHAEL STOUTE)

The next surprise was that the Russians wore blue and Chelsea red. At about 1.45 the Russians emerged. They were wearing dark-blue shirts with what appeared to be a white badge or motif. The shirt had an open neck, no buttons. I later found out the white badge was in fact the letter 'D' stitched into the shirt. Their light-blue shorts were almost Bermuda length with white piping. This was worn with green socks with white hoops. It was unheard of in those times for a team to warm up. One of the players had a camera and appeared to be wearing a military-style overcoat and snow-white tennis shoes. He turned out to be the goalkeeper, Alexei Khomich – an amazing character. Why is it that the goalkeeper was always the eccentric in the side? Khomich gave Chelsea fans the first taste of the continental keeper, a style personified by my favourite goalkeeper of all time, Peter Bonetti, and a tradition carried on by Petar Borota and more recently Carlo Cudicini. Khomich earned the nickname 'The Tiger' from the English fans. First the tiger, then Bonetti 'The Cat'.

The press had written off the men from Moscow already, describing them as a team of factory workers who lacked pace, gutsy upstarts whom nobody expected to win. At that level, they would be found out. It was said that Dynamo belonged to the Interior Ministry and the spy angle was played up. They had been training at the White City but had not impressed the watching pressmen. Only the tall, sinewy centre-forward Beskov had looked the part (Beskov later coached Dynamo and guided the Russian national team to second place in the European Nations Cup). Chelsea, with the addition of superstar Lawton, would simply be too good for them. This was a bit like the hype when Mike Tyson fought James 'Buster' Douglas, who started at 40–1, if I recall. As always, the golden rule is not to get carried away with the hype.

They warmed up till about 2 p.m. then went back down the tunnel to re-emerge soon after with the red-shirted Chelsea team. I rubbed my eyes in near disbelief.

The Chelsea side lined up as follows:

Woodley

Tennant   Bacuzzi

Russell Harris (John Not Ron) Taylor

Buchanan Williams Lawton Goulden Bain

The match referee was Lieutenant-Commander G. Clark RN. After the formalities, the national anthems were played and the Russians presented each Chelsea player with a bunch of red and white flowers. This was probably the first time that a British team were given bouquets and the Chelsea boys, faces young and sincere, seemed acutely embarrassed by it all. I looked across at Lawton, who was holding the flowers behind his back like a schoolboy smoking behind the bike sheds. Buchanan, who had narrow bones in his face and jet black hair, stared down at his boots, the flowers gripped tight in his clenched fists.

Two players guested for Chelsea: England international Jim Taylor, who had a hard-edged face, and Joe Bacuzzi, the crew cut-wearing Fulham back. The Russian line-up was a mystery to me but the Russian officials sitting next to my father spent time pointing at the winger Archangelski, who was rolling his shoulders, and the inside-forward Bobrov. He had fair hair which seemed strange at the time; I suppose I expected him to have a moustache like Stalin or a beard like Rasputin. The gimlet-eyed centre-half Semichastny was massive. He was built like one of those huge retro American fridges, with lead feet and menacing scowls.

They were ready to rumble that unseasonably cold afternoon. The Russians, attacking the Shed end tore into Chelsea straight away. They just came down field en masse, quickly interchanging passes and raining in shots. Woodley, face tense underneath his huge cap, was immediately called into action, scrambling them away for corners. Then Archangelski, a pocket of air in one cheek, cut inside Bacuzzi to fire a rip-roaring shot into the side netting. The fair-headed Bobrov got into the act smashing a shot against Woodley's right-hand post. Bacuzzi told my father after the game that Bobrov came past him so fast he almost caught a cold from the draught.

Chelsea, set back on their heels by the pace of the Russians, quickly hit back and Goulden set up a chance for Williams. With only Khomich (smaller than I had anticipated) to beat, he blasted over. My hero Peter Buchanan got into the act by firing in a long-range shot that Khomich expertly flipped over the bar. I clapped like mad. That early image of suave wing play and flash continental goalkeeping was to stay with me for ever. Buchanan scratched his cheek and looked quizzically towards Lawton.

The Russians were interchanging, the inside-forwards Kartsev and Bobrov were playing their party tricks in front of the centre-forward Beskov, who was lying deep. Today, they would describe him as playing in the 'hole'. Damien Duff gets the job in the current side. Don Revie built his playing career on that deep-lying ploy and wreaked havoc. Dynamo were the first club side to play it, though. John Harris was flummoxed by it all. Brian Clough always had a thing about that style: 'too short, too neat, too unproductive' but the Russians were getting bodies forward. The pitch was softer than that which the Dynamo side was accustomed to, but it suited the tempo of their game. I sensed a calamity was going to hit Chelsea.

Kartsev opened Chelsea up completely, skipping past Taylor to smash a shot into Woodley's chest when he really should have scored. Then Beskov hit the same post with an even harder shot that left Woodley beaten all ends up.

Chelsea broke away to score. Archangelski arrowed over a corner but Bacuzzi thumped it first time up field and it fell neatly for Jimmy Bain, who used the speed of a Gronkjaer to break away and put over a fierce cross-shot-cum-centre. Lawton charged Khomich like a rhino and the ball looped up for Goulden to thrash high into the net. The Tiger looked like he had been hit by a cable-strung wrecking ball. As the *Mirror* commented, a goal would not have been granted in Russia and probably not in the Premier League today. I can imagine the protests from the Arsenal back four if van Nistelrooy had clattered their keeper and Giggs had scored in similar circumstances.

Straight from the restart, the unchallenged Bobrov raced through the retreating Chelsea defence; it was as if he had satellite navigation. He left Harris on the seat of his pants only to hook a great chance over the bar. Chelsea scored again after the Russian defenders' nerves appeared to crack following some bagatelle in the six-yard box. A harmless back pass made the defenders freeze for a moment and the canny Reg Williams raced in and tapped the ball goalwards. Defender Stankevich volleyed a furious clearance but it rebounded off Williams and flew into the net.

Amazingly, Chelsea were two up after being totally outplayed by the cultured and mellifluous Dynamo. Instead of being ecstatic, my father took the news quietly. He started waving to the touchline. He was concerned that were Chelsea to score an emphatic victory, it would cause a diplomatic incident. The tanks would be out in Trafalgar Square. The Russians were looking anxious and a little rattled, but just on half-time defender Bobby Russell brought down the blur of movement that was Beskov in the box and a penalty kick was awarded.

Soloviev stepped up to take the kick. You would have bet your mortgage on him scoring; the press build-up had said he was a hotshot, a majestic kicker, known for zapping great goals and never missing a spot-kick. Perhaps the spellbound crowd put him off. It was so dense that people were actually touching the net and were literally almost in the penalty area. In the history of the game, no player could have had such a claustrophobic penalty kick to take. After a theatrical attempt at putting the ball on the penalty spot, Soloviev struck the outside of the post with a low, skimming drive.

In the dying seconds of the first half, Lawton had a chance to seal the match by putting Chelsea three up but Khomich made a superb save. He flung himself full length to keep out Tommy's drive. Khomich was perhaps, after Lev Yashin, Russia's greatest keeper. A case could be made for Yashin as the most famous goalkeeper ever. His graceful goalkeeping skills earned him an Olympic gold medal, a European Championship medal, a European Footballer of the Year award and the Order of Lenin. He replaced Khomich in goal for Dynamo in 1950 and stayed for twenty-two seasons, winning five Championships. A great athlete, possessing extraordinary reactions and courage, he set the standards for modern goalkeepers. Chelsea had another good one to keep goal for them in the '90s: Dimtri Kharine, who made a big contribution to Chelsea's transformation. Matthew Harding rated him highly.

The Russians trooped off, heads down. The light was already starting to fade. The tension had started to get to them but they had shown the crowd some brilliant football. I had some more ice cream in the break.

The second half opened with the Russians pouring down on Chelsea. In the space of a few minutes, Woodley had kept out two further attempts from Bobrov, who was wriggling past defenders at will. Then Chelsea broke away and Lawton smashed in a wickedly deceptive curved shot which nicked the outside of the post.

Dynamo scored eventually. By then, the sky had begun to darken. They had exerted so much pressure. It was the traditional battle of British courage and strength against continental invention and technique. Kartsev was still running the Chelsea defence ragged. He collected a searching pass from Archangelski and sidestepped Taylor to beat Woodley with a curling drive. A goal like that would have been celebrated with the full treatment today but in those days a handshake sufficed. It reminded me of the Corinthian spirit. The Russians went for the kill. Fifteen minutes from time, Kartsev drew the Chelsea defence before slipping the ball to Archangelski. The winger hammered in a cross shot which was deflected by Russell's right knee into the net. The score was 2–2. The crowd became very excited by the Russians' fight back. My predominant memory of the day was how much the Chelsea crowd were behind the Russians. They cheered every move. It bred legend, lore and nostalgia.

> The hub of some great football memories. Starting late, he would go higher and win the duel, to tap the ball smartly from that greased head to the feet of a colleague.
> John Arlott on Tom Lawton, 'Faith in Genius: Concerning Soccer', *The Footballer's Fireside Book*

Lawton emerged from his shell. He was one of those players that appeared to be lazy, never one to chase a ball he didn't think he could get. Ossie would have liked him. Semichastny had closed him down all game but as the time wore on he started to find a bit more space on the right. Ten minutes from time, the Englishman scored a classic goal. His first effort was charged down but he soared above two defenders to thump one home with that dark head of his. It was a marvellous goal; Tommy went up like the dancer Nijinsky and appeared to hover for a split second, before nodding in a superb header. The crowd were stunned. It was a feat of power and coordination unmatched in any other sport. A lot of Lawton's appeal to the crowd lay in his Olympian physique. Tommy received a brisk handshake from Goulden. Khomich picked the ball out of the back of the net. For once, even his elasticity could not prevent a goal. My father broke into a smile for the first time that afternoon. It wasn't going according to plan but this was Chelsea.

The Russians came back; the last ten minutes were totally theirs. Chelsea were tiring rapidly; the Dynamos were superbly fit, their nerves now completely calm. The Soviet deities laid on something truly special. Their passing seemed even more quick-fire than at the start of the match. The Chelsea penalty area was suddenly packed with Russians trying to force the ball home. Khomich was playing way out of his goal and set up many counter attacks with his clever clearances.

With five minutes left, in what we would call a wing-back position now, Radikorsky dispossessed the fading Goulden and put Archangelski away down the right with a pass of precise elegance. His cross flew off Harris to Bobrov, who instantly scored, ruthlessly driving the ball low against the iron support at the back of the net. He looked yards offside but Harris had played him onside. Over the years, people talked about the dubious late goal that won the Dynamos a hard-earned draw. Truth was, they had so many chances and near misses they dominated the game.

Bobrov should have won it with another clear chance as he fired against the outside of Woodley's post from almost the same position as he had just scored from. The Russians were used to a harder ball and I think their shooting wasn't as accurate because they simply weren't accustomed to the pace of it.

In the last minute, Kartsev tried to walk the ball in after Beskov had slammed a shot against Bacuzzi but the Fulham defender recovered to hack clear. Lieutenant-Commander Clark blew the final whistle with Archangelski about to fire in another cross.

The crowd poured onto the pitch to congratulate the Dynamos for their superb, kingly exhibition of football and praise the Chelsea team for their fighting spirit. The only time I saw a scene approaching it was in May 1963, the night that the Diamonds went up to the big time by thrashing Portsmouth 7–0 and the huge Chelsea crowd went delirious. That afternoon was mind-blowing, though. There were people on the pitch but it was not all over because Modern Chelsea was born that day.

TWILIGHT OF THE GODS

I wanted to go down to the dressing-room after the game but had to make do with a trip to the directors' lounge. I never saw it so packed. I caught sight of Tommy Lawton across the crowded room: it was love at first sight. He stood quietly in the corner, chatting to some Russian officials, serenely sipping lemonade and helping himself to cheese sandwiches. He saw me staring and winked back. Lawton was a Chelsea legend after two games; his hard-man reputation belied his humble and retiring nature. I looked at him and thought to myself, 'after all the fame and all the success, you're still so grounded and polite, still treating everyone the same'. I vowed to try to follow his example; I always tried to be like that – as normal as possible.

Lawton was from a lost generation: a man's man, a hero from the mould of Gary Cooper or John Wayne.

I wrote this chapter the week the papers were full of stories concerning Premiership players and an alleged incident involving a 17-year-old girl in the Grosvenor House Hotel. In a separate episode, an ex-Chelsea player had been arrested for an alleged sexual assault. A set-to between Arsenal and Manchester United players hogged the other headlines. There are still good things to report, though: Mutu made a terrific impact after a handful of Chelsea games; Rooney became a national hero.

In 1945, everyone was happy. It had been a marvellous game and nobody had lost. Lawton was a true colossus. Honours were even. Football and Chelsea had stolen my heart. Moscow Dynamo had written a whole new chapter in the history of world soccer. Total receipts for the match were £7,000 – a fortune for 1945. Chelsea took half, a fair slice of Lawton's massive fee. The Russians' cut went to the Stalingrad fund. Later in the evening, Chelsea had an official dinner at the Café Royal. I was too young to attend but my father brought us home an enamel badge. It had a white background with the obligatory red star and the 'D' that they had worn so proudly on their shirts. I kept it for years but it was stolen shortly before I decamped to America. What would it be worth today, along with the programme bearing Lawton's and Bobrov's signatures? There are some items that even Mr Abramovich's wealth cannot buy.

The papers wrote up the fascinating game like the Second Coming. The Russians were hailed as the greatest club side to play in London. I never saw another side with so many two-footed players. Chelsea were praised for their fighting qualities. Lawton's goal was the high spot of a fantastic match. The tour went on; it was as successful as the Rolling Stones in the States. Stories of the epic game at Stamford Bridge spread across Russia like a bushfire. Their next game was against Cardiff, then in the Third Division. They were younger than Chelsea and dare I say fitter. They were expected to give them a hard test. The game ended Cardiff 1, Moscow Dynamo 10 (Bobrov 3, Beskov 4, Archangelski 3). They went on to beat Arsenal 3–4 in the fog at Highbury. The Arsenal team, which included Stanley Matthews, saw victory as their birthright but Moscow were superb and once again bewitched a huge London crowd. Bacuzzi played in that one as well.

I would like to say that it all ended happily but, as so often, politics got in the way. The Russians invited Chelsea back to play a return in Moscow – what a match that would have been – but it never happened. By that time, the Cold War had started and the Russians were the enemy.

I look on that tour as similar to when the English and German soldiers fraternised on Christmas Day in 1914. They left the trenches in northern France and ended up playing football under the Christmas truce. The frozen wasteland of no man's land was soon the scene of a kickabout between the armies. When the day was over, they started killing each other again. For a short time, though, the two adversaries got to know each other, found out they were human beings and their mutual love of football gave them a point of reference. After all, that is what football is about; something that brings people together. Twenty-one million watched Lampard score for England in the Euro 2004 quarter-final.

In the last two minutes of a mediocre game at Middlesbrough in October 2003, Damien Duff conjured up a superb piece of trickery to mesmerise the Smoggies and win the game for Chelsea. Like someone crossing a stream on little stones and trying not to get his Pradas wet, Duff picked his way past several defenders before cutting back to turn and glance up. He chose Hernan Crespo as the executioner. Lucky Crespo and everyone that watched it. It was a moment that you wanted to share with your pals, the same as when guests in the boardroom raved about Lawton's header, or when fans waiting for the Tube at Fulham Broadway marvelled at the maestro Beskov's footwork. Transfers between top clubs in Russia were greatly discouraged in those days, let alone a move abroad.

Moscow Dynamo went home undefeated to a heroes' welcome. Back in the USSR. They left England invincible and unexcelled. The Soviet movie theatres were packed as they showed films of the tour. The Chelsea match was their favourite. The greatest comeback since Stalingrad, they said. Watch the grainy newsreel footage of the day and I defy Chelsea fans not to feel a lump in their throats. There is a romance in the game that is lacking today. We should have learnt from the Russians but English football blundered on in its own sweet way, refusing to take onboard the sweeping changes in tactics and methods. It was not until another grey winter's afternoon eight years later that the biggest wake-up call of all time came. It was in the shape of Hungary scoring six goals at Wembley to become the first international side to win on English soil. 'Twilight of the Gods', the headline ran in *The Times*. Lawton was plying his trade in the Third Division by then.

FIVE

THE LEAGUE
(OF EXTRAORDINARY GENTLEMEN)

> We will now discuss in a little more detail the struggle for
> existence.
>
> **Charles Darwin,** *The Origin of Species*

A decade passed before Chelsea Football Club won the title. Billy Birrell resigned at the end of season 1951–52 and was replaced by Ted Drake. The early post-war years were mediocre times for the club. Chelsea finished tenth in the Football League South in 1945–46, the season they played Moscow Dynamo.

In 1946–47, Tommy Lawton broke Chelsea's scoring record by hitting 26 League goals in just 34 games. He also scored four Cup goals: three of them against Arsenal over three epic games watched by 120,000 during January 1947. This was easily the high spot of the season – a famous Cup win over the north London giants, and the last time Chelsea were to beat Arsenal in the grand old competition in the twentieth century. After two 1–1 draws, Chelsea won 0–2 in the second replay at Highbury. Tommy scored both first-half goals to seal victory.

Lawton scored against Derby in the next round but County forced a 2–2 draw at the Bridge and eventually knocked Chelsea out in the replay with a goal in extra time. A blistering hat-trick at Huddersfield was his best performance in the League.

He could never settle in west London, though, and was unhappy at the way Billy Birrell ran things. Like Hughie Gallacher before him, Lawton was slightly past his best when he joined the club. Lawton thought Birrell was looking for a younger, more mobile model.

The next superstar to captivate the Chelsea crowd was Roy Bentley. He was that younger, more mobile model, certainly not a battering ram. The only Bentley at Chelsea in recent years has been Verón's Bentley Continental GT. There was another Bentley, though, and he was a Rolls-Royce of a footballer. He joined the club a few months after Lawton's shock departure. Roy was a tremendous fan of Tommy and had learnt a lot from studying the Pathé news footage of Lawton's championship season at Everton. They became friends and Tommy once confided that he'd been very unhappy during his time at Chelsea. Rumours of gambling problems had persisted throughout his brief stay in London. The fans had said that had he spent as much time keeping fit as gambling, they would have seen an even bigger star.

His general fitness was always in question; Lawton had not taken a proper break from the game for years and was severely fatigued. During the war, he had played for Aldershot in the low-key regional league and had registered 85 goals in 108 games. A nasty bout of food poisoning had taken the edge off his game. Chelsea wanted him to play in summer tour matches against Gothenburg and IFK Norrkoping but he refused point-blank and was banished to the reserves. He was still good enough to be picked for England, though.

Chelsea finished fifteenth in the table that season and Leeds United were relegated after years playing second fiddle to Huddersfield. The Yorkshire club's West Stand was destroyed by fire around the mid-'50s. Their debts were not so high, though.

The seeds of discontent were sown between the star striker and his manager, however. Tommy, feeling his relationship with the club had soured, asked for a transfer. Where was I to hear that one again? Chelsea fans over the years became immune to their club's idiocies and eccentric transfer dealings but to sell a player of Lawton's skill and intelligence was downright suicidal. He was such an attraction that when Chelsea played Arsenal on 1 November 1947 a crowd of 67,277 watched them scramble a 0–0 draw; across town, an astonishing 27,000 supporters watched the reserve game, featuring Tommy, between the two clubs at Highbury. He played eight first-team games in the 1947–48 season and scored four goals: match winners against Derby and Sunderland and two against Villa. His last game for Chelsea was in a return to Merseyside on 10 November 1947 when Liverpool won 3–0. It was like a steamroller against a peanut. Chelsea were pitiful. A week later, he joined Notts County, then in Division Three. The arrival at Meadow Lane of England's greatest centre-forward and pin-up was one of the most sensational happenings in the history of the game. I suppose an equivalent would be England superstar Frank Lampard joining the present Notts County set-up. The grim logical vortex that drags the smaller clubs under had by autumn 2003 almost driven County to the point of extinction. They were weeks away from being wound up.

By chance, they drew Chelsea in the Carling Cup. An appeal was made to Roman Abramovich to assist financially and the billionaire oligarch responded by literally giving them the shirt off his back. Well, not quite his back but the shirts off, amongst others, Eidur Gudjohnsen's, Jimmy Hasselbaink's and Joe Cole's back (all of whom scored in Chelsea's 4–2 win). The Chelsea shirts were auctioned to raise money to help Tommy Lawton's old side. That was the week that Roman came top in the *Sunday Times* Rich List for the highest earners of 2003. Abramovich had recently sold £4.7 billion worth of assets.

A chap called Arthur Stolley was the reason that Tommy joined Notts County despite a stream of offers from bigger clubs. Stolley was by that time managing County but he had been the masseur at Stamford Bridge. My father took an active dislike to his close representation of a key Chelsea player and following a disagreement over the physiotherapist's role in such matters, sacked him. Before his departure, Stolley asked Lawton if he would be prepared to join him if he got fixed up somewhere else. Lawton agreed but thought no more about it till Stolley rang FULHAM 3321 out of the blue to ask Tommy if he wanted out of the Blues.

Tommy joined County for £17,500 plus Irish international defender Bill Dickson. Dickson went on to play over 100 games for Chelsea. Lawton was still only twenty-eight and his decision to step down two divisions aroused disbelief. It was the marmalade dropper of the decade. He was one of those players who could put 10,000 on a gate, even in a reserve game. The combination of soaring attendances and thunderbolt headers set the town alight. Only Brian Clough was to have a bigger impact on Nottingham.

In all, he scored 103 goals in 166 games for County and won more England caps before winding down his career at Brentford and Arsenal. He died of pneumonia in November 1996. His passing marked the end of an era.

ANOTHER EXTRAORDINARY GENTLEMAN

The peerless Swiss defender, Willi Steffen, was believed to be the last survivor from the Chelsea side which beat Arsenal with Lawton's goals. Like so many things in football, his joining Chelsea was a complete accident. The records show that he only played 20 games for the Blues in

1946–47 – 15 in the League and 5 in Cup games. Not many at all but he left a lasting memory of cultured full-back play and a Taliban-style dedication to fitness and sporting values. He was the first Swiss footballer to play in England and attracted a great deal of attention from the press.

Willi was an amateur with the Swiss First Division team Cantonal Neachatel and had played for his country against England in Bern at the end of the war. Tommy Lawton was the England centre-forward that day and was impressed with the 21 year old's technique and speed. Willi had a football brain the size of Eubank's truck. He was an accomplished pilot too.

Steffen's parents had no intention of him turning professional and sent him to London to learn English with a view to going into the thriving family business. By a strange quirk of fate, his teacher was Billy Birrell's wife. After hearing of his prowess as an international footballer, she arranged a meeting with him and her husband at Victoria station. Billy quickly arranged a trial and he was pitched into a friendly at Bournemouth. Steffen passed his audition with flying colours as the Blues raced to a 0–6 victory. Willi Steffen made his debut against Derby in the League and was on the wrong end of a 1–3 scoreline. The Swiss defender was the first foreign wing-back: boy-band blond and tall with a tremendous turn of pace but he could defend. He was a cross between Michel Salgado and Dan Petrescu. The only better left wing-backs I have seen in over 50 years of watching Chelsea were Eddie McCreadie and Graeme Le Saux. Steffen was still undercooked. If he had stayed in London and been trained and coached, he could have been a world-class defender.

The fans loved him and he became another matinée idol, getting cards and letters from people who didn't even know his name. (I think Glen Campbell put it better in 'Rhinestone Cowboy'.)

In the Cup games against Arsenal, Willi was up against a lad called Ian McPherson. The Arsenal winger had a lot of pace, like our friend the Calvin Klein-wearing Freddie Ljungberg has today. Steffen stuck with him, though, and Chelsea withstood the cavalry charges led by McPherson in the second half of the second replay at Highbury.

Birrell was desperate to sign Willi permanently. His potential stood out: the Chelsea defence looked sluggish, sloppy and disorganised for most of the season. They took a savage caning at Anfield when Liverpool won 7–4. The Blues scored four at Wolves but they hit six. Stoke won 6–1 at the Victoria ground when they chucked the kitchen sink at us. After just five months at the Bridge, he had to return home to complete his military service. His last game was against Derby and Chelsea extracted a modicum of revenge for their Cup exit by beating them 3–0, Lawton scoring twice and Len Goulden bomb-shelling home one of his specials. Willi led the Blues. I never saw a prouder Chelsea captain.

Willi never came back. He played for Switzerland in the 1950 World Cup and went on to win four titles in a row with the interestingly named Young Boys of Bern. The Swiss ace always hankered to return to Chelsea. Perhaps it was for the best. His abiding memory was of the freezing winter (one of the worst on record – the season nearly went on till June). The young defender spent it in west London with food rationing and no central heating. No triple garages, indoor pools or plasma screens for him.

THE FAME ACADEMY IS CREATED

Billy Birrell had a plan. He was a man with vision. He was Mistra Know-it-all. The Chelsea boss had seen the future and it was a youth scheme producing the best talent London had to offer. Traditionally, Chelsea had always bought their best players rather than producing them. The chequebook management of the previous managers, Calderhead and Knighton, had brought a cavalcade of class players to west London but no tangible success.

Birrell wanted a structure in place to create a 'Football Factory'. He convinced Joe Mears that the days of big buying were over and that funds should be set aside to pay for a network of scouts and a coaching staff for the youngsters. In recent times, all you have is the dumbsizing of youth systems because of the availability of foreign talent.

Jimmy Thompson was appointed head scout for Chelsea. He had played in the '20s and scored 34 goals in 42 games. Some return, but whatever he did for Chelsea on the pitch his contribution off the field was incalculable. The same could be said of Dickie Foss. He was appointed youth-team manager. Dick had a moderate career as an inside-forward after joining the club from Southall. These were more players whose careers had been ruined by the war. Thinking about it, that is why they were so good with the young players: they knew all too well the brevity of a footballer's career and also, more importantly, they relived their wasted skill through the emerging talent. Together with Thompson, Dickie Spence (the oldest player to turn out for Chelsea) and Albert Tennant oversaw and orchestrated a phenomenon which spawned some of the greatest talent that this country has ever seen. Osgood, Hudson, Greaves, Venables and Wilkins were the exhilarating cream of the crop, all world-class players. There was another strata of excellent talents just below, like the fabulous Harris boys, Bonetti, Tambling, Shellito, Wicks, Langley, Bridges and Walker, who all dominated the headlines and enriched the history of Chelsea. Every youngster who joined quickly learned that only Chelsea mattered. The situation has only altered in recent years, the game awash with TV money and a huge influx of foreign talent. The Russian Revolution has taken it up another notch, into another dimension. If it is half as productive as the first set-up then Chelsea should have a golden future.

Here is my team of home-grown talent, created out of the machinery that was set up at the start of the '50s by Billy Birrell, Jimmy Thompson and his able lieutenants, Albert Tennant and the two Dickies, Spence and Foss. It is a distinguished lineage:

Bonetti

Shellito   Terry   Harris   Le Saux
Hollins   Hudson   Venables   Wilkins
Osgood   Greaves
Subs: Walker, Tambling, Houseman, Locke, Boyle, Bridges

Let me introduce the Moneybags Team. All of these players cost transfer fees and were purchased by Chelsea. I consider these to be the best signings made over the 100-year period:

Cudicini

Petrescu   Desailly   Gallas   McCreadie
Wise   Di Matteo   Lampard   Nevin
Zola   Gallacher
Subs: Mutu, Cooke, Gullit, Lawton, Elliot, Cech

We could fill up the book with teams and combinations, that is for sure. Recent events have made the selection process even more difficult, with players like Cole, Robben and Duff to include. Whatever your view, both sides would take some beating.

One of the first players to join the scheme was Joe Baker, who was part of Chelsea's ground staff as a 15 year old in 1955. The young Scot only spent a month in London before returning to Edinburgh because he was homesick. Baker, along with another Joe, the red-haired Payne, were the only players to score as many as ten goals in a British first-class football match. Baker made his mark as a centre-forward with Hibernian and it was for them that he scored ten goals in a Scottish Cup tie in 1961: the 15–1 thrashing of Peebles Rovers.

The following season, he was transferred to Italian club Torino and subsequently played for Arsenal before dying of a heart attack at a tragically young age. I wondered how it would have worked out for him if he had stayed at Chelsea.

BENTLEY REVS UP

Roy Bentley joined Chelsea in January 1948 from Newcastle for a £12,500 fee – the same route Hughie Gallacher took before the war. Bentley was instructed by his doctor to head south. Lung trouble had plagued his early career and it was felt that a move would benefit him. The same thing had applied to Tommy Lawton's wife and it is interesting to note the coincidence of Chelsea obtaining the signatures of two of the finest strikers in the game because of bronchial problems.

Roy was seen as the natural replacement for Tommy Lawton. He started off slowly, scoring three goals in fourteen games. Roy's debut was in a 2–4 home defeat to Huddersfield Town. The following week, he played in the Chelsea side that was dumped out of the Cup in extra time in a fourth-round replay at Manchester City. Chelsea languished in eighteenth spot at the end of the season, missing relegation by five points.

Bentley was the new breed of deep-lying centre-forward. Moscow Dynamo had used the tactic to such great effect in their all-conquering tour. Chelsea fans expecting a powerful player in the bish-bash-bosh style of Lawton were in for a surprise. However, his first full season in 1948–49 saw him make rapid progress as he scored 21 goals in 40 games. Chelsea finished mid-table at number 13, which was exactly where they were to finish the next season.

Roy's England record was impressive. In all, Bentley won 12 England caps during his spell at Chelsea, the same number as Jimmy Greaves in his time with the club. Tommy Lawton appeared 11 times whilst he was at Chelsea; Dennis Wise won 21 caps; Ray Wilkins was way out in front with two dozen caps while at Stamford Bridge; Frank Lampard is racking them up as I write; and Wayne Bridge will earn dozens also.

A Cup run took Chelsea to the semi-finals for the first time since Disraeli was a boy. West Brom had booted a weedy Chelsea side out the previous year but that season Chelsea were determined to make an impression. Brentford were the first team to be eliminated 0–1 at Griffin Park. Bowie scored (that's Jimmie not David). Newcastle, perhaps the best cup side of that era, were easily dispatched 3–0 in the fourth round. Bentley scored twice in the next round as Chesterfield were beaten by the same score. Chelsea were lucky to sneak a draw at Chesterfield in the first match.

A crowd of 70,000 packed the Bridge for the sixth-round clash against emerging superpower Manchester United. Chelsea won 2–0 in a pulsating match, Bentley clinching it with a thundering shot from 30 yards. A teenage Bobby Charlton must have used it as the blueprint for his wonderful gallery of golden goals. Guess who we drew in the semis? You got it. The men from Highbury. The game was to be played at White Hart Lane. Roy Bentley turned the Lane into a crucible with two goals in the first twenty-five minutes. Len Goulden, then thirty-seven, was restored to the side after being out of favour for six months. He had some good touches and calmed down the team. Chelsea looked in control. Wembley beckoned, my first visit. I could almost smell the green turf. Then the Twin Towers came crashing down.

Just on half-time, Arsenal won a disputed corner. Harry Medhurst, who was at the Bridge almost as long as me, was in goal that day. He later ended up as trainer. Freddie Cox, the ex-Spurs winger, opted to take the flag kick for the increasingly desperate-looking Arsenal. Cox was an interesting, undervalued character, a constant thorn in Chelsea's side. Like so many players, he had lost the best chunk of his career to the war. He had flown bombers and was also a keen birdwatcher. The corner he curled over defied all the rules of aerodynamics. Medhurst misjudged the flight of Freddie Cox's swerving in-swinger and could only punch the ball into the roof of the net. It was a fluke – the confidence seemed to visibly drain out of us then and there. In the second half, Arsenal threw everything at us. A thousand bomber raids battered our defence as Cox, playing like two men, rained in crosses from both wings. We held out till the last 15 minutes. Centre-half Leslie Compton grabbed an equaliser from another corner kick. This one was taken by his brother, the famous all-rounder and pin-up Denis. Joe Mercer, captaining Arsenal, waved the big defender back. Bentley was still lurking and Joe was worried about the quick break, a move Chelsea had perfected over the years. Blood being thicker than water, though, Lesley ignored the instruction and bulleted home his brother's cross. Lawton could not have improved on the header; it flew off his forehead like a rocket. On such things, cups are won and lost. We were lucky to hang on in the closing minutes. I was never so upset at failing to win a game.

The replay was a formality – our chance was gone and we all sensed it. Hamilton, purely academic. Cup-tie specialist Freddie Cox scored the only goal of a one-sided game in the 14th minute of extra time with his allegedly weaker left foot. Arsenal never had to move out of first gear. I do not know how we held out so long. We had lost it back at Tottenham in the dying seconds of the first half.

Apart from the heartbreak of the games against Arsenal (who went on to beat Liverpool in the final) another sad occasion took place with the retirement of Tommy Walker on Christmas Day 1948. Walker was another marvellous Scot, a superb player and a perfect gentleman. There was a great story my friend Brian Glanville always told about how Walker once supplied all the Scottish shirts for a wartime international at Hampden, not sure where he got them all from. Walker scored 24 goals in 104 games. The line-up of Goulden, Lawton and Walker was as mouth-watering in its day as Osgood, Cooke and Hudson or, if you prefer, Lampard and Robben. Birrell could never get them to play together at a decent tempo. I could never figure out why.

That was the day that the revolutionary new programme was issued. My father had decided that the time had come to improve the link between the club and its fans. It was the first programme to contain action photographs of the previous match and notes on the visitors. Arsenal were soon to follow suit.

Season 1950–51 was a nightmare. Chelsea stayed up on goal average. Sheffield Wednesday and Everton both had the same meagre number of points (32) but Chelsea survived thanks to a better goal average. Bentley, who finished top Chelsea scorer for eight consecutive seasons, scored eight goals. He was Chelsea captain. You did not have many centre-forwards captaining sides at that time; you still do not. Only Alan Shearer springs to mind. Bentley led by example; that was Ted Drake's style. There was very little bad language used on the pitch.

That was also the season that Bobby Smith made his debut for Chelsea. Smith later joined Spurs and went on to become a legend as Jimmy Greaves' strike partner. Funny that Chelsea supplied the pair. Fulham knocked Chelsea out of the Cup, beating them 3–0 in a fifth-round replay at Craven Cottage. They didn't just win – in the words of Tommy Docherty they 'mowed the lawn with them'. That will give you an idea of how bad it was.

The game that kept them up was the very last of the season: home to Bolton. Chelsea had to win to stay up. Bentley headed them in front after a quarter of an hour from Billy Gray's corner. In the next attack, he made it two from a free kick. Bentley did a handstand to celebrate. (Celestine Babayaro has done some good somersaults in recent times but in the cap-doffing '50s this was something!) Bobby Smith blasted two more and Chelsea stayed up by .044 of a goal.

In 1951–52, Chelsea had a better Cup run, reaching the semi-finals. Bentley scored in every round on the way to another titanic clash against Arsenal. Once again, the Cup jinx struck. The first game ended in a 1–1 draw at White Hart Lane. It was put back a couple of days due to heavy snow. The match was a turgid affair. No corners in the first hour to either side. Almost inevitably, Freddie Cox put Arsenal ahead after 35 minutes. Chelsea equalised midway though the second half through Billy Gray but two nights later, Arsenal ran out easy 3–0 winners. Cox was again our *bête noire*, scoring twice. Logie conjured an early goal for the diminutive birdwatcher which settled Arsenal's nerves. Chelsea, edgy throughout, had a considerable amount of possession but could make little impression against the unfussy Arsenal defence. Twenty minutes from time, an unmarked Cox broke Chelsea's hearts when he headed home a corner from winger Don Roper. Bentley went close near the end but Doug Lishman sealed it with another header. Cox's five goals in the semi-finals over that period remain a record.

The Bobby Smith–Roy Bentley combination was shaping up well. Young Smith hit a hat-trick against Leeds in a fifth-round replay at Villa Park. Bentley, who had moved to inside-left to accommodate the burly youngster, laid on two of the goals. The League was another grim affair – they lurched to 19th spot.

SAY YOU WANT A REVOLUTION

At the end of the season, Billy Birrell resigned, the club yet to see the fruition of his ambitious youth policy. Today, he must be recognised as the club's greatest visionary and the progenitor of the youth system. Chelsea were at a low point in their history – stranded in a sargasso sea of stagnation and ennui, becalmed. They were almost 50 years old but could not be considered as a forceful power. They were not major players because they had no major players. Only Bentley was of true stature.

Birrell was replaced by Ted Drake, who had been managing Reading. The ex-Arsenal centre-forward had lost his England place to Lawton and was winding down his sparkling career in Berkshire with the Third Division side. A bad back injury then put him out of the game altogether. He tried his hand at management and met with immediate success. Ted Drake was another playing legend. The Hughie Gallacher spirit was certainly present in his game; the problem was that he was always injured because of his uncompromising, 100 per cent, wholehearted style. Drake was one of the most powerful forwards to ever kick a ball and he played in an era when all the centre-forwards were giants. César Luís Menotti, who won the World Cup for Argentina, once told me, 'You can make an athlete out of a footballer but you cannot make a footballer out of an athlete.' Drake was both a great footballer and a natural athlete.

The former gas inspector reminded me a lot of the late, great Ian Hutchinson: both were always taking fearful risks to plunder goals and set up chances. Roy Bentley spoke of a memorable League game between Arsenal and Brentford (who for many years played in the top flight). Ted Drake was injured three times in the match and was twice carried off.

Eventually, he was stretchered off unconscious. He finished with two broken bones in his wrist and nine stitches in his head. It was said that at his peak at Highbury he could melt the legs of defenders 40 yards away from goal.

Signed from Southampton in 1934, he scored a record-breaking 42 League goals in his first Arsenal season. This has never been surpassed, even by such marvellous players as Ian Wright and Thierry Henry. His greatest achievement was seven goals for Arsenal in an away game at Aston Villa during Christmas 1935: another record and even more remarkable in that he only had nine shots – one hit the underside of the bar and the other was saved.

As Reading manager, he adopted a 'Big Ron' Atkinson-type persona of outrageous comments and brash behaviour. A fashionista to the last, Ted was an avid follower of the latest trends, dressing the part in loud suits, jazzy ties and coloured shirts. When he landed the Chelsea job, he started dressing in formal clothes in the manner of exploitative bankers in Frank Capra movies. Drake grew more introverted the longer he was in charge but he was a Chelsea man 24/7. The ex-Arsenal man hit the Bridge like a hurricane – only Abramovich had a bigger instant impact. Ted Drake was the first modern manager of Chelsea, creating celebrity, sensation and a sense of community – and he won the Championship.

Chelsea needed a makeover that even Trinny Woodall and Susannah Constantine would have found hard to pull off. Drake hated the old-fashioned image of the club. Their nickname was 'The Pensioners' after the ancient, white-bearded gentlemen you would see stumbling down the Kings Road. They were the inhabitants of the Royal Hospital, ex-army veterans who had been injured in combat. They wore distinctive bright-red uniforms and a peaked cap imprinted with the initials R.H. That represented the Royal Hospital not Ron Harris, by the way (though Harris was Chelsea's greatest-ever soldier, amassing a staggering 764 appearances). The Mears family always ensured that these wonderful, extraordinary gentlemen were always welcome at Stamford Bridge in recognition of their heroism. A pensioner could always be found in the director's box.

Ted still welcomed the pensioners but dispensed with the image and the nickname. From then on, they were to be called the 'Blues'.

In my view, perhaps Drake's greatest achievement was introducing the ageless Lion and Crozier badge – football's equivalent of the Rolls-Royce emblem. The Mears family were proud to be associated with it. After I left Chelsea, it was replaced with that revolting Millwall *Lion King* thing. When Abramovich took over, I wrote to him (even going to the trouble of translating it into Russian) asking him if he was interested in restoring the original badge. I am still awaiting his reply.

Ted Drake realised straight away that he had to have the Chelsea fans on his side and, even more importantly, on the side of his team. Chelsea fans, rather strangely, had a reputation for many years of being one of the quietest crowds in football. Perhaps it was the cosmopolitan area from which the bulk of their support was drawn in those days. Not many people owned cars and the multinational fan base from surrounding areas like Earls Court included a lot of neutrals who would just come to see a game of football. Many of the team's displays in those days would have merited an enquiry from the Office of Fair Trading. My first-ever match against Moscow Dynamo showed me how appreciative the Stamford Bridge crowd could be of the opposition. Perhaps the weather had something to do with it. In wintertime, London seemed permanently shrouded in a Jack-the-Ripper fog and a form of smog that made LA seem pollution-free. I used to go on the training jogs some mornings down to the Embankment past Cheyne Walk (which was to be Mick Jagger's address a few years later). The toxic fumes were so bad, players like 'Rabbit' Parsons and Bill Robertson wore bandannas which made them look like something out of a cowboy movie. To think Bentley and Lawton had both moved down to London for health reasons.

Ted Drake wanted the fans to be more vocal and get behind the team, even when they were struggling. He felt that the opposing team shouldn't get such vocal support. He even went so far as to write on the subject in newspaper articles and the official programme. Years later, one of my favourite Chelsea players, Joey Jones, would run onto the field and shake his fist at the fans, exhorting them to get behind the Blues. I always thought Joey was the crowd on the pitch.

Drake made sweeping changes to the personnel, both on and off the pitch. John Battersby was brought in as club secretary. Today, we have executives like Peter Kenyon and before him bean-counter Trevor Birch, who command vast salaries and bonuses. Battersby provided similar specialist services to the club without the high profile or the superstar wages. Battersby's financial acumen was perhaps his greatest asset but his superb business brain and organisational ability made it possible for Drake to focus on the football side of things.

Hardman Jack Oxberry joined as coach and immediately a much tougher training programme was instituted. Chelsea became leaner and meaner. They still had a long way to go to catch the turbo-injected 'Docherty Diamonds' of the early '60s but suddenly Chelsea were much fitter. In my view, though, the class of '65 was the side with the greatest potential ever and a match for any other Chelsea side from any era. Vialli's side in the late '90s was also superbly fit.

After a bright start that included wins over Villa and Blackpool, Chelsea faded badly and only stayed up by one point. In November, we started on our worst-ever run of straight League defeats – seven in all, with a 1–1 draw at Stoke breaking the sequence. My father was taking me to more matches as I was enjoying the experience so much, even when we lost. I recall a 2–1 win over Spurs which was an early Christmas treat for the Mears boys. It was my first glimpse of Ted Drake. He looked like a giant: hugely impressive. I always recall the strange hairstyle he had – a centre parting plastered down with Brylcreem – a mixture of all the bad haircuts of the '50s. Alf Ramsey scored for Spurs that day from the penalty spot. I remember thinking how miserable he looked throughout the game. Even when he scored, he picked the ball out of the net and strode back up the field purposefully. Little did I know how our paths would cross in the future.

Drake was a bit of a tinkerman that season, trying out 28 players in all. There were no subs either – even Ranieri would have been pushed to equal that. The best signing was 18-year-old winger Frank Blunstone, whom Drake had purchased from Crewe Alexandra. Frank Blunstone went on to become one of the most popular and influential players in the history of the club, playing 347 games and scoring 54 goals. It would have been more but a broken leg disrupted his career.

The 1953–54 season was another one of rebuilding. Chelsea finished a respectable eighth with no relegation fears. We took a bad beating at Wolves in September, being tonked 8–1. Johnny Hancock, the Wolves winger, scored a hat-trick. It is still in the record books as Chelsea's heaviest defeat. The next time we visited Wolves, though, it was a different story. Bentley hit 21 goals that season. An own goal by Ron Greenwood (future West Ham and England manager) put us out of the Cup at West Bromwich. Greenwood was approaching the end of his career but was still a polished defender. And Drake was buying for the future. The Chelsea squad was boosted by the purchase of two inside-forwards from the Third Divison South. They were John McNichol, signed from Brighton for £15,000, and Les Stubbs, from Southend for a similar amount.

Ted Drake was a great advocate of amateur football. He considered the players to have better temperaments than those of the professionals. Ted knew that they were prepared to run all day long simply because they had been given a chance at the highest level. The levels of fitness were such that the transition from amateur to professional could be overcome. Today, such a thing would be unthinkable. Drake had a vast knowledge of the amateur game and an extensive network of spies and spotters. He would spend a great deal of time attending matches and studying reports on matches and individual players. As a consequence, he signed Derek Saunders, the consistent ginger-haired defender, and the England amateur international Jim Lewis, both from Walthamstow Avenue. Neither cost Chelsea a penny piece. Avenue were a huge force in the amateur game in the early '50s but today they have disappeared off the map. Seamus O'Connell was signed from Bishop Auckland. He remained an amateur throughout his short but impressive spell at Stamford Bridge. These signings represented the top players of the booming amateur game, as important in a way as the signatures of Verón, Duff and Cole at the start of the Russian Revolution.

THE LEAGUE WON BY EXTRAORDINARY GENTLEMEN

The League of Extraordinary Gentlemen starring Sean Connery was in cinemas everywhere the autumn in which Chelsea, propelled by Abramovich's money, started their rampage. The film is an adaptation of a graphic novel by Alan Moore, which told of a group of famous late-nineteenth-century fictional characters who worked together to save the world. The group included famous names like Dr Jekyll and Mr Hyde, the Invisible Man, Dorian Gray and Captain Nemo.

The Chelsea team that won the League in 1954–55 had a captain almost as famous as Nemo – Roy Bentley. For the Invisible Man they had Frank Blunstone (no defender could catch him). The mischievous Eric Parsons was Jekyll and Hyde, capable of tearing a defence apart one moment with his electrifying pace and infuriating the crowd with a careless pass the next. Chelsea's Dorian Gray was Ken Armstrong, the veteran defender who never appeared to age in over 400 games. Ken was a forerunner of David Webb – tough and steady; if things got difficult, he could be switched up front. A tenacious, sturdy player, he filled in as centre-forward for a spell between the shock departure of Lawton and the purchase of Bentley. During that time, he scored a second-half hat-trick against Stoke.

Chelsea started off their momentous season with a 1–1 draw away to Leicester, Bentley scoring the first of his 21 League-winning goals. Parsons scored the only goal of the game in their first home match against Burnley. Bentley scored at Turf Moor in the return match to earn Chelsea a draw the following week. A solid but uninspired start. Nobody dreamt that Chelsea would come storming in for the League that season.

September was a topsy-turvy month for Chelsea, even by their standards. Cardiff, who just missed relegation, grabbed a hard-earned draw at Stamford Bridge. In the next home match, Preston won a close game 0–1. Their Scottish international, Tommy Henderson Docherty, dominated the match and was the best player on the field. Docherty was a fast-talking, highly competitive player who seemed to spend a great deal of the game arguing with officials, John Harris and most of his team. The Chelsea crowd were not used to such an extrovert display and voiced their disapproval.

Roy Bentley headed a fine goal against Manchester City at Maine Road to earn Chelsea a point. It had to be a fine goal because ex-German prisoner of war Bert Trautmann was in goal for City. Johnny McNichol, slowly starting to exert his influence on the side, shot the winner at Preston to earn some revenge. After the match, the boiler system developed a fault and the only water that was available was scalding hot. The players had to have a 'monkey' bath, lowering themselves into it going 'ooh, ooh, ah'.

McNichol scored again at St James' Park the following week and Roy Bentley chipped in with two smart goals against his old club.

October opened with a 3–3 draw with West Bromwich. Bobby Smith, playing one of his best games for Chelsea, laid a goal on for Roy Bentley. That was the only point we were to glean that month – hardly Championship-winning form! Huddersfield scraped home by a solitary goal in our next away trip.

The next game saw us score five against Manchester United. The trouble was they scored six times. The amateur Seamus O'Connell made his Chelsea debut and scored three. Imagine that today, an amateur scoring three against United on his debut. As flash as a fighting cock, O'Connell just turned up one day and then he was in the team.

United beat us again at Old Trafford in the last match of that momentous season. They were the only side to do the Double over Chelsea. We did not mind, though, because we had already won the League. The loss at home was the turning point. We had played so well Drake was convinced that Chelsea could push on and win it. My father said that if the game had lasted another ten minutes, we would have won. He must have been the only one because Chelsea lost their next two games: away to Blackpool and at home to Charlton. Chelsea were shocked by the Charlton result. It was their fourth consecutive defeat by an odd goal. Eddie Firmani, perhaps Charlton's greatest-ever player, scored both the Robins' goals as they snatched a surprise win. The Charlton fans had this great club song: 'When the red, red robin goes bob, bob, bobbing along'. They sang it when they scored the winner. They still play it at the Valley. Chelsea wanted to sign Firmani but he was on his way to Italy, where he had a successful career. The Italians were just starting to cast their eyes over the talent available in the UK.

Sunderland was the next port of call for the Ted Drake roadshow and Chelsea fought out a 3–3 draw, Johnny McNichol scoring twice in near-arctic winds. That point lifted Chelsea to 12th place in the table; most fans would have settled for a spot mid-table by then.

The following week, in early November 1954, Chelsea narrowly beat Spurs 2–1 in a bump-and-grind match. Bentley scored the first with a shot that took the loopiest of deflections. As so often happens, a streaky win can propel a team on to an unbeaten run. The Blues' next five games produced four wins and a draw. The most significant victory was the 3–4 away win against the defending champions, Wolves.

SNATCH

Wolves were the team of the '50s. Managed by the patriarchal Stan Cullis, their old gold-and-black colours dominated the era like red did the '90s. Cullis, a military man, ran the club like it was his own private army. He knew everything from top to bottom. His foul temper was known throughout the game. Even my father, a Royal Marine and generally fazed by nobody, was wary of Cullis. He hated Chelsea; I don't really know why. Perhaps it was the London thing. Clough was the same.

The game was played on a mud heap of a pitch under a slate-grey sky and the odds seemed stacked against the Blues throughout the match. Johnny McNichol, making Lampard-size improvements in his game each week, shot Chelsea ahead after a quarter of an hour. Wolves equalised immediately through Peter Broadbent, their emerging England star. Roy Bentley restored Chelsea's lead seven minutes after the break. Parsons, who was the man of the match with his ceaseless running, hit the angle of bar and post with a speculative long-range shot that deceived Wolves goalkeeper Williams. The ball rebounded straight to Roy Bentley who ran it into an empty net.

Swinbourne equalised for Wolves when he crashed home Leslie J. Smith's cut-back cross. The referee, J.W. Malcolm, disallowed three Chelsea goals. One of them involved a Wolves defender clearing when he was standing in the back of the net almost. When Wolves scored with a debatable late penalty to take it to 3–2, it looked like game over.

Swinbourne had gone down in the box after a challenge from John Harris, and Malcolm had pointed to the spot. I later called them 'Anfield' penalties: when a Liverpool forward would go down in the penalty area in the closing minutes and a penalty ensued. Incensed by the decision, Chelsea swarmed around the referee, protesting in the most vigorous manner.

Malcolm took some names and the ball was booted off the spot. There was pushing and shoving. Eventually order was restored and up stepped the diminutive Johnny Hancocks. The Wolves winger smashed the ball high into the roof of the net over the diving Robertson. Wolves to all intents and purposes had the points in the bag and would stretch their lead at the top even further. The history of Chelsea is full of improbable events, though, and two Chelsea goals in stoppage time tore the game out of Wolves' grasp.

It could be said that the title was won in those dying minutes. Only Chelsea could have fashioned it like that. Straight from the kick-off, Parsons picked the ball up and tore down the wing. The fans called him 'rabbit' because of his lightning surges. Sometimes he was as nervous as a rabbit. (It was an apt name but football fans are good like that.) Not this game, though. He tore past the Wolves defenders, finding it increasingly hard to move in the cloying mud. It was raining again as Parsons crossed and Les Stubbs scored easily. The score was 3–3. The Molineux fans made for the exits but the game had one more twist. Wolves came forward in a last assault but Yorkshireman Ken Armstrong won a desperate challenge with Leslie J. Smith just outside his own box and sent a Jonny Wilkinson kick towering into the Wolves half. It dropped just right for Roy Bentley, instantly seizing upon it and racing through a Wolves defence caught painfully square. All he had to do was draw the unprotected Williams from his line to score. It ended 4–3 to the good guys. It did enormous psychological damage to the champions and laid to rest the ghost of the previous season's 8–1 beating.

When the final whistle blew, Bentley looked across at the disbelieving Wolves defender Ron Flowers, a brilliant footballer and an England teammate who won 49 caps. Flowers' face had turned ashen white – a vital game had been snatched away from them in the dying seconds but the most terrifying prospect was returning to the dressing-room to face the apoplectic wrath of Stan the Wolves man.

The week before Christmas, Chelsea beat Leicester City 3–1 and the most bizarre goal ever scored at Stamford Bridge was witnessed by the 33,215-strong crowd. With the Blues leading 2–1, Johnny McNichol, the man of the moment, cracked in a shot from Blunstone's cross. The ball hit the underside of the bar and bounced down onto the goal line – a similar scenario to Geoff Hurst's legendary shot for England's second goal in the 1966 World Cup final. However, on this occasion there happened to be two City defenders, Stan Milburn and skipper Jack Froggatt (no relation to Selwyn), almost on the line. There was an element of comedy, though, because as Johnny and Roy Bentley raced in for the kill *both* Leicester men tried to hack clear. In an amazing coincidence, they simultaneously connected with the ball but could only volley it hard into the net. It is the only recorded joint own goal in the history of soccer. To this day, the stats record that the third goal scored by Chelsea was a unique own goal credited (if that is the correct word) to Milburn and Froggatt. I searched the archives for a picture of the extraordinary occurrence but there was no photographic evidence. It was good to know vaudeville was not dead. After all, we were the music hall team. It was always at Christmas that these things seemed to happen.

Tommy Lawton of all people ended Chelsea's unbeaten run on Christmas Day 1955. Thanks, Tom. The big guy was then at Arsenal and scored the only goal of the game with a first-half header. Vintage Lawton, though the gaps between goals were getting longer. Arsenal had signed him as a short-term solution. He had been struggling as player–manager of Brentford. Lawton loved the chance to sample the glamour of being attached to a top London club again. Until the Lawton goal, it had been a very even contest. Two days later, Arsenal came over to Stamford Bridge for the return. Seamus O'Connell scored a second-half equaliser to cancel out Tapscott's well-struck effort. Tapscott's chance was set up by Lawton's chested-down pass. Tommy got revenge for his unhappy spell at the Bridge.

New Year's Day 1955 was celebrated with a 2–5 win at Bolton, always a gruelling fixture for Chelsea. Bentley notched two as his greatest year began to unfold. He followed that up with three goals against Newcastle, who gave their ex-striker far too much space in the exciting 4–3 home win. Chelsea fans were convinced they had a title-winning side for the first time ever.

That year was one of those landmark years where earth-shattering events happen. Elvis Presley made his television debut in the States in 1955 and James Dean died. Chelsea won the League title. I suppose that shook a few people, particularly in north London and Manchester.

Notts County, Lawton's old side, knocked Chelsea out of the Cup in the fifth round. I am not sure if Chelsea donated their shirts at the end of the game. Chelsea bounced back the next week, whipping Huddersfield 4–1 with Blunstone in stunning form. The blue juggernaut lost at Villa by the odd goal in five but that was to be the last defeat they were to suffer before they won the League. Chelsea won their next four away games in convincing style: 2–4 at West Brom, 0–2 at Charlton, 0–1 at Cardiff and 2–4 at Tottenham.

The win at Cardiff took them top for the first time that season, with O'Connell's goal the clincher.

Peter Brabrook also made his debut at Tottenham that season. What a player! He went on to play for England and ended up at West Ham. He was still there, last I heard, working in the youth set-up. Brabrook was very influential in the shaping of the careers of Lampard, Joe Cole and Glen Johnson. Good espionage work, putting him into West Ham as a 'sleeping agent' all those years ago, then activating him to unearth all those prospects. Then we got the Russian to buy them all. John le Carré, eat your heart out.

THE LONG GOOD FRIDAY

It was around Easter in 1955 that Chelsea clinched the title. In those days, the clubs would play on Good Friday, the next day as a normal Saturday fixture and then again on the Bank Holiday Monday. Three games in four days – the real acid test of a team's fortitude. Drake had cleverly brought forward the game against West Bromwich, originally scheduled for the Bank Holiday Monday.

Chelsea's first game was against Sheffield United on Good Friday. The Blades were mid-table and Chelsea really should have done better than a mundane 1–1 draw. Nerves got to them, though. England winger Colin Grainger laid on a first-half goal for Sheffield centre-forward Jack Cross to give them a deserved lead. Eric Parsons, the only man to play to form, grabbed the equaliser to save a point for the Blues. Parsons, along with the efficient Derek Saunders, played in every League game. Twenty-four hours later, it was the same place, same time, for the biggie: the visit of champions Wolves. Drake made two changes, bringing Seamus O'Connell in for the youngster Brabrook and the rugged Stan Willemese in for the veteran John Harris. This involved Peter Sillett switching to right-back. Sillett turned out be the unlikely match winner. A crowd of 50,978 had turned up on Good Friday to see Sheffield United but the Wolves clash attracted 75,043 – support of Dynamo proportions. The huge bank of terracing which stood where the West Stand is today was absolutely packed. To the players running out of the tunnel, it must have been simply awe inspiring.

Wolves smothered Chelsea for three-quarters of the match and the game looked to be heading for a draw. That was their plan. Seamus O'Connell had other ideas, though, and smashed in a tremendous shot that the Wolves and England skipper Billy Wright handled. Sillett scored from the spot after 75 minutes with a shot that threatened to uproot the netting. Peter might not have been the most stylish of full-backs, compared to say Glen Johnson, but he possessed one of the hardest shots in the game. He had no nerves whatsoever that day.

Wolves staged a late onslaught as they could see their title slip-sliding away. Chick Thompson had replaced Bill Robertson in goal and he earned Chelsea's undying gratitude with a wonder save from Swinbourne. It was the only chance the Wolves danger man had in the match. Chelsea centre-half Stan Wicks kept him quiet all game. Wicks had a tremendous season for Chelsea. When Drake had brought him from Reading, it had raised a few eyebrows but what he lacked in skill he made up for with great pace and tremendous fitness. The Blues hung on to take the points and clinch a remarkable double over the champions. Chelsea won the title on the four points they obtained from Wolves.

On the run in, we held Portsmouth to a goalless draw and clinched the League with an effortless win over Sheffield Wednesday, who were relegated. Bentley scored at Old Trafford as United scraped a narrow win. It did not matter, though, because Chelsea, despite their limitations and stylistic conservatism, were already champions!

Looking back, it seems an unreal period. There was a national newspaper strike at the time and Chelsea never received their fair share of coverage. Nobody was impressed with them. In the 1930s, a popular music hall song was 'The Day That Chelsea Won the Cup' (a satire, as in the Americanism 'any time soon', generally used to denote something unlikely). I don't recall them writing a follow-up when Chelsea won the title. Chelsea lived in their own fantasy kingdom that year, the same one that Disneyland was created. They were always seen as the nearly men of football, as effete pushovers, either 'southern softies' or, more recently, spineless foreign mercenaries, forever yo-yoing up and down the table. It was a lot fairer then, far more equal. With Bosman, team spirit died. In those days, everybody had a fair chance, the squads were the same size. (Ranieri had to conduct 13-a-side training sessions at the end of 2003 so swollen with world-class players was the Chelsea squad.) Everyone was on the same basic wage and bonuses were equal.

Portsmouth won the title in 1950, Tottenham the year after. Realistically, what chance have those teams in the twenty-first century? Today, there is a nostalgia for a Chelsea that probably never existed but survives in many memories, mine included. I suppose it is for the values that existed in the days before the monetarism and the moronification of certain sections of the support. Bates ached to win the title but never could. That year did have an extraordinary significance for the club: it was the 50th anniversary of the founding of the club by the Mears family, halfway through this current history.

My father gave an impromptu speech (which he had started to prepare after our win at Tottenham) at the end of the Sheffield Wednesday game.

The crowd spilled onto the pitch to congratulate the players. Bentley was mobbed and it took him ages to get through the back-slapping fans. It was low key, though, no cuddle puddles, open-top buses or victory parades. Afterwards, the players caught the Tube home.

SIX

HOW DRAKE'S UGLY DUCKLING BECAME THE GREATEST SWAN IN THE HISTORY OF CHELSEA

We are English, that is one good fact.
Oliver Cromwell to Parliament, 17 September 1656

The invite read:

Thursday, 30 October 2003, Chelsea FC
(The Galleria, Stamford Bridge)
The Jimmy Greaves Dinner with extra guest Ian St John
Arrive 7 p.m. for 7.30 p.m.

The night before Hallowe'en, some of the people present were already in the mood. What scary masks. I assume they were masks. This was the week after Chelsea had narrowly beaten Lazio at the Bridge, two days before Chelsea had a tricky League visit to Everton, followed by the return against Lazio in Rome.

Speaking of Romans, at the time the press carried reports of the arrest of Mikhail Khodorkovsky, Russia's richest man, at gunpoint on a Siberian runway. Khodorkovsky's business links with Abramovich led to speculation that the Chelsea owner could be the next target for Kremlin hardliners.

A small, tubby middle-aged man in an ill-fitting cream summer jacket started his stand-up routine. The vast room was packed with tables of similarly aged men in lounge suits having a good time, not-so-good food, good booze and then a good laugh.

'First, I would like to thank Ken Bates for the use of his office.' Wearing a proper smile and a crumpled shirt, he looked scruffy as usual but carried his confidence like a hod of platinum bricks. Fidgeting to his right was Ian St John, a man who survived a tackle from Ron Harris at Villa Park in 1965 that would have felled a rhino. St John was wearing a light-grey suit, double-breasted and straight out of *Minder*. He pointed a finger decorated with Garrard rings at the crowd. Tugging on his lairy retro Versace, the speaker started into a rap about Rio Ferdinand. The Manchester United defender was still at odds with the drug-testing authorities and had recently been dropped from the England team.

'Rio was brought up in Peckham, times were tough and he didn't have a pot to piss in. Still doesn't.'

The room erupted; the little chap allowed himself a look through the thick, plate-glass windows. He saw only darkness. The structure called the Shed had stood there once. I wonder how many of that night's more affluent fans had stood in the Shed when it was overseen by Mick Greenaway and his noise-merchant chums. The afternoon they had, that famous one with Tottenham and their donkey-jacketed crew, springs to mind. St John must have been sitting near the spot where the Bovril gate was located. The cost of a table for a forthcoming Chelsea pitch-owners' dinner was a mere £7,000. Even Russian Roman blinked at that one. I suppose you could say it was a bit rich. Sloaney gits with Sloaney git friends: privileged, bumptious and unremarkable. Far below was the pitch, the same pitch where the same little man once scored the bulk of his 132 Chelsea goals in 169 games. Jimmy Greaves had come home . . .

1955 AND ALL THAT

On 20 August 1955, Ted Drake awoke to another Chelsea morning. The first day of the 1955–56 season and his team were the champions of England. The future at the elite level must have seemed so bright he could have been forgiven for wearing Ray-Bans. There lay a goldmine of opportunities ahead.

There is a marvellous scene in *The Producers*, a film in which everything depends on the two anti-heroes staging the largest Broadway flop ever. Max Bialystock (played by the monstrous Zero Mostel) turns to his accomplice Leo Bloom (Gene Wilder) and bemoans the unlikely success of their musical about the Third Reich, 'Springtime for Hitler'. 'We chose the wrong play, we chose the wrong director, we chose the wrong Hitler. Where did we go right?'

Ted Drake chose the wrong players and the wrong tactics, yet Chelsea won the League and virtually everything else they had entered. Where did he go right?

Chelsea should have gone on to play in the first-ever European Cup. My father Joe Mears was also president of the Football League. He was bullied out of competing in Europe by the League's secretary, Alan Hardaker. He was very strict and opposed to any form of foreign competition, always clad in an ill-fitting blazer. Full of moralising outbursts, Hardaker had a morbid dislike of foreigners. Like the House of Lords, FA committees and blazers acted as guardians of what they regarded as 'traditional values'. I can only speculate how Chelsea would have performed in the Euro contest. They had fared well in numerous friendly fixtures against top-class foreign sides. Chelsea were drawn against Djurgaarden of Sweden but the tie never took place. Real Madrid won the European Cup in its inaugural season and they liked it so much they retained it for the next five years. They still have a major say in it today, with Beckham, Carlos and Zidane. I would love to have seen Chelsea play against the most successful club team of all.

The press made much of the rivalry between the youngsters in the Manchester United and Chelsea sides. United were known as the 'Busby Babes' after their mentor Sir Matt Busby. The Chelsea side were known as the 'Ducklings' – I don't know who actually coined the phrase. Busby had a magnificent side crammed with brilliant youngsters but the incomparable Duncan Edwards was the jewel in the crown. The new England centre-forward Tommy Taylor was another huge prospect. I had seen him score two breathtaking goals in United's incredible 5–6 win at Chelsea the previous autumn. The much-vaunted Manchester United youth set-up was the envy of the game, still is – Best and Charlton through to Beckham, Scholes and Giggs.

Bolton ruined the party for our opening game by winning 2–0, their winger Doug Holden running the game. Holden, who had the face of a boxer and the gait of a drag queen, made one goal and scored the other. I had a feeling that it was going to be a tough season and for once I was proven correct. Tommy Lawton, still a muscular penalty-box presence, scored again for Arsenal as they held us to a draw at Highbury. Portsmouth came to the Bridge and scored five as they walked over the champions. The crowd were as silent as a Vermeer picture. (Later in the season, the pair fought out an exciting 4–4 draw at Fratton Park with Blunstone, firing on all cylinders, notching a beautifully executed hat-trick.)

The dismal run continued with away defeats at Blackpool and Sunderland. Wolves gained revenge for their Championship-costing double defeat, winning by the odd goal in three at Molineux. Eric Parsons seemed to reserve his best performances for Wolves and scored a neat goal but it was not enough. There was a perpetual tension between Stan Cullis and Ted Drake, similar to the discord between Wenger and Ferguson today.

With O'Connell's brief tenure at Chelsea over, Bobby Smith forced himself back into the side and scored four goals in a short run, one of the goals a crackerjack against Tottenham who signed him shortly afterwards. My father was reluctant to sell the teaky striker but Ted Drake was growing impatient. His youngsters were blossoming but they needed time. Even in those days it was the most valuable commodity in the game. Drake was keen to sell Smith to bankroll an attempt to sign a youngster called Alick Jeffrey, whom Jimmy Thompson had spotted playing for Doncaster Rovers. Jimmy deserved his spotter's badge for that one.

Jeffrey was one of the greatest young footballers this country has ever seen. Wayne Rooney reminds me a great deal of him with his bulky build, intense focus and bloody-minded hunger for goals. Scouse Rooney is actually a throwback to the golden age of burly strikers. Jeffrey made his debut at the age of 15 for Rovers, who at that time were a competent Second Division side. He became the hottest property in the game with two Cup goals against Aston Villa. Matt Busby wanted to sign him for United and integrate him into his Babes troupe alongside Tommy Taylor and in front of Edwards. There was great rivalry between the two sides as to who could sign the best youngsters. Busby's Babes were in direct competition with their southern counterparts. It was an unwritten law that United had the best kids from the north and vice versa. If Chelsea could have signed Jeffrey, born in the pit village of Rawmarsh, it would have outraged United even more than when Peter Kenyon defected.

Despite preliminary enquiries and a good offer from us, it was soon obvious that Busby had already secured a deal with Jeffrey. Alick was lining himself up for a full England cap as well. He was just 17. You know what I mean.

His youth was taken away, though, when in the opening minutes of an England Under-23 match against France he smashed his right leg in two places. It was a horrific collision and ruined his career. Alick received £4,000 after his catastrophic injury and ended up on the dole.

The story did not end there; he broke his leg in his first comeback game in non-League football and subsequently emigrated to Sydney for a time. He eventually came back in the '60s to play for Doncaster, a testament to his unflagging desire to play again, coupled with strength and courage. Plagued by weight problems and with only limited use of his right leg, he was still good enough to finish top goalscorer in the Football League in 1965. That was his last stab at the big time because the next year he suffered appalling injuries in a car crash which ended his chances of a decent comeback. He died in 2000, a stark reminder of the dangers involved in playing football. I often wonder what inspiration he would have given to Chelsea Football Club had events taken a different course.

THE LONGEST CUP TIE EVER

All that remained for Chelsea that season was the FA Cup. Marooned in mid-table, it was their only chance to salvage some respect in a wretched season. In the third round, they scrambled a 0–1 victory over Hartlepool thanks to an own goal. A fourth-round draw took us to Burnley. The tie turned into a five-match soap opera which ran for over nine hours – the longest-ever Cup clash in the history of Chelsea. Shortly afterwards, the Government introduced extra time in an attempt to reduce workers' absenteeism caused by attendance at replays.

The Lancashire side were seen as an emerging power in the top three and their growing youth system was producing a crop of famous names for the future. Their star player was the Irish schemer Jimmy McIlroy. It was he who engineered the first goal with a towering centre for Peter McKay to put Burnley ahead in the first half. Eric Parsons equalised from Bentley's pass for Chelsea in the second half. Parsons' head-down dashes and crosses set up enough chances for Chelsea to win comfortably. Two days later, the pair reconvened at Stamford Bridge where the closely contested game was played on a bone-hard pitch. The players struggled to keep their footing on the treacherous surface. Frank Blunstone put Chelsea in front only for the classy Burnley winger Brian Pilkington to level it up with a soft goal early in the second half. That was how it was to stay, even after extra time, although the ever-dangerous McKay almost stole it near the end with a long-range shot that hit Bill Robertson's post with the big man stranded.

Wolves played a League match at Chelsea on the Saturday and won 3–2 to do the Double over a weary Chelsea that season. The following Monday, Chelsea met Burnley again at Birmingham's ground. A terrific match ended 2–2, aet. McKay put Burnley in front early on. Then came a Peter Sillett equaliser with a thunderbolt spot-kick after Peter Brabrook was tripped in the box. Brabrook went down like a giraffe on a skateboard. As always, Sillett showed unflinching nerve when the stakes were high. McIlroy shot Burnley's second but Roy Bentley slid in to equalise with 15 minutes of normal time left. Extra time was bedlam; Robertson pulled a muscle but made a string of great stops despite his obvious distress. Ron Tindall's effort was kicked off the line when it looked like he had won it. Chelsea won the toss to decide where the neutral ground venue would be.

A week later, they met at Highbury in a third replay which remained scoreless after two hours. This was the first match in which Chelsea had the edge, the ex-schoolboy boxer, Bentley, going close on a couple of occasions. Finally, it was resolved two days later in the fourth replay of the fourth-round tie. Again played in north London, thanks to another lucky Chelsea call, this time at White Hart Lane, Chelsea won 0–2 on the arctic wasteland of a pitch. The promising Duckling, Ron Tindall, catapulted himself forward to score the first after a great run by Brabrook. Jim Lewis wrapped it up near the end with a simple goal. It was the only time in the series that one of the sides had been two goals up.

The stats from the five matches made good reading. Chelsea used 17 players and made 11 changes – not a lot compared to the Ranieri era but let us not forget that there were no subs and no squad of global superstars. A total of 163,446 fans watched the games (I saw them all, the Birmingham game was the best) and receipts were £23,809. The team captains, Bentley and Tommy Cummings, tossed for ends eight different times. Three different refs employing ten linesmen officiated. It was the only Chelsea tie to be played on five different grounds.

Perhaps it was going to be Chelsea's year for the Cup after winning through the marathon tie against Burnley. That is what we told each other. It was not to be, alas. Three days later, the Cup draw took them to Everton. Chelsea were exhausted – it was their third game in five days and their eighth in three weeks. No respite in those days. Now, the fellows would need a week in Florida to recuperate. A battle-fatigued Chelsea went out of the Cup to a solitary Everton goal in front of 61,572 supporters. Burnley quashed us 5–0 in a League match up there a few weeks later, Pilkington grabbing three goals.

NATURAL BORN BOOGIE

The season that had promised so much became a story of yesterday's dreams. Bobby Smith scored for his new employers Tottenham Hotspur as they thrashed us 4–0. The incomparable Johnny Brooks also scored two brilliant goals. Brooks was later to join Chelsea in exchange for another promising youngster, Les Allen. Promising youngsters, we had so many.

Runaway leaders Manchester United also scored four at the Bridge. The Babes ended up with sixty points, a massive eleven points (don't forget only two for a win) ahead of Stan Cullis's outfit. We trailed in sixteenth, only six points clear of bottom club Sheffield United.

The following season, 1956–57, saw the Championship side break up. Drake knew that they were past their sell-by date. Also, the assembly line of youngsters was now spilling out of the warehouse of talent that was the Welsh Harp ground in Hendon. That was where the Chelsea youth side played. They had previously been known as the Tudor Rose. The season opened with a 2–0 defeat at Burnley (not them again) and Chelsea only won two of their first eleven games.

Roy Bentley was the first to leave the club, joining neighbours Fulham in the autumn. In 10 seasons he scored 150 goals in 347 games: only Bobby Tambling and Kerry Dixon scored more for Chelsea. Funnily enough, Peter Osgood scored exactly the same amount but he took twenty-nine more games (and four subs) to do it. Who was the most stylish of the duo? Nothing in it, really. Only Zola, as a footballer, and the intrinsic talent of Jimmy Greaves could really stand comparison with the pair. Roy captained Chelsea to the title, though, when he was on £8 a week. The bonus for winning the League was a new suit.

At Fulham, the ex-Chelsea skipper switched to centre-half and played successfully for five years before joining another London side, QPR. He ended up at full-back for the Rangers and later managed Ted Drake's old side Reading. At the time of writing, he was still living down there and avidly following the Blues' glorious repeat of his achievement. The knighthood is long overdue.

Stan Wicks, the defensive stalwart of the Championship season, took over the captain's armband from Bentley. It was short-lived, though; a bad knee injury sustained in the September 0–0 draw with Sheffield Wednesday put an end to his career. Peter Sillett missed the start of the season with knee problems and struggled to regain his fitness. Eric Parsons was next to go, joining Brentford. Eric was the quintessential Chelsea player. His unique relationship with the besotted Stamford Bridge crowd was the template for similar complex relationships enjoyed by players like Peter Houseman and Dennis Wise – players that started off being hated by certain sections of the support but were later loved because of their dedication to the cause of Chelsea. These particular players were all clever enough to realise that they carried the hopes and aspirations of the fans. In the '80s, Joey Jones was the most popular player at the club because he enjoyed a relationship with the fans similar to that of Wayne Rooney and the England fans in Portugal 2004.

Ken Armstrong was another outstanding performer from that mould. For years, he was Chelsea's talisman and a rallying point when things got tough. He retired and emigrated to New Zealand after setting a record for the number of League games played. Later, this total was surpassed by Ron Harris.

Further tragedy hit the club when Frank Blunstone smashed his leg in the fourth-round Cup tie at Tottenham. It was a bleak day for Chelsea. They were swamped 4–0. Bobby Smith and Tommy Harmer, later to play a significant part in Chelsea folklore, were amongst the scorers.

In March, Chelsea played their first game under floodlights at Stamford Bridge in a friendly against Sparta Prague. A crowd of 30,701 watched the lights being switched on and Chelsea win 2–0. In 2003, Sparta returned to the Bridge in a Champions League match. They played so deep they were almost in Chelsea Harbour and ground out a 0–0 draw. The point was enough to guarantee Chelsea qualification into the last 16, though.

Easter was another interesting period. On Good Friday, they won 1–2 at Newcastle and made history by becoming the first Football League side to fly home. (Up until then, the League had banned air transportation for clubs. My father once told me that the League was afraid of one of the top clubs being involved in a crash. With Europe opening up and fixtures becoming more congested, however, flying was becoming essential. The advantages of using the planes soon became obvious.) The next day, Chelsea put five past Everton and on Easter Monday won the return with the Geordies by 6–2. Brabrook was in peak form in all three matches, causing pandemonium with his pace and quality passing.

Chelsea finished in 13th spot, not too unlucky as Jimmy Greaves was about to take centre stage.

ASK GREAVES

'Jimmy Greaves, Chelsea FC was it, and only 18, a wonder striker, idol to me and all blue-and-white scarved Stamford Bridge lads. I was there August '58 when he woofed five goals past Wolves.'

Andrew Loog Oldham, former manager of the Rolling Stones, *Stoned*

Greaves was, in my view, Chelsea's greatest-ever player. Better than Lawton, better than Bentley, even Osgood or Zola. Fans identify him more with Tottenham, where he was to spend the best and most successful part of his career. He showed enough in his Boy's Own Adventure at Chelsea, though, to convince me of his priceless ability to score goals – a neglected art these days but surely a highly important one. Greaves was the most instinctive goalscorer in the history of football and its finest finisher. Nothing fazed him; he was the most complete two-footed player I had ever seen. Playing for the Chelsea youth side, he scored over 170 goals in his first 2 seasons, honing the skills that would make him the supreme striker. People would have you believe that strikers are born, not made; that goalscoring is an art that can't be taught. Greaves was a natural. Drake just had to pick him for the opening game of season 1956–57 against

Spurs at White Hart Lane. Seventeen-year-old Jimmy scored Chelsea's second-half equaliser and was on target again four days later when he made his home debut against Manchester City. It was the start of a seemingly never-ending stream of goals scored with dead-eye accuracy. By the end of the season, he had accumulated 22 goals in 35 League games. Jimmy was the original 'ugly duckling' in baggy shorts with unruly hair but he left the Bridge the golden boy of soccer with a Jonny Wilkinson persona.

After just three months in the first team, he was called up as reserve for the full England team against Ireland. Jimmy would have been England's youngest-ever player if the tousle-haired Manchester United striker Tommy Taylor had not passed a late fitness test. Taylor looked to have made the England centre-forward spot his own with his remarkable displays.

The most memorable match that season was against Portsmouth on Christmas morning 1957. It will live on in the memory of anyone who was lucky enough to see it. Drake had rested Greaves in an attempt to deflect some of the hyperbolic publicity that he was attracting as the first flashbulbs of fame exploded in his face. Ted wanted to rest him, too, from the rigours of the game. Chelsea were as unpredictable as ever, flamboyance coming in instalments. In Greaves' absence, they had won the battle of the 'young guns', with a 0–1 victory at Old Trafford. The next week, Tottenham hammered Chelsea 2–4 at the Bridge. They were up and down more times than a gondola on the London Eye.

Jimmy repaid him by scoring four goals in a Christmas bonanza game that ended in a 7–4 goalfest to Chelsea. It was the last game that was ever played at Stamford Bridge on a Christmas Day and more fun than an *Only Fools and Horses* special. Jimmy struck after 15 minutes, scoring with a first-time low drive from long range. It was a rarity for him to score from outside the penalty area. It was almost worth the admittance money for this alone. The goal deluge had started, with ten more to follow. Ron Tindall popped in the second and a crazy own goal made it 3–0. Then Greaves sandwiched a Chelsea own goal, more bizarre than Pompey's, between his two solo goals. It stood 5–1 at the break. The fans must have thought Christmas had come early, except it was Christmas already. Derek Dougan, one of the era's most colourful characters and also a terrific player, set up a second Portsmouth goal. Back came Greaves to score instantly for Chelsea, a goal bearing his hallmark, appearing from nowhere to neatly steer in Lewis's cross. Sillett made it a magnificent seven with a toe punt from nearly forty yards that sailed into the roof of the net after a one-two with Greaves. The fans trudged home for their Christmas dinners shaking their heads. Pompey strolled through a non-existent Chelsea rearguard to pick up their Christmas gifts and score two late goals. No match better typifies the Chelsea team of the Greaves era. Superb goals, simple goals, bizarre goals, slipshod defending. No ostentatious celebrations, just fun, fun, fun. The next day, Chelsea travelled down to Portsmouth for the return game. They lost 3–0.

A few weeks later, Third Division Darlington came to the Bridge in the fourth round of the Cup. They shook Chelsea by storming to a 0–2 interval lead. The Blues eventually scrambled a 3–3 draw. Worse was to follow in the replay. Chelsea were ignominiously dumped out of the Cup 4–1 after extra time. Greaves was dropped for the replay but was soon back in the team and celebrating with a hat-trick at Sheffield Wednesday.

A few days before, on 6 February 1958, one of the greatest tragedies in the history of the game occurred. The plane carrying the Manchester United team back from a European Cup tie in Belgrade crashed, killing most of the passengers. Amongst the victims were seven of the players who had played against Chelsea at Old Trafford just before Christmas: Roger Byrne, Eddie Colman, Mark Jones, Duncan Edwards, Billy Whelan, Tommy Taylor and Dave Pegg.

The greatest players of their generation, wiped out in a terrible disaster. It took the game a very long time to recover from this palpable loss; perhaps it never fully did. Alick Jeffrey always used to say that if he had not broken his leg, he would have been a United player and on the BEA Viscount when it crashed in the snow.

Ironically, in the last League match of the season, Chelsea played Manchester United at the Bridge. Only one player, the indestructible Billy Foulkes, remained in the United line-up from the team that had gone down to a Ron Tindall goal only four months earlier. Foulkes, along with the amazingly resilient Bobby Charlton, were to win European Cup winners' medals ten years later.

David Cliss scored Chelsea's opener in a meaningless 2–1 victory. It was a terrible experience even watching that game. I kept looking for Taylor and Edwards. It was eerie and so spooky: the crowd watched in silence. Chelsea finished eleventh, two places behind United. It was Cliss's only League goal for Chelsea. At one time, he was regarded as the most exceptional of all the talents that passed through the Welsh Harp. Greaves was in awe of his ability when he first arrived at Chelsea. Cliss was just that far in front of his peers when it came to skill. His right foot was sweeter than a Mars bar washed down with treacle. For whatever reason, though, he was unable to harness it. One has to sympathise with his short term on the wheel of stardom. At the top of the ride, it is all blue skies but at the bottom the wheel drags you through a pool of urine. His career was thwarted, just as Jeffrey's was by injury, or Edwards's by fate. Only a handful ever scrambled into the big time, unbowed and unscathed. Jimmy Greaves was one who made it all the way to the very top. It is a matter of course that every story written about Greaves and his problems after he quit the game is required to mention that once upon a time he was a great footballer. As a matter of truth, he was the greatest goalscorer ever.

THE FA YOUTH CUP

Chelsea took part in their first-ever Youth Cup final against Wolves, played over two legs. It still is. The Blues had stormed through the ten ties with future England centre-forward Barry Bridges scoring twenty-four goals alongside Greaves. It was the seventh year of the competition; Manchester United had won it the first six times, but now their all-conquering Babes had sadly departed.

Chelsea won the first leg 5–1 at home with Greaves and Bridges amongst the scorers. The second leg appeared to be a mere formality but 50,000 Wolves fans turned up to support their wolf cubs. Greaves scored in the return but the problem was Wolverhampton scored six. To the seemingly invincible, overblown Chelsea youth side it was a huge setback. They had met with nothing but intoxicating success and this reverse was demoralising. Panic had spread through the young Chelsea side like a virus in a John Wyndham novel when Wolves started getting back into the game. Greaves learnt from it, though, never to take anything for granted and that he was only as good as his last goal. That is what drove him.

CHELSEA IN EUROPE (THE FIRST TIME)

Season 1958–59 was another scoring spree for Greaves. Young Jimbo played in every League game, all 42 of them, and plundered 32 goals. He took particular revenge on Wolves early in the season. The Youth Cup defeat burnt in his mind. He felt that he had let down Thompson and Foss and that somebody had to pay. This game was against the big boys who also happened to be champions of England, not the class of '57. Jimmy, at his most blissfully sublime, scored five in a 6–2 win. He took each goal like a Stalingrad sniper: cold and remorseless.

Newcastle were beaten 6–5 a few weeks later, with our hero scoring twice. He followed that with a hat-trick against Nottingham Forest. This was a bright start to the season but the creaking defence shipped water. Some heavy defeats at Burnley 4–0, Man City 5–1 and West Bromwich also 4–0, saw Chelsea slide down the table quicker than a lap dancer down a pole in the Spearmint Rhino.

It was the first time that Chelsea entered into European competition in the curiously named International Industries Fairs International Cities Cup. Chelsea had been selected to represent London. Tottenham got the gig first but Chelsea ended up in Europe. It had some weird rules, one of which was that three players from other clubs were allowed to play, provided they were from clubs in the same city. Drake stuck with his own squad, though my father was keen on loaning Danny Blanchflower from White Hart Lane and Danny Clapton from Highbury. Drake was the first manager to obtain reports on the opposition. The information for the first match against BK Frem from Copenhagen must have been sketchy though. Guess who scored the first-ever goal in Europe? Jimmy Greaves, in a 1–3 victory. Interesting to note that the return crowd, who saw Greaves score two in a 4–1 win, was only 13,104. A massive 57, 910 attended a home League match against Arsenal the following week. (See, this foreign rubbish will never catch on. Hardaker was right all along!) The game ended in a 0–3 win to Arsenal. Greaves was marked out of the game by the volatile Tommy Docherty, one of the fiercest tacklers in the League. The 'Doc', as he called himself by then, had joined Arsenal from Preston earlier that season. Drake was keen to sign him for Chelsea after Docherty had requested a transfer following a row over his World Cup appearances for Scotland in Sweden.

Christmas was its usual schizophrenic self. Greaves scored in a 0–3 pasting of Blackburn Rovers on a sunny Christmas morning. Boxing Day saw the decorations come down, though, as Rovers won 2–0 at the Bridge. Floundering in mid-table, the Cup was again the only avenue open. A brilliant 1–4 win in the third round over Cup titans Newcastle signalled that maybe, after all those years, it was going to be Chelsea's year. Newcastle had lifted the Cup three times in the '50s and were formidable opponents. Greaves had scored the second in the first half to open up his Cup account – a marvellous strike, collecting a long throw from centre-half John Mortimore and weaving himself into a shooting position 20 yards out before scoring with his left foot. Fans numbering 57,038 witnessed it – 10,000 fewer than when one Hughie Gallacher had returned there nearly 30 years before.

Greaves scored again in the next round against Aston Villa but the Midland side knocked out Chelsea 1–2.

ALL THE YOUNG DUDES

Once again, the season was over in January but Drake was still blooding the youth-team players. The Championship side was being replaced by youngsters who were emerging in their dozens. Johnny McNichol left to join Crystal Palace. In February, Chelsea beat West Ham 3–2 at Stamford Bridge. Two debutants scored in that game for Chelsea: Barry Bridges and Bobby Tambling. Inevitably, it was Jimmy Greaves who scored the other. It was the day Chelsea played their youngest-ever forward line, the average age being eighteen years and five months. The line-up is interesting because in my horribly unfashionable opinion it was one of the greatest five-prong attacks in the history of the club:

David Cliss   Jimmy Greaves

Peter Brabrook   Barry Bridges   Bobby Tambling

They were all English-born players and, except for the enigmatic Cliss (technically the best player of the five but a classic example of the finite nature of football), became full England internationals. Brabrook was a better jockey than Kieren Fallon. He could make space out of nothing by cleverly manoeuvring. This enabled him to beat his defender or, as Drake would say, to 'jockey' him. His distribution of the ball was impeccable and even today Lampard and Joe Cole, whom he later coached at West Ham, have the indelible stamp of accurate passing in their play.

Barry Bridges was blisteringly quick. Osgood later overshadowed him but, in my view, Barry never received the praise he deserved. In his day, Barry was as fast as the majestic Thierry Henry; the problem was his fame and bank balance never grew at the same rate. Bobby Tambling ended up as Chelsea's all-time top scorer with 202 goals but he was no Argos version of Greaves. At his peak, Tambling was a sensation, a synthesis of speed and cunning. Tambling also had a harder shot than Greaves. Jimmy did his damage from close range, while Tambling was a sharpshooter. Hasselbaink at his very best reminded me of Bobby. What a famous five – Crespo and Mutu had a lot to live up to.

The season ended tamely, Chelsea finishing 14th. A robust Birmingham beat the Blues 4–1 in the final League match. Chelsea had conceded 98 League goals to establish a worst-ever record and, generally speaking, the defence had a woeful time all season. There was no organisation. A Fairs Cup tie against Ville De Belgrade wound things up. A team of Johnny-no-stars, we all thought. Brabrook scored the only goal of the game in the anaemic home leg but Chelsea were soundly beaten 1–4 in the return.

Greaves was on top of the world, though, as the goals flowed quicker than Father Thames. The Hainault-born striker finished joint-top goalscorer in the division, a title he shared with burly Bobby Smith, now the Spurs and England number 9. Jimmy also pulled off the neat trick of smashing the club scoring record set 48 years earlier in the Second Division by Bob Whittingham.

Season 1959–60 was of uniform mediocrity once again, with Chelsea finishing 18th.

Jimmy had spent the summer touring with the full England team. He kept his unbelievable record of scoring in every senior debut game he ever played by netting in May 1959 against Peru. Perhaps the first cracks started to appear in his relationship with Chelsea then. Greaves realised that the world did not stretch the length of the Kings Road. Chelsea missed relegation by three points and conceded over ninety goals again. Only Greaves' 29 League goals (plus a Cup goal) kept them afloat. The pressure on him to score week after week must have been immense. Chelsea were simply aiming to avoid relegation until the youngsters could be welded into a cohesive unit.

The Preston matches typified the situation. In the first game of the season, the clubs drew 4–4 with Greaves scoring a hat-trick. In the return (the last match before Christmas), Greaves scored all five as Chelsea crept home by the odd goal in nine. In the two matches, Jimmy had scored a total of eight goals whilst the defence conceded the same amount.

Drake stuck with the traditional 3-2-2-3 formation, called the 'WM' system. The four players who formed a square in the midfield (usually Brabrook, Johnny Brooks, Frank Blunstone and Stan Crowther) did almost all of the running up and down the field, whilst Greaves and his centre-forward (either Tindall or Charlie Livesey, signed from Southampton) stayed up. The defenders, usually the 'Fabulous Sillett Brothers', and centre-half John Mortimore stayed back. Well, that was the plan. Drake took the training sessions but his influence on the team seemed to wane, particularly with the youngsters who found him aloof and unapproachable.

For the second year running, Aston Villa put paid to Chelsea's Cup hopes with an identical 1–2 fourth-round victory at Stamford Bridge.

The youth side was once again the beacon of hope – for the fourth successive season they won the South East Counties League. Their biggest honour, though, was landing the FA Youth Cup for the first time. They beat Preston over two legs to erase the disappointment of the Wolves debacle. The first leg at Chelsea ended in a 1–1 draw but Bobby Tambling scored a hat-trick at Deepdale in a 1–4 victory. Two more Chelsea legends made their League debuts that season: Peter Bonetti in goal and Terry Venables in midfield.

The season ended with a 1–5 drubbing from Wolves at the Bridge. Stan

Cullis's men were bidding for their third League title in a row. Burnley denied them at the death by taking the title by a point. Tottenham finished third and might have won it but for losing 1–0 to Chelsea at home on Bank Holiday Monday. Jimmy Greaves had deprived them of the League by scoring the only goal of the game. White Hart Lane was a lucky ground for him. It had not escaped the attention of Spurs manager Bill Nicholson (then as financially omnipotent as Chelsea are today) that Greaves was the greatest marksman around. That summer, the press was full of speculation that Chelsea were terminally ill and Greaves would soon be on his way with a golden bungee jump to Tottenham.

THE LONG GOODBYE

The '60s opened with the departure of Greaves after one more goal-drenched season. The 1960s swung, everybody said. Nobody swung more than Chelsea.

Greaves scored 43 goals in his final season, 2 of them in the newly created League Cup. Just as well, because the defence conceded a ton of League goals – they're still in the record books.

Life was never dull at the Bridge. Greaves scored five against West Bromwich in a 7–1 thrashing, the best-ever First Division score by a Chelsea team. (I recall Gordon Durie scoring five at Walsall in a 0–7 romp in the Second Division in 1989.)

It was raining goals in season 1960–61. Greaves notched hat-tricks against Blackburn and Manchester City in 5–2 and 6–3 home victories. Other high scores were a 6–1 win over Cardiff and a cardiac-arresting 4–4 draw at Burnley. On the debit side, they took some bad beatings: a 2–6 loss at home to the champs Burnley sticks in the mind. This was followed by an appalling Christmas with a 6–0 caning at Manchester United on Boxing Day, followed by a 6–1 defeat to Wolves on New Year's Eve. Happy New Year, Stan. Drake never looked so angry with his players as after that one.

The bitterest pill he had to swallow, though, was a 1–2 home defeat to Fourth Division Crewe in the third round of the Cup a few days later. Even after the bumper catalogue of humiliations Chelsea had suffered in Cup competitions over the years, the Crewe defeat ranks as one of the worst. Ted Drake was under pressure; the press had already marked his card. The fans, long suffering as always, were unhappy, particularly with the constant rumour of Greaves' departure. The media backlash exerted on a manager today is far more extreme than it was 40 or more years ago. The focus on Drake was microscopic compared to what Ranieri had to put up with in 2003–04 or what Glenn Hoddle had to contend with in the last few months of his unhappy spell at Tottenham.

The Crewe match was a nightmare. They caught Chelsea napping to steal a two-goal lead. Blunstone scored against his old side in the first half to reduce the deficit. On an appalling pitch, Crewe withstood non-stop pressure to hold out for a shock victory. Greaves decided after that defeat that his future lay away from the club. Drake knew in his heart that his time was up. He had taken Chelsea as far as he could and his dream of producing a team of home-grown players to emulate his Championship side perished.

The celebrated youth system was still turning up trumps, though. The Ducklings' latest line-up retained the FA Youth Cup, beating Everton 5–3 on aggregate. The Everton side featured future stars like Kendall, Royle and Harvey, which made the achievement even more remarkable.

Greaves was by then in negotiations with AC Milan. Rumours abounded that Chelsea needed the money. Greaves, with his eye to the main chance, played it shrewdly. To this day, in his heart, I am convinced he never really wanted to leave. He is still a Blue and his happiest memories were linked with Chelsea, who were his roots after all.

THE LEAGUE CUP

Tucked away amidst all the dramas was the start of the League Cup. Chelsea's first game was away to Millwall. They won 1–7 with Greaves notching two. A good score at the old Den. If they had played it five years later, though, I think the Chelsea side and their fans would have been glad to leave in one piece.

Chelsea scored another seven at Doncaster in the next round. Alick Jeffrey's old side could have done with their favourite son. Greaves missed the game through injury but Brabrook, Blunstone and the rapidly improving Tambling scored two apiece.

Once again, hopes were high for a Cup run but Portsmouth ended the dream by putting them out 1–0 at Fratton Park. Around that time, Alan Harris broke into the first team at left-back. Harris was a ferocious tackling defender but the word was his younger brother Ron was an even harder nut.

LOST IN THE FOREST

Greaves still had a few treats left for his fans. They went up to Newcastle and won 1–6. He scored four goals as Chelsea equalled their best-ever away performance. Ron Tindall scored the other two. The partnership between him and Jimmy never really gelled but, just sometimes, the hard-working Tindall looked like bacon against Greaves' eggs.

After months of speculation, Greaves announced he was signing for

AC Milan and more lira than he could count. Chelsea received £80,000 for a player that had cost them £10. After only a few strife-torn months, he quit Italy to join Spurs despite Chelsea's attempts to buy him back. The whole business was hideously complex. Strict currency controls almost wrecked the striker's return. The case of Greaves' transfer even reached the desk of Selwyn Lloyd, Chancellor of the Exchequer in Harold Macmillan's Tory Government. Eventually, Treasury officials got around the problem, which limited the amount of money which could be taken out of England, by saying he should be treated as 'luxury goods'. To Chelsea, he was anything but a luxury.

Greaves' last game for Chelsea was at home to Nottingham Forest. He scored all the Blues' goals in a 4–3 win.

SEVEN

TRUST ME, I'M A DOCTOR

Get out of my way, son, you're using my oxygen.
Jack Nicholson in *One Flew Over The Cuckoo's Nest*

Amid all the hullabaloo of Greaves' sad departure in February 1960, Tommy Docherty joined Chelsea. If Jimmy's transfer marked the passing of one era then the arrival of the Arsenal defender signalled the start of another. Tommy Docherty's six action-packed years at Chelsea were in complete contrast to the fun-filled, laid-back period of chewing-gum-for-the-eyes football that Greaves and his fellow Ducklings enjoyed – tasteless, repetitive, disposable. All the great teams of the past are yesterday's roses – the memories of elderly men. When the white-haired octogenarian Roy Bentley attended Chelsea's narrow victory over Manchester United in November 2003, he was amazed at the warm reception he received from the fans. He mentioned that you would have to be in your 70s to have seen him play.

People ask me what was the best Chelsea team ever. Who can really tell? It is a matter of personal opinion, generational mainly. Bentley's team won the League. The Osgood–Hudson partnership won the FA Cup for the first time and followed it up with European success. Yet, the Doc's lads were potentially the best footballing side in Chelsea's history. They fell short but paved the way for the glorious success of the early '70s. They opened up a new phase and raised the standards. Beyond talent, in front of technique even, the invisible power of every great team stems from their need to capture the imagination of their fans. Docherty's passion for football and his desire to succeed connected with his young players and released a bewildering energy. The Stamford Bridge crowd were previously aloof and fickle. They had expectations woefully at odds with the skills of the previous management teams and the abilities of many of the players. This time, though, the fans surrendered to the idea totally. Chelsea became a state of mind, a collusive sense of intimacy. The Docherty side was unique in that it was the first one that demanded emotional loyalty. It had a soul.

In a television documentary, Docherty referred to his young charges as his Diamonds – it stuck. Even today, we have diamonds at the Bridge, the complex formation employed by Ranieri to include the disparate talents of players like Verón and Joe Cole. After the home win over Lazio in the Champions League, Ranieri was quoted as saying: 'Against Lazio, the sides of the diamond were Frank Lampard and Juan SebastiánVerón. While both can play at the top of the diamond, I prefer to use them on the sides of the diamond because it gives them more freedom to move around the pitch.'

Docherty's Diamonds were shiny, sharp and bright. There is a pigeon-blood ruby that was the greatest ruby there was. Count Basie compared Sinatra to it. Terry Venables was the pigeon-blood ruby in the collection of jewels mined and polished by the Doc. For a short time, the pair almost defined the perimeters of the modern game. Then they fell out.

FOR EVER CAME TODAY

If Docherty had not broken his ankle whilst playing for Arsenal against his former club Preston in October 1959, then he probably would have never joined Chelsea. Docherty never fully regained his fitness and lost a little of his tremendous enthusiasm for playing. Ted Drake, who had dropped his compass and lost the map, recruited him as first-team coach. It was his last gamble as Chelsea chief and he hoped that the Doc's dynamic personality could rejuvenate the club. History proved him correct but Drake just ran out of time. After nine years in charge, he was sacked at the end of September 1960.

The most exciting decade of the twentieth century was under way. John F. Kennedy was the youngest-ever President of the US, and the first episode of *Coronation Street* was shown.

The Doc had a nose for trouble, a head for heights and was out to consume the football world. Of all the managers I dealt with, the Doc was my favourite; his charm was irresistible. He flew low to avoid the radar. The Scot possessed the same work ethic that was the byword of the other famous Caledonian managers – Jock Stein, Bill Shankly and Sir Alex Ferguson. Docherty was a complex character in many ways and a great chameleon.

Tommy was appointed chief coach and then in January promoted to team manager. The problem was Chelsea were in free fall throughout 1961–62. Drake's last game was a 4–0 defeat at Blackpool. They started badly and it got worse.

In an early game, 'Pancho' Pearson of Manchester United scored the winner against us at Old Trafford. Mark Pearson obtained the nickname 'Pancho' because of his distinctive sideburns which made him look like a Mexican bandit from the big hit film of the day *The Magnificent Seven* (not a film of the Christmas Day Chelsea v. Portsmouth, Jimmy Greaves, chestnuts-roasting-on-an-open-fire extravaganza). Not many players have nicknames today, I notice.

Chelsea won the return with goals from the teenagers Bridges and Tambling, who were to be the mainstays of the attack. The incandescent David Cliss had eight games that season but could make no impact as the paraphernalia of fame got in his way. I have a picture of him on my study wall in a team group from that season. Perhaps his Teddy boy haircut was to blame – his sideburns were not as large as Pancho's though. If you liked Lampard with his showbiz smile, you would have loved Cliss – he looked like Billy Fury, if you remember him.

Sheffield United were thrashed 6–1 with Tambling, revelling in Greaves' roving role, notching a hat-trick. It was one of the four League games that Docherty played in that season. By October, Chelsea were rooted at the bottom of the table and stayed there.

Docherty was one of the first managers to use his players to the maximum. Thirty-one different players appeared at various junctures during that disastrous season; thirteen of them made their full debut. Of the whole squad, 19 were products of the youth academy. The stats indicated that the only season that saw the use of a higher number of different players was the relegation season of 1909–10. The turnover of players was phenomenal. Docherty's new office should have had revolving doors. The old guard were decimated – the Fabulous Sillett Brothers, Ron Tindall and Johnny Brooks (idolised by a young Venables) were amongst the casualties. The classy Graham Moore was purchased from Cardiff after the Welshman had given a dazzling performance in a 5–2 savaging of the Blues. With his crisp passing and exceptional touch, Graham should have been another legend – the implication being that Chelsea failed to realise his potential. Who do you get angrier at, the club or the player for squandering obviously formidable talents?

New faces included Albert Murray, Ron Harris and Frank Upton who were all to play large parts in the coming seasons. Ian St John (last seen acting as straight man to Greaves in The Galleria) scored twice in the first half of the third-round Cup tie at Anfield. Liverpool, managed by Bill Shankly, were running away with the Second Division. The club were on their way to a date with destiny that would make the Merseyside doomsday machine the most powerful side in the land for decades. The Reds led 4–1 at the break but Chelsea made a tremendous fight back and clawed themselves up to 4–3. Shankly watched his team scrape home, impressed with the spirit of the young Chelsea team. Bobby Tambling was a player he particularly coveted. It was first blood to Liverpool in a series of titanic Cup clashes that would continue over the years.

The second half of the season saw no real improvement, though. Chelsea only won four more games as they nosedived towards the Second Division. Inevitably, the papers' delight with the young team soon curdled and Chelsea were depicted as underachievers and playboys. What's changed?

Docherty led the charge out of the Second Division in 1962–63. It was merely a whistle stop for the Blue express, but they almost missed their destination. The swinging blue-jeans days should have been better named after the swinging blue shirts from the Kings Road.

Tambling was in deadly form – he should have worn a Superman costume and cape instead of the number 8 shirt. Chelsea hit the front and stayed there till the end of the year. A tremendous run of ten wins and a draw in the last eleven games of 1962 gave them a six-point lead. Like most campaigns, it looked like Chelsea were going to be home before Christmas.

SLIP-SLIDING AWAY

Then England suffered the worse winter in living memory, even more severe than the winter of 1946–47 when Swiss Willi Steffen almost froze his nuts off. That was in between helping the Blues knock Arsenal out of the Cup. It was the all-time freeze up. Even the polar bears wore overcoats and Burberrys.

Chelsea's last home League game before the icebergs floated down the Thames was against Rotherham United. They were trounced 3–0 (Bridges, Blunstone 2) on 15 December. It was not until 2 March that Chelsea played again at the Bridge and lost 1–2 to Huddersfield Town. The only League matches played in the interim were two defeats in Wales at the hands of Swansea and Cardiff. The slide became even more slippery. They lost their next five away games followed by a shock 0–1 home defeat to relegation-bound Walsall. Only a few scrambled home victories kept them in the hunt. With just three games left, Stoke and Sunderland occupied the top two spots. We had to play them both in a quirk of the fixture list that media companies lust over. (In those far-off times, only the top two were promoted and play-offs were unheard of.)

Chelsea appeared to have blown it conclusively when Stoke clinched the title by beating us at home. Jimmy McIlroy, architect of our downfall so often at Burnley, scored the only goal of a tepid game. Chelsea still appeared to be frozen in some sort of suspended animation, brought on by the extreme winter conditions, no doubt.

Drastic action was called for and the Doc took a scalpel to his wobbling team. Out went the youngsters Murray, Bridges and Moore. He stuffed his forward line with the combat-hardened veterans Frank Upton, Derek Kevan and Tommy Harmer. Tommy had been signed from Watford to coach the youngsters and provide impetus for their further development. He was a particular influence on Terry Venables, who had watched him from the terraces at White Hart Lane when 'Harmer the Charmer' was in his pomp.

Docherty knew that, above all, football was to do with mental attitude. He picked a side with a specific job in mind: to win at any cost, and win they did. Harmer scored the only goal of the fevered game midway through the first half, Tambling's cut-back corner flying into the roof of the net, rebounding off part of Tommy's lower anatomy that shall remain anonymous.

Sunderland battered Chelsea for the rest of the game but the Blues defence played magnificently and they hung on to take the priceless points. Ron Harris (even criticised by some of the older Blues fans for his demonic treatment of the middle-aged Stanley Matthews in the Stoke defeat) was outstanding alongside Peter Bonetti.

Chelsea then needed to beat Portsmouth in their last game to go up. On a beautiful, early summer's evening (it was late May by this point because so much time had been lost, the darling buds of May-be) a crowd of 54,558 watched Chelsea score seven without reply. (The last time Chelsea had hit them for seven, they had at least managed four in consolation.) Chelsea went up on goal average, which was how they quaintly worked it out in those days. The margin was 0.401 of a goal. It was calculated with an algebraic formula that would blow your laptop; actually, working it out by goal difference (the twenty-first-century way) gave Chelsea a comfortable ten-goal margin.

It was Tambling's benefit night as he scored four times to take the Blues back to the big time in a match of high drama. Some of his skills were breathtaking that night. Bobby was completely throwing his markers with audacious tricks and penetrating runs.

Not far behind him in skill was Terry Venables, who played in every match that unforgettable season. Venables was my unequivocal favourite, so underrated as a player he would be a sensation today. I am reminded of him a lot by the unshowy Lampard in the current team of Abramovich all-stars. Lampard, like Venables, is essentially a self-made player as opposed to a naturally gifted player like Beckham or Hudson. Lampard quickly moves the ball on from the centre of the Chelsea midfield with those neat, diagonal passes that Venables invented.

DR KNOW

Season 1963–64 went better than expected, with Chelsea finishing in fifth place. This was a highly creditable performance. Finances did not allow us to sign anybody. A solid, tight-fisted defence was the key with only 56 goals conceded. Bonetti was in superb form, playing behind the best pair of backs Chelsea ever had: the England international Ken Shellito and the Scottish international Eddie McCreadie. Ken was a youth product from the same area as his old friend Jimmy Greaves; Docherty bought Eddie for a bus fare from East Stirling. Both men had their careers blighted by injury and both were to later manage the club. At their peak (as they were that season), both were incredibly pacy and very dependable. They also had what so many defenders lack today – positional sense. Today, with players like Glen Johnson, the greatest problems arise not when the ball is on their flank, but when it is on the other side of the pitch. It is because their positional play is poor that they get caught in possession in no man's land. When the play is on the opposite flank, then the full-back has to do two things. First, cover his central defender. Second, don't play the opponents onside. The primary function of the twenty-first-century wing-back is to attack: Docherty's defenders had a fine balance and appreciated the full extent of their responsibilities. They could play up against the touchline. Johnson and Ferreira, the right-sided wing-backs at Chelsea, always look better players when they have space to play in but are ill at ease in a confined area.

Shellito was so highly rated he was included in the squad for the prestigious England v. The Rest of the World (FIFA) game to mark the centenary of the Football Association. The Rest of the World team included a galaxy of stars like Eusebio, Di Stefano and Gento with Yashin in goal. Pelé was due to play in the match but pulled out at the last minute. Ex-Chelsea goal aces Greaves and Bobby Smith were in the England team, along with Bobby Moore, Gordon Banks and Bobby Charlton. England won 2–1.

The high spot of the season was putting Spurs out of the Cup in the third round after a 1–1 draw at Tottenham. The Bridge accommodated over 70,000 that night. Bert Murray, whose goal earned the draw at White Hart Lane, was on target again and the pantherish Tambling wrapped it up. Jimmy Greaves was adjusting to life at the decaying Tottenham and was ruthlessly policed by Ron Harris in both games. A Cup run was on the cards but Huddersfield surprisingly knocked them out in the next round at home.

Tambling cheered the fans with all four goals in Chelsea's 2–4 hammering of Arsenal at Highbury. Ex-Chelsea junior Joe Baker, now rehabilitated at Arsenal, was amongst the scorers. Young Peter Simpson, a Double winner in subsequent years, was given a baptism of fire, having to mark the free-scoring Tambling.

Players from the Blues' star-processing system who made their debuts that season included a 17-year-old John Hollins and winger Peter Houseman and, in addition, one of the Doc's shrewdest signings, Marvin Hinton from Charlton.

If that was a stabilising, highly experimental season, then 1964–65 was the pivotal moment of the Doc's turbulent reign. It was the season they switched to the all blue strip with numbers on the shorts. He had that spark and belief in his team and being a perfectionist he pushed them to their limits. Tommy was a taskmaster and he drilled the defence like a platoon. Ranieri, it has been reported, insists on complete command of the dressing-room. On the flip side of his joke-filled eccentric Italian persona exists a *Master and Commander* dark veneer. Docherty was the same and ruled with a rod of iron. He expected the players to be on time, obedient, well groomed and grateful. The difference between the two men is that Ranieri has a Machiavellian approach to things. Docherty was headstrong, impetuous and reckless, anxious to wipe out any trace of the Drake era.

George Graham, who became another manager from the same mould, was purchased from Aston Villa for a minuscule fee and he immediately fitted in. The goals flowed with another top striker in the line-up. The team for most of the games was the classic Diamonds line-up of:

Bonetti

Shellito (until his injury)   McCreadie

Hollins   Mortimore/Hinton   Harris R

Murray   Graham   Bridges   Venables (captain)   Tambling

I would still back that line-up against any other team that has appeared for Chelsea in any season, past or present – a favourite amongst favourites. It's interesting to see that Bonetti, McCreadie, Hollins and Harris formed the backbone of the Cup-winning side of the early '70s.

1965 AND ALL THAT

I have always been of the opinon that consistency is the last refuge of the unimaginative.

Oscar Wilde, *Pall Mall Gazette*, 28 February 1885

Venables was the mainspring of the side. His brief apprenticeships with old hands like Brooks and Harmer, together with the productive Foss, had given him a wonderful education. Every time he played he had an 'I will show them what I can do' attitude. The Doc had moved him into his most creative role, scheming off the strikers: Bridges, Tambling and Graham.

By 1965, his apotheosis as a Chelsea icon was complete. The young pretenders stormed to the semi-final of the FA Cup. On the way, they butchered Northampton and Peterborough at home and also knocked out Tottenham for the second year running. Bridges scored the only goal of the game and a solitary goal from Tambling was enough to defeat West Ham at Upton Park. The Hammers had won the Cup the year before and it was a great performance to knock them out on their own ground. They had put in their most sustained bid for the title and remained in contention throughout the season. Liverpool knocked them out of the Cup in the semi-final at Villa Park 0–2. Chelsea were favourites to win as Liverpool had even more of a fixture pile up. (That season, Chelsea played a total of 56 senior games: League, FA and League Cup – a record.)

It was a watershed moment, a real melodrama. A timid Chelsea seemed to freeze on the day and Docherty, despite cajoling, admonishing, scolding and pleading, could do nothing. Their nerves were shot to pieces. Before the game, some players were literally shaking. It must have been as demoralising a defeat to them as the FA Youth Cup defeat to Wolves had been to the Ducklings.

Ten days later, Chelsea won their first and only piece of silverware under the Doc – the League Cup. In those days, it had rather less standing than it has today, if such a thing were possible. It was played over two legs and in the first at home Chelsea won 3–2 against Leicester – the winner coming from an amazing 'Roy of the Rovers' jinking solo effort from Eddie McCreadie, who was playing as an emergency centre-forward. A 0–0 draw at Filbert Street was enough to clinch the Cup. Perhaps the fairy tale was still attainable?

This should have been the springboard for a late run on the League.

Docherty was still fretting over the semi-final defeat and he saw Venables as the donkey on which to pin the tail of his frustration. The Doc saw some of the players' understated style as being lackadaisical. Rumours of discord in the dressing-room abounded. In January, Dave Sexton, the club coach, had quit to take up the job of manager at Leyton Orient. The cerebral Sexton was very popular amongst the players and acted as a buffer between them and the volatile Doc and his one-liners. Hindsight is a wonderful thing but looking back, the departure of the ascetic Sexton destabilised the team at a crucial moment. Sexton had always hankered after managing his own team but it seemed a bewildering move.

Things came to a head at Blackpool where the team were staying in readiness for two vital away games at Burnley and Blackpool. Docherty sent eight first-team players home, including Venables, Graham and Murray.

It made front-page news, although compared to the drug-fuelled antics and lurid hotel incidents we read about in the twenty-first century it seems pretty trivial. Eight Chelsea players sent home today would keep the tabloids in business for some time. One story circulating the Fulham Broadway bars was that a high-profile member of the team had become too friendly with a female friend of the Doc and, through spite and silliness, the whole thing exploded.

The dynamic of the relationship between the abrasive Docherty and the team, particularly Venables, altered. The humour changed – it became more vitriolic and Venables' forceful wit and mimicking of his boss became less comical. The Docherty grand plan was to remain out of reach.

A patched-up team, including reserves and youngsters, was brutally slaughtered 6–2 at Burnley with Andy Lochhead scoring five of them. They lost the last match of the season 3–2 ironically played at Blackpool (tangerine dream becoming a nightmare), and finished third, five points behind Leeds and champions Manchester United. United had done the Double over Chelsea during the season, so it could be argued that the title was lost in those games, in the same way that the four points gleaned from Wolves gave Chelsea the title in 1955.

Both of these Docherty seasons were glorious, heroic failures but the football Chelsea played during them and the drama that unfolded as the Docherty–Venables marriage foundered was incredible. The new West Stand was built at a cost of £150,000, if I recall – the cost of a few sticks of furniture in one of the Millennium Suites today. What is the Joni Mitchell song about nothing lasting for ever? Well, the West Stand has been long since torn down but the memory of some of those ebullient games remains as a monument to the team.

Season 1965–66 was my favourite ever, with the Diamonds maintaining their momentum. We won nothing but it merits a book of its own. We played 60 games: 42 in the League, 6 in the FA Cup and 12 in the Fairs Cup (their high-league position won the Blues a spot in the latter).

They had two ties against Italian sides which were as unforgettable as Michael Caine in *The Italian Job*, the definitive '60s Rule Britannia, 'England-swings-like-a-pendulum-do' flag-waving movie. The first match was against Roma and Venables scored a hat-trick in Chelsea's 4–1 home victory. It was one of the finest performances of his career and confirmed his status as an England player. The return in Rome was a stormy affair, Chelsea showing great resilience in grinding out a chancy 0–0 draw. Carlo Cudicini's father Fabio played in goal for Roma that night and late in the game denied Barry Bridges a winning goal. Enzo Matteucci had kept goal in the first leg but Roma brought in young Fabio to try to stop the freewheeling impudence of the Chelsea forwards. Fabio went on to have a magnificent career in the Italian game and won a European Cup winner's medal.

The 0–4 romp over Lazio in November 2003 was commemorated in 'The Gladiators' T-shirts which showed Lampard, Crespo and co. brandishing swords as victors at the Colosseum. On that October night in Rome in 1965, Chelsea faced a hostile reception on and off the pitch. After the match, the furious Roma fans even attacked the Chelsea team bus. Good times.

Around then, Docherty introduced Peter Osgood to the first team, although he had made his debut the season before. The gangly youth had scored both goals in a 2–0 victory over Workington on Chelsea's way to their League Cup triumph. This time, though, he was given an extended run in the side, replacing the England centre-forward Barry Bridges, who was shunted out to the wing. Osgood started slowly and nervously but soon justified the Doc's faith in him. He scored his first Cup goal in Chelsea's epic 1–2 win at Anfield in the third round of the FA Cup. Chelsea obtained swift revenge for their semi-final defeat the previous spring. Liverpool had gone on to lift the Cup with a narrow win over the emerging Leeds, our friend St John scoring the match-winning goal. For the second year running, Chelsea had knocked the Cup holders out on their own ground. Ron Harris had replaced Venables as captain and was a towering figure in Chelsea's defence. Venables masterminded the winning goal, headed home by Bobby Tambling. The defence had been changed to attack with one wonderful diagonal pass from Terry. Chelsea were the first team to silence the Kop. We left the champs face down in their home-town ring, their fans streaming for the exits like the place was on fire. We should have taken the belt. It was that close. Shoulda, woulda, coulda as they say in *Will and Grace*.

Tambling shot the winner in the next round as Chelsea dumped out Leeds at Stamford Bridge. That was the day the Doc christened his team the Diamonds amid a fog of hyperbole. Not for the first time, Peter Bonetti deprived Leeds of victory with a string of breathtaking saves. The Chelsea midfield worked harder than a Texan chain gang to subdue the dangerous Leeds side.

In the midst of disposing of the previous year's FA Cup finalists, Chelsea found time to knock AC Milan out of the Fairs Cup. The powerful Milan won the first tie 2–1 in the San Siro, watched by a tiny crowd of 11,411. Graham gave Chelsea a lifeline with a late header and repeated the trick with an early goal in the return match, Venables creating both of them. Shortly afterwards, Osgood scored possibly the most spectacular goal of his career, blurring the ball home after roasting the Milan defender Karl-Heinz Schnellinger. The blond Karl-Heinz was the Schumacher of German football. The ex-Roma defender had more decorations than Field Marshal Erwin Rommel and had played in the Rest of the World team at Wembley. To be beaten so comprehensively by a youngster with only a handful of senior games under his belt, gives you some insight into just how good the Windsor-born striker was and the quality of that Chelsea side. My memory serves me all too well. Milan pulled a goal back on the break as Chelsea coasted for the whistle. The Italians won the coin spin for the replay venue, so it was back to the San Siro.

The media made great play of Chelsea's 2003 win over Lazio as being their first victory on Italian soil. They got it wrong, because Chelsea went through after extra time in February '66. Barry Bridges burst through early after turning two defenders. He found himself alone in front of the Milan keeper, Luigi Balzarini, and tried his favourite option – the lob. Liverpool goalkeeper Tommy Lawrence had stood his ground a few weeks previously and deprived Barry of a hat-trick. That day, though, the Italian went down and Bridges spooned in a shot to put Chelsea ahead. That is how it remained till the dying seconds. Giuliano Fortunato scrambled home a fortunato goal for Milan. Extra time went the distance. The unlikely match winner was Ron Harris, who called correctly when the ref spun the coin in the centre circle. No golden goals or penalty shoot-outs in those days.

Chelsea fought on three different fronts as the season wore on. In the League, they ultimately finished fifth, ten points behind Shankly's Reds. The cups were the real dramas. They reached Villa Park for the second season in succession. The games piled up. Hull took them to a replay in the quarter-final which they won two days after knocking out TSV

Munchen 1860 in the Fairs Cup. Substitutes were introduced for the first time that season (Albert Murray was the first Chelsea player to be used in that capacity) but rotation and large squads were as distant as mobile phones and DVD players.

The Chelsea team was overwhelmed by the sheer weight of fixtures and the heavy pitches added to their growing exhaustion. Venables, hyperactive as always, was driving them on but the pressure on him was growing. Sheffield Wednesday bludgeoned them out of the Cup by the same score as Liverpool, 2–0. Docherty insisted on Chelsea wearing the Inter Milan strip in that fixture. The Blues' trips to Italy had a big effect on him and his idea was to reinvent Chelsea in the mould of Inter. I never thought I would write that Chelsea were a bigger side than Milan but Abramovich's cash enabled them to buy their star striker Hernan Crespo. Chelsea's only similarity to Milan in 1966, however, was the strip. It brought them no luck, though, and it was never worn again.

All that remained was the Fairs Cup. The semi-final draw paired them with Spanish aces Barcelona. Bonetti played superbly in the Nou Camp to restrict Barca to a two-goal lead. It was to be Venables' last game for Chelsea. Docherty had decided to break up the band. Barry Bridges had already played his last game in Chelsea Blue, a glacial Docherty sending him home from the airport en route to Barcelona. A few days later, he joined Birmingham. The cavalier Charlie Cooke was bought from Dundee and pitched into the return at the Bridge. I was in the dressing-room when Docherty showed him round. Venables looked at him uncomprehendingly. Alan Harris was re-signed from Coventry and deputised for the injured Eddie McCreadie, sorely missed at Villa Park. By now, Shellito's career was in ruins, a succession of knee injuries destroying his brilliant future. The wonderful partnership between him and McCreadie, such an integral part of the Diamonds' tactics, was no more. I found it oddly moving when I would watch him training alone in the afternoons, trying to rebuild his knee and his life.

Chelsea won the home leg against Barca 2–0 thanks to two bizarre own goals to level the tie. Barcelona staged the play-off (Ronnie could not call it right every time) and crushed the Blues 5–0. The game was about as one-sided as your average game of solitaire. So, the season that promised so much, ended in bitter tears.

THE YARD WENT ON FOR EVER

Venables left to join Tottenham, Warhol released *The Chelsea Girls*. I expected a mass exodus of talent as the Doc decided to rebuild. There were only two types of player, he once told me: 'the good ones and the bad ones'. The problem was, his view of what constituted a good player and a bad player changed from match to match.

Terry Venables, the coolest man ever to play for Chelsea, joined their biggest rivals. Sorry to be cantankerous here but you can keep your Adrian Mutu and John Terry, my Terry was the real deal. He was about liberation and fun, about the working classes running their own game before the moneyed participants took centre stage. It broke my father's heart to see the young team torn apart. Terry's parting shot to my father was the classic: 'The trouble with Docherty was he blamed the scapegoats.'

My father started expressing concerns about Docherty's judgement – to lose a great, visionary player like Venables made no sense at all. Dick Foss, the manager of the highly successful youth system, was also axed by the Doc. Venables saw it as a political move because of Dick's close friendship with him. The Chelsea board, when chaired by a Mears, always gave 100 per cent support to the manager. As we shall shortly see, this was possibly not always the wisest course of action but some standard of ethics had to be maintained. When I look at how Ranieri was treated, I wonder.

Joe Mears died a few weeks before England won the World Cup in the summer of 1966 – that incredible summer of Hurst's hat-trick, Greaves' disappointment at missing out on it, The Beatles, The Stones, hot pants and miniskirts. The centre of gravity had moved from Carnaby Street to the Kings Road. London became the cultural capital of the world and the Kings Road the cultural centre of London. Chelsea Football Club could be added to the rich roll-call of star names that left their mark in that amazing period.

My father's sudden death at that time devastated the club from top to bottom. Once again, Chelsea started the season brightly going unbeaten in the first ten games. Charlie Cooke scored on his League debut at West Ham after nutmegging World Cup winner Bobby Moore. Chelsea led the League into early autumn. An imperious Bobby Tambling scored five goals in Chelsea's 2–6 win at Aston Villa. The crowd were singing 'Hey, Mr Tambling Man', a parody of the Bob Dylan song made into a worldwide hit by The Byrds. Shortly after that, Bobby smashed Roy Bentley's Chelsea scoring record with a goal in the 1–4 testosterone-charged demolition of Manchester City at Maine Road.

The fans argued that perhaps the constant upheavals at the club could be justified by the continued rip-roaring action. In the next match, Osgood smashed his leg in a League Cup game at Blackpool.

Chelsea dropped down the League. The Doc, with his very own 'English Patient' in Osgood, acted quickly and smashed Chelsea's transfer record to buy Tony Hateley from Aston Villa. The Bonobo-faced Hateley had scored against Chelsea a few weeks previously in the Tambling jamboree game. The whole side had to be restructured to accommodate him. Now they were playing long to the big striker. No Venables to bind things together amongst the myriad changes and the clique-ridden dressing-room.

George Graham left to join Arsenal after a row with Docherty. Tommy Baldwin moved to the Bridge as part of the deal. Graham had a fairy-tale relationship with the Gooners for many years and ended up leading them to championships as both player and manager. On the Matthew Harding Stand the fans still sing Baldwin's name in the wonderful ditty, 'His name is Tommy Baldwin and he is the leader of the team'. Tommy became a Chelsea legend but he was the makeweight in the deal and Graham was a huge loss.

Peter Houseman was back in the reckoning after a long period in the wilderness. He was not Docherty's cup of tequila but an orthodox winger was needed to provide the crosses for Hateley. That was the plan, anyway. Five straight draws and three consecutive defeats blew any chance of the title. New Year's Eve saw the Blues crash 1–6 at Hillsborough, home of Sheffield Wednesday, who had become our *bête noire*.

Once again, the Cup was the only thing left to play for. Chelsea stumbled to Wembley with a series of narrow victories and close shaves. Tambling scored the winner against Huddersfield in the third round. Brighton held Chelsea to a draw in the next round but two more Tambling goals in the replay contributed to a 4–0 victory. He was on target once more against Sheffield United and in the next round their neighbours, Wednesday, were drawn in the quarter-final. Wednesday came for the draw and were within seconds of forcing it when a Chaplinesque goal from Baldwin gave us revenge for their shock exit at Villa Park. That was exactly where Chelsea travelled to in their third consecutive semi-final.

Leeds were the opponents and Hateley won the game with one of his trademark headers. He had struggled to replace Osgood but in the semi-final he got to be a hero, just for one day. Leeds had a perfectly good goal disallowed in the dying seconds. Twice in those times, we had played them in the Cup and twice stolen it.

Chelsea reached a Wembley FA Cup final for the first time in their history. It was also historic because it was against Tottenham Hotspur and the first-ever cockney Cup final.

Spurs won 2–1 in a huge anti-climax of a game; Chelsea were lost in a blizzard of white shirts. It was an agonisingly awful afternoon of unmitigated incompetence between two sides whose problems should not have been inflicted on the public at a Cup final. The only bright spot was in the closing minutes when, trailing two goals from Robertson and Saul, the Spurs keeper Pat Jennings punched a cross against Tambling's head and the ball flew into the net. A multiple anti-climax.

It was a total non-event and failed to rage across the pages of Chelsea history. By this time, Docherty had lost the dressing-room. Money was the root of it all. The Doc had promised generous bonuses to the team if they won the Cup. All this was news to Bill Pratt, the new chairman. Their League form suffered and Chelsea eventually finished ninth, marooned in mid-table

Season 1967–68 was the last hurrah for the Doc and it started badly. The squad was unbalanced, almost a bootleg version of the Venables outfit. The Doc was playing both ends against the muddle. Hateley was sold to Liverpool and Osgood, clearly overweight, was back in the side. I will hesitate to say he was fit because it took about another 18 months before he even approached the form he had shown before his injury. The defence performed abysmally and in one week at the end of August conceded eleven goals: five at Newcastle and six at home to Southampton. The Doc's last game was a tepid 1–1 home draw with a robotic Coventry. The sound of the crowd booing was the death rattle of the Doc's patients. The board sacked him in early October – the scent of dissent in the dressing-room had become unbearable.

EIGHT

JOHNNY ENGLISH

John Hollins was my childhood hero. I used to wear the No. 4
shirt for England in one-day internationals because of him.
Alec Stewart, former England cricket captain

John Hollins was the kind of player who makes you thank God for the
Chelsea of the '60s and early '70s. That was truly his time and it fit him
like a Kings Road suede jacket. If you were lucky enough to see him play
in that era, you would need no reminding that he literally never stopped
running. His tremendous versatility and wonderful temperament, plus the
fact that he was so pleasing on the eye, made him a firm favourite with the
Stamford Bridge faithful: a confrère to Hudson, Cooke and Osgood, a
peer to Butch Wilkins, a disciple of Venables and a forerunner of
Lampard. His unfortunate spell managing the club in the '80s detracted
from that wonderful relationship but it is well worth reminding oneself of
just how great he was when he was a superstar.

Hollins's looks certainly fitted in with the time: his sweet, cherubic
choir-boy face and bright blue eyes. A razor blade dipped in cream.

When the players' choice, Dave Sexton, replaced Tommy Docherty in
the autumn of 1967, Hollins was already a hardened professional. A few
days after playing in the cockney Cup final in a number 4 shirt, he had
returned to Wembley to wear the number 11 shirt for England against
Spain. Jimmy Greaves, who was quitting Chelsea when Hollins joined the
groundstaff, scored that night. It was John's only England cap; he should
have won dozens. John was overlooked by everyone – the selectors, his
teammates, the fans. I would like to put the record straight.

Hollins came from a footballing family. His father played in goal for Wolves and Stoke. His elder brother Dave was also a goalkeeper and was good enough to play for Wales and Newcastle. The Hollins family moved from Wales to Guildford and John qualified to play for England. Young John captained Park Barn secondary school in Guildford and that was where he was discovered by Jimmy Thomson. He won six England Youth caps. Football-crazy John also played for the sea cadets where he used to go fitness training. This included plenty of running and he built up his endless stamina at a young age. Frank Lampard is the hardest running of the current Chelsea squad and his keenness and energy is a constant reminder of the young John. Surely it is reasonable to expect that, at this point in Chelsea's evolution, the benchmark for midfield greatness might be set higher than an ex-West Ham player doing John Hollins impressions?

The day after Docherty's Chelsea managerial career was toast they travelled to Leeds and were crushed 7–0, their worst beating in living memory and that takes into account the grim tide of Chelsea history in the '80s. Four adrift at the break, Leeds extracted maximum revenge for their unlucky dismissal at Villa Park a few months before. Eddie Gray, who managed the spirited Leeds side in their 1–1 draw with Chelsea in December 2003, was the mainspring of the victory. The Leeds fans crowd-surfed as Eddie sauntered through the ruins of the Chelsea defence to score a wonderful solo goal and had a hand in three others. In his day, only the swaggering Charlie Cooke was in his class. They talk about Zinedine Zidane's drag backs but Gray's mastery of the art was easily the best.

Chelsea were rock bottom morale-wise, with a titanically dire defence and heading out of the division. With the myriad problems of the end of the Docherty regime, there had been a drop in the physical and psychological state of the players. The term 'Blue Funk' springs to mind. Sexton, Chelsea's seventh manager, steadied the ship and by the end of the season he had taken Chelsea to a comfortable sixth in the table. His first victory was a 3–0 home win over Sheffield Wednesday and it was fitting that Hollins opened the scoring. It was a freezing cold November afternoon and a few snowflakes were falling as John drove the ball home.

A fourth successive visit to Villa Park for the semi-final beckoned when Chelsea were drawn away to Birmingham in the quarter-final. Barry Bridges was starring for the then Second Division team along with fellow Diamond Albert Murray, now converted into an early type of wing-back. Birmingham edged Chelsea out by one goal. Hollins played in the number 2 shirt that game. Sexton saw him as playing in a deeper role to help fill the gap left by Shellito. Charlie Cooke wore Hollins's number 4 shirt for a spell and Osgood had a run there. Neither had the jaunty energy of Hollins or the pace to make those Olympic surges up field.

It was a bitter defeat for Chelsea but the next day Hollins married his sweetheart Linda following a whirlwind romance. They are still married to this day. I used to see her at the Bridge a lot in those days. Bridges was one of the guests at the wedding, along with Terry Venables, another lifelong friend of his. Hollins's marriage was the only one that lasted out of that side.

The Doc's adversary, chairman Bill Pratt, died around the time of our Cup exit. Vice-chairman Len Withey took over as chairman and I moved into his role. Sexton was tinkering all the time and had added some Sheffield steel to the team by buying Alan Birchenall from Sheffield United. He later acquired David Webb from Southampton, who was to become one of the most colourful characters that ever played for us.

Season 1968–69 was another one of transition. Chelsea finished a place higher than the previous year and Sexton was adding the finishing touches to the Chelsea team's grand design. Ian Hutchinson arrived almost unheralded in the summer, signed from Cambridge United of the Southern League. On his home debut against Ipswich Town, he stunned the crowd with his extraordinary long throws. One of them completely flummoxed the Ipswich centre-half Bill Baxter who headed it into his own net.

The Blues had a very short excursion into Europe, going out on a spin of a coin (can you believe that they were still deciding games that way in 1968?) to DWS Amsterdam.

West Bromwich knocked Chelsea out of the Cup at home in the sixth round. It was to be the last Cup game we were to lose for a very long time.

Hollins was Chelsea's best player again that season with his infectious, uncomplicated style and total commitment. Alongside him, he found an able partner in David Webb, who played in every game. Webb, in those days looking like an extra from *The Lord of the Rings*, was teaching him how to walk tall and talk back. The Stepney-born defender opened his scoring account for Chelsea with a hat-trick at Ipswich on Boxing Day.

A goal he scored the following season was to prove to be the most important ever scored by the club.

HOLLY, HOLLY, HOLLY

'Holly, Holly, Holly' was a war cry often heard from the North Stand when its favourite number 4 had the ball.

Chelsea won the Cup for the first time in their chequered history in 1969–70. David Webb scored the winner against Leeds in the first-ever replayed final. It was staged at Old Trafford and was one of the most exciting Cup games ever played. The full story has been well chronicled in books focusing on that unique period. Who did the most to help Chelsea lift the Cup is a perplexing question. I made a strong case in my first book for Peter Houseman. His match-winning performances against Burnley in the fourth-round replay and in the semi-final against Watford saved Chelsea from almost certain defeat. Yet Osgood scored in every round (still the last player to do so). His historic late equaliser at Old Trafford paved the way for Webb's winner in extra time.

Peter Bonetti was brilliant at Wembley in the first match, simply defying the Leeds forwards who at times threatened to overrun the outgunned Chelsea defence. In the firestorm of a replay, he played even better after being crocked early in the game. Yet despite all these claims, the indispensable Hollins dominated the season. John easily won the Joe Mears Memorial Trophy, which was the annual award for the Player of the Year as nominated by the supporters' club. For good measure, he won it again the following season. John Hollins was without a doubt the most consistent player Chelsea ever had. He played in every game of that marvellous season; a smile passed my lips when I read of Lampard being substituted near the end of the home defeat by Bolton in December 2003. After the match, Ranieri said: 'Some of my players looked tired in the second half. Frank needs more rest but it is difficult to play without him.'

Frank Lampard had, by that stage in the season, played 23 League and cup games. 'The game is faster today' I hear you say, but Hollins at his peak would have had an Olympic selection committee drooling. Over the season, he would have left Frank an ageing burnout. The East Ender, for his part, has more discriminating distribution and had a great Euro 2004 competition.

In the League, Chelsea finished third, their highest-ever position and equalled once more by Vialli's side in the '90s. Two away defeats in the opening games slowed their progress but injuries and loss of form to the older guard forced Sexton to bring in the youngsters. The autumn of 1969 saw the emergence in the team of Ian Hutchinson and Alan Hudson, both destined to be players of mass destruction in every sense of the word. Both immediately established themselves in the side and Chelsea started the FA Cup competition as one of the fancied teams.

An easy 3–0 win over Birmingham in the third round gained revenge for the Cup defeat inflicted upon Sexton in his first season in charge. Hollins scored Chelsea's second goal early in the second half against Burnley in the fourth round. This appeared to put the game well out of the Lancashire side's reach. Hollins had scored in his previous two League games and his shooting, always powerful but a little wayward, was improving immeasurably. Burnley hit back though with two late goals and forced a replay at Turf Moor which they very nearly won. Only a late solo goal from Houseman took the game into extra time. Goals from Baldwin and another from Houseman took them through eventually.

Away ties in London to Palace and QPR were easily dealt with as Chelsea headed for Wembley. The gritty Hollins was exceptional in both games, stifling dangerous attacks and setting up chances for his goal-hungry strikers. Watford, another southern side, were the semi-final opponents at White Hart Lane. Webb gave Chelsea an early lead but a stubborn Watford side quickly equalised and gave Chelsea numerous problems for a long spell. Inspired by Houseman, a devastating, late four-goal burst took Chelsea to Wembley against their hated adversaries Leeds United.

We have seen how in that era Chelsea's two previous narrow Cup victories (particularly in the 1967 semi-final) had exacerbated the existing tensions between the two sides. It seemed to me that Leeds had the upper hand in the League battles (for example, 7–0 the day after the Doc left) whilst Chelsea had the better of the Cup exchanges (earlier in the season, Chelsea, with Charlie Cooke in unstoppable form, knocked Leeds out of the League Cup after first drawing at Elland Road). In the League, though, Don Revie's side did the Double over the Blues. They won 2–0 at Elland Road and then administered a 2–5 drubbing at the Bridge.

The pounding continued at Wembley as they swarmed all over Chelsea on a diabolical pitch. It was to blame for both of the first-half goals: a soft header from Jack Charlton and a snap shot from Houseman that Sprake, the Leeds keeper, should have saved comfortably.

I watched the game from the Royal Box. I was now chairman, following the sudden death of Withey. Alan Hudson missed the Cup final games through injury. He built his myth on the 35 League and FA Cup games he played that season. In my view, he was never the same player when he returned. To compensate for his loss, Houseman switched from the flanks into the undermanned midfield and Hollins played in a more advanced role. The problem was that it left the fragile defence even more exposed.

Claude Makélélé received rave reviews from the press for his early performances as a holding midfielder when he arrived at Chelsea from Real Madrid for £16.6m in September 2003. Most of his game is spent about ten yards in front of his back four intercepting, tackling and harrying opponents. This gives the Chelsea defence another shield of protection and less talented players, like Terry and the much-touted Bridge, valuable time. Hollins relished playing in this type of role for most of his career. Sexton preferred to play him even deeper, being acutely aware of both Harris's and particularly Webb's lack of pace. Dave thought long and hard about playing Webb in a number 2 shirt, particularly as he was marking Eddie Gray. Webb was exceptional in the air, though, and Sexton knew that Leeds would be attacking the near post using Charlton, Clarke and Jones.

Eddie Gray was in the form of his life, allying his high-speed dribbling with shrewd passing. A few weeks earlier, I had gone up to Elland Road on a spying mission with Sexton to watch our fellow finalists play Burnley. The Scotland winger scored two bamboozling goals to win them the match; the second goal a mesmerizing run through the entire Burnley defence. I watched the young Burnley defenders (which included Tommy Docherty's son, Michael, and Colin Waldron, who had a short, unhappy spell at the Bridge) being undone by their inexperience. They went plunging in time after time and Gray picked each one off. Manchester United's Cristiano Ronaldo reminds me of Gray's grace.

Eddie Gray dominated the second half of the Wembley final. The term roasting has taken on another meaning in the football world but Webb took more heat than a King Edward next to the Sunday joint. Gray's smooth drag backs with the sole of his left foot saw David flailing for a ball that was no longer there. Time after time he committed himself unnecessarily and was sent skidding all over Wembley as the Leeds winger picked his way through. The tackling became more brutal as the game wore on. Norman Hunter's tackle almost splintered Hutchinson's shin but he got straight up. Even when he was cruelly hurt, he never showed it.

Jones scored near the end and, to paraphrase the words of commentator Kenneth Wolstenhome, 'They thought it was all over'. One man didn't; his name was John Hollins. He had spent the second half patrolling the centre of midfield. He could do nothing to subdue the quicksilver Gray and stop his complete mastery of Webb. Hollins had stopped Bremner from exerting total midfield domination by denying him space. The perceptive Houseman had been trying to plug the gaps around Webb.

With four minutes on the clock, Houseman went to take a free kick out on the right but Hollins waved him back. He spotted the inattentive Leeds players already mentally celebrating their Cup final victory and saw that the defensive wall wasn't fully deployed. It was about then that Ian Hutchinson started to gallop towards the Leeds box. Harris rolled the ball sideways and John crossed instantly to the near post.

Hutchinson had worked as an apprentice for Rolls-Royce in his native Derby. He was released as a youngster by Notts Forest and then schlepped around with Burton Albion. Apart from the effects of the horrific tackle on him by Hunter, Ian played at Wembley with a cortisone injection in his hip. He could barely stand but near the end of the most savage Cup final ever he came in at the near post. Scorning Jack Charlton's granite forehead, he leapt to equalise. It was the bravest goal I ever saw. Lawton's goal against Moscow all those years before flashed across my mind. Crespo nodded a nice one against Fulham just before Christmas 2003 but Hutchinson's was a killer. Leeds were stunned. In their hearts, they must have known they could not beat that Chelsea side.

Hutchinson died in September 2002 at the age of 54 after a long illness. Football killed him as certainly as pop music killed Elvis. To me, his tragic death was marred by comments in the tabloids questioning what that Osgood–Hudson team did for Chelsea Football Club. What did *they* do for Chelsea?

THE CUP AT LAST

The rest is history. Being in the Royal Box, I couldn't even celebrate Hutchinson's glorious equaliser. They show it on TV sometimes, usually buried amongst a montage of nostalgia-sodden clips accompanied by something by Mahler, or is it Radiohead?

Mr Abramovich and his pals created a stir at the opening game of the 2003–04 season when Chelsea won at Anfield. The directors' box was a sea of sycophants high-fiving and screaming when the boss's team grabbed a late winner. The salvation army almost. I wanted to drop him a line and advise him about the violations of protocol. There have been others in Chelsea's past who couldn't understand these matters nor grasp the concepts of the folklore of the club. Someone should tell Roman.

Hollins had a brilliant game at the Old Trafford replay. Sexton detailed Harris to mark Eddie Gray. And mark him he did. An early challenge flattened the Scot and we never saw him in the game again. For the rest of the match, the teams whaled each other worse than they did at Wembley. Leeds went in front after Bonetti was savaged by their Rottweiler strikers. The second half, though, saw Chelsea play the best football of the contest. Hollins, probing, passing, always running, started creating pretty patterns in the centre of the field.

Osgood's equaliser is probably my favourite-ever Chelsea goal. It just meant so much. Leeds were running down the clock but a compelling move involving Hollins ended with Osgood diving full length to head a wondrous goal. I liken it to the famous Ali–Foreman fight in Kinshasa, Zaire. Heavyweight champion Foreman dominated the early stages of the fight and Ali for long periods looked to be heading for a loss. With defeat staring him in the face, he walked back at the end of the fifth round to his corner. At that moment, he must have looked inside himself and found some extraordinary power.

He raised his fist and did the famous Ali Boom Bah Yea chant. The fans, subdued and apprehensive, responded. Ali went on to knock Foreman out in the eighth round. That night, trailing to the brutal Leeds side, Chelsea looked inside themselves and found something.

Webb bundled in the winner at the right-hand post from Hutchinson's famous 'windmill' throw in.

HAD ME A REAL GOOD TIME

The glory continued in 1970–71 as Chelsea won the European Cup-Winners' Cup, beating Real Madrid. This was also after a replay and by the same score: 2–1. The competition was of a much higher standard than when Chelsea won it again in 1998. The following year was the last year it was held. It was subsequently replaced by the UEFA Cup, itself a dumping ground for Champions League rejects and sides that did not even make the cut.

Madrid were in a state of rebuilding, not the roster of world-class talent they are today but still a formidable, highly experienced side. Madrid's aim today is to be the world's best team with the best players available. Osgood scored in the first game but a mistake by Webb let in Zoco for a last-minute equaliser. Again, it went to extra time but nobody could break the deadlock.

Hollins missed the replay two nights later with a knee injury and Charlie Cooke played in the number 4 shirt, Tommy Baldwin coming into midfield. Centre-half Dempsey smashed them in front from a half-cleared corner. Osgood made it two with a scintillating goal. Ossie had beaten Georgio Benito with various ploys all evening. This time, as the Real defender rushed in to tackle, the Chelsea centre-forward timed his push of the ball perfectly and skipped over the lunge before rolling the ball to Baldwin. Tommy ran towards the byline and with time to spare checked before hitting a low return pass to Osgood. Peter didn't wait for the ball; he ran across the box, losing his marker, and sent a first-time rasping shot past José Luis Borja. It was 2–0. We were too strong then for anybody to give us a two-goal start and catch us.

Madrid dominated the second half and pulled a goal back but Bonetti, after a difficult season, denied them. I suspect Chelsea fans would settle for a similar result in future European finals against the haughty aristocrats from Madrid.

HOW HOLLINS SCORED THE GREATEST GOAL EVER SEEN AT THE BRIDGE

Arsenal won the Double that season, with George Graham playing no small part in it. They only lost six games in the League, all away, one of them to Chelsea. In that match, Hollins scored what a subsequent programme described as the greatest goal ever scored at the Bridge. It was certainly the most spectacular, if not the most important goal ever scored there. Put simply, John ran onto a long clearance from Ron Harris and accelerated through the retreating Arsenal defence to crack a fierce shot against the bar. He then seized on the rebound to swivel and drive it into the net. You should have seen it, though – perhaps you did. That goal confirmed Hollins as one of the all-time top five Chelsea greats.

Zola's back heel against Norwich in the FA Cup, the increasingly likeable Lampard's roof-smashing volley in the home tie against Lazio and Eidur Gudjohnsen's overhead kick against a Leeds side managed by Terry Venables stand out as the most memorable goals in Chelsea's recent past. Of course, it is purely taste. When people gather in a bar after a game, the football talk invariably turns to goals, the lifeblood of the game. Sometimes, goals stick in the mind for no particular reason other than their excellence. How about a Kerry Dixon goal savagely struck against Arsenal on the opening day of the 1984–85 season? Roberto Di Matteo's volley at White Hart Lane maybe? Hollins scored sixty-four goals in total for Chelsea, a figure equalled by David Speedie and one more than Durie.

Hollins's goal was an amalgam of his continued hunger and drive for success. The problem was not all of the players had his spirit or desire. Hudson returned from injury but, like Osgood after his leg smash, he had changed, become withdrawn and moody like some Percy Bysshe Shelley character. He grew his hair and was always surrounded by hangers on. The European win disguised poor League form – Chelsea traipsed in a distant sixth. They never came close to taking the Championship. Nor, sadly, did it occur to any of us that they might.

Manchester United put us out of the League Cup with Best scoring a wonderful solo winner. If Hollins's goal against Arsenal was the greatest ever scored then perhaps George's was the greatest goal we ever conceded. John had scored in the United game also and it had looked enough to earn us a replay. The team from the other side of Manchester knocked us out of the FA Cup 0–3 on our own pitch. The warning signs were everywhere. What also concerned me was that Ian Hutchinson missed half the season with injuries.

SEASON 1971–72

This was probably John Hollins's best-ever year in a Chelsea shirt. Raiding deep from midfield, he scored over twenty goals in all competitions, half of them coming in the first two months of the season. His only low spot was when he missed a penalty in the second-round Cup-Winners' Cup tie at home to Atvidabergs. Chelsea could only draw 1–1 and we went out on away goals. In the previous round, we had annihilated Jeunesse Hautcharage 21–0 over two legs, which I believe is still a record for a European competition. Osgood totalled eight goals in the games. Sexton had transfer-listed him earlier in the season for lack of effort. It was patched up but there was an uneasy peace in the dressing-room.

Hutchinson, desperate to resurrect his career, broke his leg in his comeback game and didn't play for a season and a half. Keith Weller left Chelsea after a brief stint in Blue. Sexton signed him after the Cup final victory but after a Mutu-type start, he too faded. Hollins was one of the few consistent players and I was pinning a lot of hopes on him to win us a cup. Finances were a problem. A bizarre goal from Hudson knocked out Spurs in the semi-finals and took us back to Wembley for a League Cup final against unfancied Stoke.

The week before, Orient had sensationally knocked us out of the FA Cup. At 2–0 up, through the famous Cup firm of Webb and Osgood, the defence caved in and ended up conceding three pitiful goals. None of them in the class of Best's. What a mess. After the game, I saw groups of shocked Chelsea fans standing around in disbelief. The police were moving them along ('there's nothing to see here people, please keep moving'). Stoke continued where the Os left off, Conroy scoring a jammy goal early on to give the Potteries side a huge lift. Osgood equalised just on half-time and it appeared to be business as usual. Hollins ran the second half but, as so often with Chelsea games and honours they should have won, it slipped through their fingers.

The veteran Eastham scored a late winner and Chelsea's dream of a hat-trick of Cup victories died. There was to be no reason for hanging bunting in the Kings Road.

It was to be 24 years before they reached another major final.

NINE

THE RAT PACK

Go, go before you break my heart
Go, before I go down on my knees and beg you 'please don't go'
Gigliola Cinquetti, 'Go'

The Osgood rows, Hudson leaving, the nightmare of the stand, relegated, the whole thing was a nightmare.
The late Matthew Harding

Football's rubbish now – maybe they was boozing, gambling womanisers in the '70s, but they was Chelsea through and through.
Ron Manager, *Marvellous, Isn't It?*

Chelsea were drawn away to Brighton in the third round of the FA Cup in January 1973. It seemed to be an easy tie but then so did Orient. Brighton were rock bottom of the Second Division after ten straight defeats. Houseman missed the match with a strained calf. Osgood scored both Chelsea goals in a 0–2 stroll. The first goal was scored after 15 minutes from a Hudson free kick; the second was a close-range effort from Baldwin's cut-back centre.

Those three players were the Chelsea 'Rat Pack'. I previously compared Venables to Sinatra. Well, Hudson was also a huge Francis Albert fan. For a short while before his brilliance faded, Alan was guv'nor at the Bridge. Osgood could have been Dean Martin; Baldwin, his compadre, Peter Lawford, the 'fix it up' guy. I'm afraid Chelsea had nobody suitable for the

152

Sammy Davis role. For the Sands Hotel, read the Speakeasy or the Bag O'Nails.

Ron Harris was sent off at Brighton for throwing a roundhouse punch that would have pole-axed Lennox Lewis; John Boyle had been sent off six years before on the same ground, for the same offence. Must have been the sea air.

Ipswich were the visitors to the Bridge in the fourth round. They had beaten us comprehensively 3–0 on Boxing Day at their place. It was Chelsea's biggest defeat of the 1972–73 season. The tractor boys normally played in blue so both sides changed for the tie – Chelsea were resplendent in their new strip of red shirt, white shorts and green socks for the first time at home. They had worn the kit at Brighton, Sexton finally tiring of the bilious yellow shirt and blue shorts (especially after the nightmare Cup exit at Orient – they call it mellow yellow). I notice Arsenal wear that combo now, almost obliterated with mobile phone logos.

Bill Garner, who I think looked a little like a walking voodoo doll, scored both of Chelsea's goals in another moribund match. The first was via a long pass from Harris, the second almost straight from the kick-off after half-time. On an arctic February afternoon, the 36,491 crowd could have had a warming drink of Bovril for just 5p and a packet of biscuits for 3p. (For the home game against Portsmouth at Christmas 2003, a cup of undrinkable tea was £1.20. The teabag must have dated from around the time of Garner's goals.) Wagon Wheels were also available at 4p, whilst peanuts were 6p.

After the game, I went into the dressing-room to congratulate the lads on getting through but Hudson and Osgood emitted a blast of iciness as cold as anything felt on the terraces. It seemed out of character for the pair. I did not think much about it at the time but in hindsight it was a truly revelatory moment. Both players, in my opinion, displayed an attitude that seemed to say: 'I am more important than Chelsea and don't you forget it.'

This attitude was soon to tear the club apart. Times have changed. Now you don't talk so loud, now you don't seem so proud.

The fifth-round draw took us back to Hillsborough, then seen as a modern, safe ground. It had been used in the 1966 World Cup and had been considerably revamped. A crowd of 46,410 packed inside the stadium to watch a thrilling game. Chelsea had the Leppings Lane end of the ground and packed it to capacity. Wednesday took an early lead with a jaw-dropping shot that went over keeper Phillips' head. Chelsea equalised after 38 minutes when Osgood flicked a Hollins free kick across the face of the goal. Peter Houseman was standing on the left, out by the corner flag but he instantly returned the ball into the box. It was a quality cross with great variation and it completely fooled the extended Wednesday rearguard. Garner easily prodded in the equaliser. Osgood later won it for Chelsea with a header of great power. It was like a Shaolin monk smashing a slab of marble with a single head-butt. On the way home on the coach, he seemed arrogantly vague about this act of wonderment when I attempted to engage him in conversation.

The quarter-final draw gave us Arsenal at home. Harris was suspended following his fisticuffs at Brighton and Webb was injured. After some early midfield skirmishing, Osgood volleyed in a goal on a par with anything he ever scored. That was his greatest-ever season for scoring phantasmagoric goals. Despite the overall decline in the side, Osgood had reached almost monumental stature. To the fans, he just scored shed loads of great goals. This effort was scored after 15 minutes when he thundered in a shot from 25 yards from John Hollins's deep centre. Bob Wilson could only watch it fly past him; I swear that there was a hissing sound as it hit the back of the net. Nowadays, Bob commentates on goals in his media capacity but that must have been one of the greatest ever.

That goal deservedly won the BBC *Match of the Day* goal of the season award. Osgood at his peak never did things by half and also won ITV's award (then the other major channel of the day) for a goal scored against Derby on New Year's Eve, 1972. Osgood really had it in for Derby (and their manager Brian Clough) that year. By autumn, he had scored a thunderous winner against them in a 3–2 League Cup victory.

The League Cup proved to be another embarrassment to Chelsea. After stumbling through to the semi-final, they were outplayed in both games by a workmanlike Norwich City. I am not sure if Delia was around then.

In the Arsenal quarter-final, Osgood's dazzling goal went to Chelsea's heads and they lost their early grip on the game. Arsenal hit back with two goals in as many minutes. Alan Ball, the feisty World Cup winner, cranked up the Arsenal midfield and quickly headed home a corner to level. Then, with the Chelsea defence still suffering from the Orient Cup sleeping sickness, Charlie George sashayed up and slammed them in front. Charlie was soon to burn out but at that time his addictive charisma made him the adored idol of the North Bank in the same way Monsieur Henry is today.

Barely had the excitement died down when John Hollins equalised for Chelsea. The goal came from an overlap by Gary Locke, an exciting young prospect who had recently forced himself into the side. The crowd went berserk and the jackboots stomped in the Shed. Arsenal fans tried to invade the citadel. Gallons of red paint were sploshed about. Paint chucking was fashionable that season.

That was how it stayed. The second half was more heavy duty – it could never live up to the heart-stopping mayhem of the first half hour. The pitch was a disgrace. Chelsea pressed hard for the winner. Steve Kember, bought by Sexton the previous season to replace Hudson (or at least provoke him into better form), almost scored near the end. It was all down to the replay at Highbury three nights later. A point of those times was the proximity of the matches. There was no cooling-off period between games. The police never had to rearrange their overtime schedules. As I walked down from Finsbury Park, I thought of the match against Moscow which had an even larger crowd.

It was estimated 10,000 fans were locked out as the mighty steel gates of Highbury slammed shut on 62,746 supporters, eager to see the sequel. They were lucky to witness a great clash between the schizophrenic, subtle skill of Chelsea and the improbably aggressive persistence of their north London rivals. It was all very abstract. I realised for Chelsea that night it was make or break. The critics had written them off and the bookies put Chelsea at long odds to progress in the Cup.

Peter Houseman put Chelsea in front after 20 minutes. Hollins hit over a long diagonal cross that Garner headed across the face of the goal. Houseman jumped highest to nod downwards across Wilson and into the net. It was to be his last-ever Cup goal for Chelsea. A sense of inescapable tragedy overcame me then. At the time, I never knew why.

TOO MUCH OF NOTHING

Boosted by the goal, Chelsea dominated the first half and scared the life out of Arsenal. For the first time since the Cup-Winners' Cup games of '71, we showed flashes of the old Chelsea troupe. The North Bank was transfixed as Chelsea pushed the home side back and Hudson bossed the game. Arsenal ran into cul-de-sacs whilst Chelsea carved out pretty patterns in the midfield. The old buccaneers appeared to be in total command but just on half-time (as when Orient scored) fate struck another direct hit.

Kember was playing in the Hollins number 4 shirt with John switched to right-back. The ex-Palace skipper clashed with George Armstrong, who went down as if hit by a carbine. Sadly, George died of a heart attack at a young age. The late Geordie Armstrong was football's answer to Norman Wisdom. Where Wisdom had built up an entire career on looking daft and falling over, Armstrong had built up an Arsenal career on looking daft and falling over. At first, the ref gave a free kick outside the box. In the next few moments, he was besieged by a posse of protesting Arsenal players who were insistent that the offence occurred inside the box. The referee was Gordon Hill, an experienced official but a controversy waiting to happen. That night, refereeing abandoned the laws of common sense.

Amazingly, Hill changed his mind and gave a penalty kick from which Alan Ball gleefully scored. The Chelsea team were disgusted that the referee had been coerced into altering his decision. The Chelsea fans, who had taken over the Clock End, would have garrotted the oaf in black. To be fair, the television evidence did later prove conclusively that the tackle took place in the penalty area. Tackle as opposed to a foul. The significance of it was that the Arsenal team had bullied the official into changing his mind. Had Hill consulted the linesman before he gave the first free kick, he would have avoided a great deal of controversy. Today, people talk about the cynicism of the modern game: the moral of the story is we live in a time without morals. Mind you, in the last Cup competition of the twentieth century, the Arsenal boss Arsène Wenger actually had his side replay a Cup tie against Sheffield United after a controversial goal had enabled his team to win. In March 1973, Arsenal didn't ring me with an offer to replay a game we had forfeited in similar circumstances.

The heart seemed to go out of Chelsea at that point. The sheer effrontery of the Arsenal players astounded me but they still had the hunger and passion to win despite having already won the Double. Alan Ball was the difference in the sides. He almost had the sublime skill of a Hudson but was tactically more advanced and far better disciplined. The ginger-haired Gooner had the stamina of a great miler. That night, early in the tense second half, he took his Blue markers on three or four runs of over seventy yards. Then he really started to play. Ball rabble-roused his teammates to greater efforts. Hudson sulked.

The Gunners steamrollered Chelsea in the second half. Ray Kennedy scored the winner with a booming header from Eddie Kelly's flawless centre but by then Chelsea seemed almost resigned to their fate. It could be said that they had actually outgrown their present circumstances. Possibly, Chelsea had used up their quota of luck winning the cup finals against Leeds and Madrid. Both were technically superior sides who had been edged aside by Chelsea's uncompromising force and determination. It was karma because, in my view, players like Osgood and Hudson were not convinced deep down of their own huge potential. That is why they clung together in the Rat Pack. In the matches against Atvidaberg, Orient, Stoke and Norwich they were beaten by vastly inferior sides. However, they had all worked much harder than Chelsea to secure the victories. There followed a further Cup defeat against a side Chelsea had outplayed for long periods in both matches. It was all downside. Would they have won the Cup if they had gone through at Highbury? We will never know. Sunderland, then in the Second Division, won it that year after knocking out the mean machine of Arsenal in the semi-finals. Ian Porterfield, who managed the Blues from 1991–93, scored the Cup-winning goal. Some people would suggest that is the only reason he was given the job.

Chelsea's soul was now poisoned. The odyssey was almost over; it had all gotten so very much worse. Chelsea slumped to 12th in the League, their lowest placing since the Doc revolutionised the club. The writing was on the wall with a Braille translation for the partially sighted.

The season ended with a trip to Tehran of all places. It was quieter then. In the autumn of '73, Peter Houseman was awarded a testimonial against Fulham. Mr Fayed, a local shopkeeper, was not connected with them then. Osgood scored twice in a 4–1 win with one apiece from the old road warriors Webb and Hutchinson. The crowd of 9,927 watched Ian Hutchinson win the half-time 'London long throw' competition with a giant lob of 112 feet. There is no record of how much Peter took on the night. When Dennis Wise had his testimonial match in the summer of 1999 he spent a colossal £50,000 of the kitty on watches and pens for the players and staff in top West End jewellers Cartier. The difference between the two lifestyles could not be better illustrated. Of course, Wise proved what a great club man he was when he demanded a transfer after being dropped by Ranieri. He later withdrew it when faced with the tears of the Stamford Bridge tea lady and the prospect of a transfer to Blackburn.

I attended one of the events organised for Houseman's testimonial: a dance at the Mecca in Reading on a wet Monday evening in midwinter. Tickets were priced at 75p each. Peter's testimonial committee were organising coaches to take supporters back to Stamford Bridge at a reasonable charge. I recall how he was always the perfect gentleman and personally thanked everybody who made the trip. There was not a Cartier watch in sight. Houseman didn't have to buy anybody, though.

Around this time, Chelsea's star continued to wane. They were sixth from bottom with only four wins in fourteen matches. The side was so one dimensional that if you revolved them they would disappear. They had been dumped out of the League Cup by Stoke, who were disturbingly making a habit of it. It was a horrid winter with a fuel and travel crisis caused by an oil shortage and the miners' and railwaymen's disputes. The Heath Government was enforcing a three-day working week to meet the power emergency.

Chelsea had their own energy crisis. The Rat Pack were partying like it was 1999 and working what seemed to be a one-day week. The only club they were interested in was Dolly's on Jermyn Street where they spent many an evening. The real Rat Pack drank whisky sour, the lads liked vodka. Tommy Baldwin was the pick of the forwards; he led the League's scoring charts by racing to nine goals. For early November, that was some going but only the foolhardy bet on Chelsea. Still do. Baldwin had adopted a new image: stylishly bedraggled barnet and a somewhat foolish-looking beard; the combined effect made him look like a slimmed-down Jim Morrison. Osgood and Hudson had both occasionally sported beards from some doomed warrior culture which they doggedly developed over the months. Osgood had carried Chelsea on his back for the previous two seasons. His goalscoring was in steep decline but he had far fewer chances to take by then.

> One of the most talented footballers of his generation. Car was now up to his armpits in decline; and he was only 25.
> Martin Amis, *Yellow Dog*

Cooke, the player most capable of thrashing a defence and setting up goals, had left for Crystal Palace. Tambling had ended up there as well when injuries finally halted his conveyor belt of goals. Hudson's form had deteriorated to such an extent that there was a real feeling within the club that his best days were behind him. He was like a character in a Martin Amis novel. There were shock waves in paradise for him. Like so many players, the chase for the dragon proved too much. Alan Ball had delivered on his promise, the other Alan never did. Houseman had been plagued by injury and bedevilled by the constant abuse from the Shed. Hutchinson was losing his long and painful fight against injury. He had the dubious reputation of being the most-battered striker in the game. Only his massive powers of endurance and stoicism had carried him that far. It was all held together by a piece of tissue paper, namely Sexton's vibes.

Christmas 1973: the empire, collapsing for so long, finally fell apart. Leeds had won 1–2 at Chelsea on 15 December to complete the century's record start of 20 games undefeated. Arsenal beat it later, I think, when George was in charge and again in 2004. Joe Jordan, the Scotland international centre-forward, proved to be the match winner. Another lapse on half-time allowed Jordan (a brontosaurus of a player) to head home the late Bremner's swirling corner. The bearded Osgood equalised with a powerful header from Houseman's corner to raise the Shed's hopes but it was short-lived. Jordan deftly set up Mick Jones to blast the winner. Chelsea were brushed aside by the Elland Road team; in midfield, Hudson and Kember were simply obliterated. The bitter, unpalatable truth was Chelsea couldn't hold a candle to Revie's side. Both teams contained seven players who had slugged it out in the Old Trafford replay but the message was clear: Leeds were the top dogs. They won the title by a distance that season. Chelsea had tumbled a long way down from the upper echelon. Even in London town, they were no longer numero uno: Arsenal reclaiming a crown which they continue to wear and QPR making threatening noises. The Rat Pack were on their uppers, though they still spent a fortune in the Chelsea Cobbler on the Fulham Road.

In the next match, Wolves, a team of has-beens and hopefuls, beat Chelsea 2–0 with John Richards, a player Sexton was desperate to buy, scoring both. The poison that was running through the system was finally kicking him. A virus called Tourette's syndrome was about to strike. Tourette's causes the sufferer to act spontaneously and unpredictably, sometimes uttering obscenities and generally causing a disturbance.

On Boxing Day morning, West Ham visited Chelsea for a vital match. The Hammers were rock bottom of the League and had only won two games all season. Leonardo Di Caprio had better survival prospects at the end of *Titanic*: like the real ship, Chelsea were building up momentum before the crunch. At half-time, Chelsea were 2–0 up. The fans and players were looking forward to a nice Christmas lunch then putting their feet up by the fireside and getting stuck into the eggnog. Goals from little Ian Britton (the '70s Morris without the baggage) and a fine solo effort from Hudson had put them in a strong position. West Ham looked down already. The rest is history with a small 'h'. The game and Chelsea Football Club's future took a colossal shift.

Dean Martin died at Christmas in 1995; the Chelsea Rat Pack died 22 Christmases before. In the second half, Chelsea's defence fell apart. Frank Lampard Senior (father of the England midfielder with the face of a Calvin Klein poster boy) walked through the left-hand side of the defence, skipped a couple of half-arsed tackles and crashed the ball home. Frank Junior owes Chelsea big time for the sins of his father. Soon afterwards, a clean-shaven Osgood (he must have got a Remington for Christmas) nearly crashed the bar down on Hammers keeper Mervyn Day with a first-time volley from Houseman's cross. The rebound was punted up to Bobby Gould (whom I later employed as an assistant manager) to fire home a shock equaliser. It was one of the most bizarre goals ever seen at Stamford Bridge. The only one comparable was the unique half-share own goal scored by the Leicester players in our championship season.

Television presenter and football power-broker Trevor Brooking set up the leviathan Clyde Best for two further goals as the Chelsea fans looked on in horror. Nowadays, Brooking appears on BBC (wearing what appears to be one of the Duke of Windsor's old sports jackets) and we see yet another middle-aged hack with his portfolio career. In 1973, though, he was a midfield player with lovely technique, great dollops of skill and a brilliant tactical brain. Clever Trevor didn't miss a trick that Boxing Day. The Hammers must have thought it was Christmas two days running as they romped home 2–4. (Sad to report, they avoided the drop and finished level with us on points.) Chelsea, so classy early in the game and then going down in ignominy, served up a better Christmas pantomime than anything at Wimbledon Theatre that day. The Shed had to eat a skip of humble pie as the East Enders had a knees-up under the North Stand.

A fight broke out in the Chelsea dressing-room after the fiasco. Actually, it wasn't so much a dressing-room as a Portakabin. The rebuilding of the ground that was to almost destroy Chelsea was well under way. The East Stand looked like Wembley after the bulldozers turned up and the conditions added to the stress and discontent. I walked into the room with my head down. Sexton was pink in the face and trembling with poorly suppressed fury. Straight away he launched into Osgood and Hudson like a missile leaving Houston. I knew this was going to happen at some point but the ferocity and bile even shocked me as the gossamer web of relationships finally collapsed. Dave argued that Osgood and his accomplice should have given far more of the ball to Houseman. It was Houseman's 300th first-team game and two days past his 28th birthday. There was no party, though. Sexton was adamant that the Battersea-born winger had the beating of the West Ham back, Coleman. Dave was ranting that the Rat Pack duo had selfishly indulged in intricate passing movements between themselves rather than feed Houseman. The pair protested that it was not them at fault but an unspeakably bad defence that had caved in so dramatically. Only Marmite benefits from being spread very thin – the duo's talents did not. It raged for ages. The atmosphere was awful – worse than the dressing-room rows after the Villa Park semi-final defeats under the Doc.

Three days later, Liverpool visited the Bridge in what was the last-ever Chelsea game with Osgood and Hudson in the line-up. They could not have had any sterner opposition. Liverpool were second to Leeds in the pecking order, though not yet the superpower that laid waste to the top flight in the '80s. Like Leeds, they had the edge over Chelsea in the League but the FA Cup was a different matter.

Mickey Droy, then trading as much on his physiognomy as his ability, was restored to the heart of the Chelsea defence. Droy was tough – he hurt players just by breathing on them. (Speaking of which, in the Boxing Day bust-up, Sexton said that he could smell whisky on Hudson's breath).

I once met Bruce Dern, the Hollywood actor who was living in Chelsea whilst making a film. He became a fan and was impressed by Droy, who he always referred to as being the sort of guy you saw 'in jail'. This was long before it was considered fashionable for movie stars to attend matches. Emmanuel Petit (who sounds like a porn film himself) introduced actor Mickey Rourke to Chelsea shortly after Abramovich took over. Rourke, the wild man of Hollywood, would have been ideal as Hudson if they ever made a movie of that era. *The Chelsea Story*, I can see it now. Chelsea life president Attenborough as himself, Kenny Rogers as Ken Bates, John Malkovich as Vialli . . .

In 1973, Kevin Keegan was Liverpool's ace. The double 'K' danced around Droy's size 11 boots to set up Peter Cormack to score the only goal of the game. Like Chelsea fan Michael Caine said in *Get Carter*: 'You're a big man, but you're out of shape.' Chelsea were simply awful: a mixture of sloth and gut-wrenching predictability. I was in utter despair. In our last three home games, Chelsea had been outclassed and outfought. They had gone close to the flame one too many times. I saw Bill Shankly in the tunnel at the end of the game. The legend that was Bill usually had a wisecrack or a smile but he just nodded over, almost embarrassed by it all. It was like an exhibition match.

Football is as much about accepting defeat as winning. The team Sexton put together in the early '70s had been seen as the great counter-punchers of the post-war game. They had in previous seasons performed most effectively after they had taken severe punishment – Leeds at Wembley, the first Cup-Winners' Cup final against Madrid – but now there was to be no way back as the egos erupted. The disease was now an epidemic.

ASHES TO ASHES

I was so concerned about things, I phoned Dave Sexton at his Brighton home and persuaded him to have lunch. I drove down to the south coast. He was paranoid, not wishing to lunch on the Kings Road for fear of being spotted. Eventually, he poured it all out to me, his growing discontent with the two superstars of Stamford Bridge. There was a struggle for control of the dressing-room and he was losing. Too many duvet days when they were too tired or hungover to train. He felt that their actions had gone beyond the bounds of reasonable behaviour. Sexton was keen to dump them both but feared the reaction of the crowd, particularly the Shed.

Sexton was speaking like the psychobabblers before they were fashionable. He talked of the issues around Osgood and Hudson. He even quoted the Roman Emperor Marcus Aurelius Antonius: 'All is ephemeral – fame and the famous as well.'

Dave was probably the best-read manager ever. He loved the game so much and could not understand how players could abuse their fitness through high living. In his view, it impaired their ability to compete at the highest level. Now into his 70s, Dave is a venerable figure in coaching circles and at the time of writing was the senior statesman on Eriksson's coaching staff. I told him the board would give him full backing but warned him the club was haemorrhaging money because of the ground improvements. In the end, I told him to exercise caution in his future dealings with the pair.

A few days later, the Rat Pack of Osgood, Hudson and Tommy Baldwin, along with the less acrobatic Bonetti, were dropped from the club's trip to Sheffield United. It was New Year's Day 1974. Chelsea's re-shaped team crawled out of the ashes to come away with a 1–2 victory, courtesy of some questionable goals from Kember and Hollins, the United goalkeeper John Connaughton looking badly at fault for both strikes. Sexton could scarcely conceal his delight at getting an away victory without his refuseniks. It crossed my mind that he was making plans for the future that did not include the malcontents. I had heard of downsizing but this was dumbsizing.

Sexton kept the same side for the home FA Cup tie with QPR, who were now about to go into overdrive. Rangers were the new kids on the west London block. It seems unthinkable now, but just then they were the top club in the capital. The main reason was Stan 'The Man' Bowles, the greatest Chelsea-style player that never played for Chelsea. Stan was on fire that season. Sexton wanted to swap him for Hudson but the Rangers fans would have demolished the ground brick by brick. Bowles always played with a discernible direction. In any match he stood out like a split skirt at the Hunt Ball. Ron Harris tried to use his studs to conduct acupuncture on the QPR striker's shins but Stan refused to be intimidated. Bowles' instantaneous reflexes and extraordinary agility proved too much even for Harris. I saw Bowles at the end of the game with a huge grin on his face. He looked like he had barely broken a sweat.

John Phillips saved a Gerry Francis penalty in the match to deny QPR the victory they deserved. Stan Bowles scored the only goal of the tie in the 65th minute of the replay. Continuing industrial disputes meant that there was still a ban on the use of floodlights, so the game had to be played on a midweek afternoon. Rangers, with Bowles in unstoppable form, dominated from start to finish. Shorn of the skill of Osgood and Hudson, Chelsea were about as creative as Pablo Picasso (Picasso being dead). Sexton's side were already on their way to Palookaville. As Steve Tyler, the lead singer of Aerosmith, once famously sang: 'There is no substitute for arrogance.' Chelsea were to find this out to their cost.

After a training ground bust-up and some silly macho behaviour, Osgood and Hudson were placed on the transfer list. Hudson was the first to go, surprisingly signing for Stoke. Most Blues fans scratched their heads in bewilderment or dropped their marmalade when the London sharpie joined the Potteries version of *Dad's Army*. A place like Stoke seemed like anathema – a million miles from Blaises in Queensgate or the Cromwellian on the Cromwell Road. Osgood's departure dragged on and for a time it looked like he might stay at the Bridge. All he had to do was knock on my door and maybe we could have patched it up. Dave could have had his say over a cup of tea and there may have been some workaround. Osgood never did knock on my door – perhaps he wanted me to push the peanut forward and go after him, talk him round. It didn't work like that, though.

To this day, I think he still blames me. After my beloved wife June died in the summer of 2003, I rang Peter to ask him if he wanted to come to the funeral. Despite our differences and all that had happened over the years, I wanted the chaps to know. June had done a tremendous amount to help shape the careers of so many of those young men. She was never part of the arguments and had only ever shown (to Osgood in particular) kindness and support. When I told him the sad news, Osgood slammed down the phone, snarling, 'What do you want me to do about it?'

Chelsea Football Club broke Osgood as surely as it did Hutchinson. The reason why Peter never really made it in any walk of life after football is best summed up in that painful story. He always lacked the casual charm of Hudson; there was a malevolence that crept into his soul around that time.

Some saw the jettisoned Hudson as the sacrificial lamb. No religion could flourish without sacrifices. Hudson, chucked on the bonfire of vanities. There were even press reports of the board siding with Osgood and sacking Sexton. What really happened, though, was when I quizzed Sexton on his real motive for selling Hudson he stood up and walked out of the board meeting. Dave was later spotted on the pitch telling players and journos that he had been sacked. Such was his free-floating anxiety about the whole matter, the slightest thing set him off. I had a golden chance to retrieve the situation and could have sacked Sexton. I could not accede to the player power which had diluted the magic of that team, though. No matter what star power the players had. Recent events have shown that the players can in some cases be bigger than the manager. Vialli and Gullit were both unseated by players and backroom staff despite their haul of trophies.

The truly big clubs always back the manager, though. That is why Ferguson sold Beckham to Madrid despite his image as the most famous athlete in the world. That is why United are still the biggest club in the world. Even Abramovich's billions cannot buy class and integrity. Selling Hudson and Osgood ultimately cost me everything: my club, my job, nearly my life but I would do it again because in my heart I know I did the right thing.

Because I did it for Chelsea Football Club. I did it for the guys that stood in the rain and spent their last pounds supporting us. In those times, following Chelsea could get you seriously hurt. You were taking your life into your hands visiting places like Newcastle and Liverpool in a blue scarf. Chelsea only survived because of the spirit those people showed. You cannot cheat those people; they know. They know the players that would run through brick walls for them – names like Joey Jones, Webb, Mickey Thomas, John Bumstead and Zola. They knew the players that took the money and ran. That is why the diehards still meet in a stand named after Matthew Harding and others are soon forgotten.

Then 1973–74 was a season of glass. The bulldozers were still hard at work outside my office but were the truth to be known, the club was already flattened. Throughout the whole sorry affair, Dickie Attenborough had supported my decision to transfer Osgood and Hudson. For this role, he adopted the persona of the character he played in John Sturges's 1963 film *The Great Escape*. He kept on about letting the other chaps down and how it was all about fair play, discipline and duty. At any moment, I expected 'Biker' McQueen or 'Digger' Bronson to enter the room! It was stiff upper lips all round. Yet, I took the heat in subsequent years and Attenborough was the 'go-to guy'.

Attenborough was something of a figure of fun to the Rat Pack. They were always taking the mickey out of him. Every Christmas, they would show the film of the mass Stalag breakout. The Rat Pack would make a point of watching it because Attenborough's character was machine-gunned down by the Gestapo at the end. This was a source of great amusement to them and they spent a lot of time whistling the catchy theme song whenever Dickie was in the dressing-room.

Attenborough and co. were constraining and demanding. Cracks were appearing everywhere. The board felt morally obliged to support the manager but doubted the wisdom of selling the team's best players. It was corporate hara-kiri.

After a difficult Christmas in 2003, Mr Ranieri told the press: 'When Chelsea win, Mr Abramovich wins. When Chelsea lose, Ranieri loses.' I do not remember Dave Sexton ever saying a similar thing about me when Chelsea lost. Eventually, after threatening to quit the game, Osgood joined Southampton. The notoriety of the pair had frightened many of the top clubs from signing them. Clubs like Everton and Liverpool preferred their heroes to be untarnished and in their prime. A northern giant who moved in for Hudson had their potential acquisition vetoed by their chairman. It was not so much a question of 'You will never eat lunch in this town' as 'You will never shake a cocktail'. A fellow London manager told Sexton that he was of the opinion that the rebels were like Siamese twins: one could hardly survive without the other. Despite signing Osgood, Southampton were relegated that year. They had a learned helplessness about them. As a vehicle for Osgood's career, Southampton was a hearse. To this day, no top side has let its players go in such a manner. It started as a farce but ended as outrage. Nobody paid a higher price for it than Chelsea. They were talents that overwhelmed the imagination. Tommy Docherty was by then managing Manchester United, who were also relegated that season. It had been the Doc who had discovered the Rat Pack (and signed Baldwin). He was quoted as saying at the time that he would 'sooner swim the Atlantic than sell players of that quality'. He could never accept they had been sold.

Osgood went to the Dell for £275,000, Southampton smashing the transfer record set a few weeks before by Hudson's move to Stoke. It was another strange choice, in my view. A curious bunch of players and personalities were at the Hampshire club. Osgood was like the character Lord Snooty in the *The Beano*, a wannabe Sloane toff exiled on the coast. Peter lost the power to astound when he left the Bridge. It would be fair to say that he never reached the heights he scaled at Chelsea. Both the rebels' careers drifted aimlessly when they left the Bridge. Hudson had the occasional game at Stoke when he played as well as he did before his serious injury. More often than not, though, he strolled through games as if they were his right. If the truth be told, Alan had hitched his star to a very ordinary side: it was like Jude Law acting in *Emmerdale* or Eric Clapton joining a pub band.

THE SIMON DEE OF FOOTBALL

Simon Dee was another Kings Road dandy – a suave, sophisticated television host who epitomised the cool face of swinging London. Like Hudson, he was the bloke who had it all – charisma, good looks, on-screen presence and the ability to make his job look effortless. But he was always hideously pleased with himself and by the mid-'70s he had virtually sunk without trace. After his fall from grace, I used to see him walking down the Kings Road near the Chelsea antique market or the Countdown boutique where he used to buy his Paisley shirts and flash suits. Like Hudson, he blended disillusion and defiance, mockery and self-mockery so very fashionably. Both chucked away their careers. It was a cautionary tale because nobody was allowed to have that much fun again.

After his career fizzled out, Hudson's personal life span out of control and he ended up a bankrupt, pathetic figure, horrifically injured in a road accident. I was sad that no one in the game he had graced had thought to help him.

STRANGE DAYS

In a political move, Charlie Cooke boomeranged back from Palace for a small fee. Cooke's career had stalled badly in south London. There was none of the dizzying success he had enjoyed with Chelsea. Rumours of alcohol abuse circulated but the old showman's swagger never left him. The talent was still there: nobody could go round a defender like Cooke, not even Pat Nevin. Charlie had a sense of belatedness in his play then. Bobby Tambling had left Palace as well, in his case to pursue religious work in Ireland.

On 13 March 1974, Burnley came to Chelsea for a League game. Once again, the floodlight restrictions meant it was a midweek daylight fixture. Attendance was 8,171, the lowest for a League game since the war. I wonder how many of the fans were in the 41,932 crowd who watched the victory over Manchester United 29 years later in 2003? The fans were staying away in droves; also few could afford to miss an afternoon off work. The loss of the Rat Pack, punished for an act of insurrection, was a massive blow to the average Shed fan and disillusion was setting in fast. The absentees missed an interesting little afternoon, however, as Chelsea cantered home 3–0. Houseman headed the second from 16-year-old John Sparrow's cross, the boy making his debut for Chelsea. Sparrow was another player who should have made it to the big time but injuries hampered his progress.

This leads inexorably to Hutchinson, who came on as sub just before half-time when Garner went off with concussion (sometimes, Garner would head the rival defenders more often than the ball). It was Hutchinson's first game since September. To some, he was all but forgotten. He scored Chelsea's third goal with a zinging left-foot volley. It briefly reminded the small band of loyalists of better days and emphasised the criminal waste all around them. It set off a mighty roar from the fanatics lost inside the dank, empty stadium. Hutchinson scored again at the Bridge the following Saturday, the winning goal against Newcastle. I can picture him leaping like a springbok, almost as high as the crossbar, to nod home. Crespo reminds me a little of Hutchinson. I wish he wouldn't wear that stupid garden twine in his hair, though.

Hutchinson only played a handful more games as his ravaged knee wore him down. The injury worsened as the cartilages were torn and ligaments inflamed. He was taking eight tablets a day just to keep going. In spite of that, he still scored vital goals to keep Chelsea in the top flight.

For a vital match at Tottenham, Houseman was switched to number 9. Osgood's shirt was coveted by every forward in the club. If he had left on better terms, maybe we would have retired the number. Sexton's choice of the flexible Houseman was a fitting accolade. It brought a cynical response from its original owner, however, who wore a ubiquitous half-sneer in his last days at the Bridge. Osgood was about to join Southampton as the transfer deadline day neared. Stoke had come in for him and Hudson was keen to get him up there but Osgood declined. He hated the north.

In an extraordinary match at White Hart Lane, defenders scored all the goals in a 1–2 win to the Blues. They trailed to an early strike from Bobby Evans but big Mickey Droy levelled it up. Mick looked the size of Canary Wharf that night and equalised with a simple header from Charlie Cooke's corner. Tottenham was always one of Charlie's favourite grounds and in short, sharp bursts he played as well as ever. Holding back the years, as the man sang. Ron Harris scored the winner from a long way out. It was with a low drive that spun over the diving Jennings. It was as unlikely a winner as Hudson's freak free kick in the League Cup semi-final on the same ground a few seasons before. That win kept Chelsea up with the big boys for one more season. I honestly think if we had lost at Spurs we would have gone down. In the end, we stayed up by one point.

Making his full debut that night was a raffish 17 year old called Ray 'Butch' Wilkins. I do not know where he got the nickname, I never asked. With the self-belief of Robbie Williams, the tactical brain of Venables and the shooting power of the notorious Dillinger Gang, 'Butch' was born to be a star. Ray's older brother Graham had already played at left-back earlier in that hellish season. Graham had broken the fibula of his left leg at Old Trafford in an exciting 2–2 draw (Rat Packer Tommy Baldwin scoring a brilliant goal to save us a point).

For Ray, that game was the start of a marvellous career. The Shed were enraptured by him. They were desperate for a new idol on account of their old favourites being sold. Wilkins did not let them down, quickly ascending to an artistic midfield plane and going on to play for England. He left us for Manchester United and subsequently played for AC Milan, Glasgow Rangers, QPR and Millwall. He later went into management and was back at the Bridge for a spell as assistant to Vialli. This was while Graham Rix was in prison. Then he assisted Wise in managing Millwall and he helped take the club to the FA Cup final in 2004. Sexton saw Wilkins as the ideal replacement for the shimmering brilliance of Hudson. Arsenal were later to see Rix as the player to replace Hudson when he quit Highbury for America.

Hudson returned to the Bridge with his new side, Stoke. It was the last game of the season and the local lad was in tremendous form. The influence of his manager and his spiritual guru, Tony Waddington, banished his inner demons (albeit temporarily). If Waddington had told Alan he could walk across the Thames under Chelsea Bridge, he would have attempted it. One of Alan's showbiz pals was the actor Dennis Waterman, who was a loyal Chelsea fan. I always think of Waterman's hit theme tune to the television show *Minder* called 'I Could Be So Good For You'. It should have been the theme song for Waddington and Hudson.

Fittingly, Hudson scored the only goal of the game, a snap shot that flew over Phillips. There was a wonderful symmetry to it.

TEN

THEM'S THE BREAKS

Never trust the artist. Trust the tale.

D.H. Lawrence

We got the bill for the '70s in the early '80s. Boy, was it high. Chelsea were by now sinking into the morass of debt that was to haunt them until the appearance of their saviour Roman Abramovich.

The club was relegated at the end of season 1974–75. Osgood and Hudson had the last laugh. The defence was as thin as Ryvita. The midfield lacked strength and invention, negligibly au fait with concepts like subtlety and style. The attack struggled to score goals without any recognised strikers. The conceit of the new stand was that it started to rust. It looked like a tramp steamer on its way to the scrapyard. Chelsea fans looking at the debris of their team prayed that the East Stand could be scrapped and compressed into a cube comparable to the size of Sexton's Ford Escort. The club had started to die.

Every generation of a football club has its *nouveaux pauvres*. For Leeds, it was their early twenty-first-century incarnation. For Chelsea, it was the last quarter of the twentieth century. Eventually, the level of debt and the subsequent financial embarrassment incurred by the exorbitant cost of the East Stand led to my departure from Chelsea. The dream of the futuristic stadium is commonplace now but 30 years ago it was visionary. Some of the circumstances that brought about the situation were foreseeable, others not. The shortage of cement and the builders' strike could not have been predicted by anyone. The rising costs were triggered by the absence of penalty clauses and fixed prices. The decline in the team, caused by the internally combusting problems between Sexton and some of his stars, sent the gates tumbling.

That summer, in the new pina colada dawn of hope, I was responsible for signing David Hay, the Celtic midfielder, for £225,000. After his success with Scotland in the World Cup, we were looking for the Paisley-born star to give Chelsea moral and physical leadership. David, nicknamed 'The Silent Assassin', was in the same mould as Johan Neeskens – part BMW, part armour-plated wrecking machine. Today, he would be a cert for *Robot Wars*. Hay was a jack of all trades: an awesome tackler, creator, imaginer and goalscorer. The feeling north of the border was that he was on his way to even greater things. In his first full season in London, a cataract was discovered in his right eye. For the sake of the struggling team, David postponed a vital operation, though it affected his natural game. The fans never realised the full extent of his problems. Two seasons later, in Chelsea's promotion season, he received a bang which displaced his retina. The doctors were of the view that he would never play again but, like Hutchinson, he battled back. His cause was helped by some marvellous surgery and the management's faith in him. Hay met further adversity with a serious injury to his right knee. Only a triumph of will kept him going for so long. I cannot stress what a great, great player David Hay was and his loss to Chelsea was incalculable.

John Sissons joined Chelsea in August 1974 from Norwich, in another attempt to bolster the shrinking squad. Sissons started his career at West Ham and was heralded as one of their brightest-ever prospects. He was a naturally left-footed player (a rarity those days) and quicker than a Ferrari with exquisite ball control and a hammer shot. Shankly once remarked that he was so good 'they used to mark him in the kickabouts'.

Somehow, he never lived up to his potential. Joe Cole reminds me of him a great deal: a huge array of gifts but little end product. Sissons 'The Wunderkind' had seen the world from the rocket ship but, like Chelsea, he was falling fast. He had one great flaw: a lack of balance in his running meant that he was too easily injured. John-boy failed to make any impression at Chelsea and only played ten League games.

Carlisle were the visitors on the opening day of the season. It was the big moment when we unveiled the new East Stand but the party was spoilt by the Cumbrian side squelching us 0–2. Ten years previously, Carlisle had been in the Fourth Division – they were the classic rags-to-riches-to-rags side. After winning their first two games, they headed the table but that was as good as it got and they eventually went down with us.

THE FIRST OF THE GANG TO DIE

I could hear the death knell sounding somewhere. If you were to have asked any Chelsea fan sitting in the luxury of the East Stand, they would have swapped their plush seats for a place on the rain-lashed terraces provided they could watch players of the calibre of the mesmeric Rat Pack.

At the start of the season, within two months of the East Stand opening, Sexton was sacked. Chelsea were in a tailspin towards bankruptcy and he was perceived as having lost the plot some time before. Having backed Dave to the hilt over the player-power matter, it seemed like poor timing. As Hudson was to comment years later: 'In the end, nobody won.' Least of all the punters. Chelsea took some fearful hammerings that season. Stoke scored six in our seemingly annual League Cup defeat at their hands. After the match, a terrific row erupted on the train home. My cousin Leslie Mears started tearing a strip over some of the team. He was later removed from his position on the board.

In the League, Newcastle slammed home five goals and Wolves, reviving memories of the previous decade's goal sprees, managed to put seven past us. Birmingham knocked us out of the Cup at home.

The exodus continued: Kember, Webb, Chris Garland and even Hollins were all part of the giant car boot sale of the old guard. Peter Houseman left Chelsea to join Oxford United in May 1975 but within two years he was dead, tragically killed in a road accident. The first of the gang to pass away.

Season 1975–76 was one of stabilisation. Chelsea finished 11th in the Second Division as McCreadie started to blood the youngsters. They included Gary Stanley, Kenny Swain, Teddy Maybank, Steve Wicks and Steve Finnieston, who were to form the nucleus of the promotion side.

Ian Hutchinson quit the game that season after four years of terrible injuries, which included two broken legs, a broken arm, a broken toe and appalling knee injuries. Eddie McCreadie was by now Chelsea manager and spoke glowingly of his ex-teammate: 'I watched him struggle with great courage for years of terrible injuries where no one else would have survived. As his friend, I am relived that he will not have to suffer any more.'

The 1976–77 season was one of my favourites, despite the awful financial pressure on the club. Our gates had dropped by half. The East Stand had been built on the basis that the club would have continuing success and consequently be able to afford the huge repayments on the loan. That was the plan. Roman Abramovich was then just 11 years old and a poor orphan.

We won promotion, finishing second to Wolves and narrowly missing out on the title. Brian Clough's Nottingham Forest finished three points behind us and within two years had won the European Cup. Some League! Stronger than the Nationwide League we have today, which seems to merely provide the following year's relegation candidates as cannon fodder.

Steve Finnieston spearheaded the attack, scoring 24 League goals. The young Scot was ably supported by Scouser Kenny Swain, who chipped in with 13 goals. Perhaps our best performance was a 2–1 win over Forest on the run in. Martin O'Neill gave Forest a first-half lead but goals from Ian Britton and Finnieston won us the points. Ray Wilkins, the playmaker, dominated the season with his classy performances from midfield; he was the coolest kid on the block.

Suddenly, the future looked brighter. We had the best crop of youngsters at the club since the Diamonds were shining on brightly with Venables and his pals. The hottest young manager in the game was Eddie 'Mac', a budding Diaghilev of the Kings Road. If only we had had some money to spend strengthening the side with experienced players that could have helped the Sonic Youths, Chelsea could have been a real force again.

Then McCreadie quit over a pay dispute – a matter I regret to this day. McCreadie has never been back to the club he served so brilliantly, first as a world-class defender and then as the most charismatic manager since the Doc. If he had stayed on, I am convinced he would have been Chelsea's greatest-ever manager. Ranieri has a propensity for high-profile mistakes but Eddie was almost perfect. Ken Shellito was appointed in his place. A good coach but in my opinion not forceful enough for the demands of the job. It was a thankless task following Eddie.

We were too good for the lower League but many of the youngsters were not yet the finished product. We needed what no Chelsea manager has ever had – even more so today – time. In season 1977–78, we finished 16th, which, considering the small, inexperienced squad we had, was a highly credible effort. Two magnificent victories over Liverpool at the Bridge will always live in my mind: a 4–2 win in the FA Cup and a 3–1 League victory. This dented their chances of catching the runaway Forest. We had beaten Clough's team in the autumn as well, thanks to a goal from Trevor Aylott. Clever Trevor had scored the winner the week before on his debut as well. The burly striker looked set for a bright future. In 26 first-team games, though, he didn't score any more goals and faded out of contention.

FATHER TED

Shellito lasted half of the 1978–79 season before resigning. Danny Blanchflower was appointed as the next Chelsea manager: legendary, venerable and, as it turned out, entirely inappropriate. At the time, it seemed like one of my better ideas. I had to make a quick appointment as we were lying stricken at the bottom of the League. Danny boy, the ex-Tottenham captain, had done well with Northern Ireland but they had Pat Jennings in goal. We had someone called Bob Iles.

Frank Upton, at the time a coach, was manager for a day. I remember him storming into the dressing-room like a regimental sergeant-major, telling the players that it was going to be different now he was in charge: training was going to be harder and the young scruffs would all have to wear club ties and blazers. Upton also insisted that the players address him as 'Boss', not Frank.

Within 24 hours, Blanchflower was appointed and Frank was back in the ranks. Gary Stanley happened to be walking into the main entrance with me the next morning when we spotted Upton marching across the car park (about where that Arkles restaurant is situated nowadays). 'Morning, FRANK,' Gary said, his cheeky grin in evidence. Frank glowered back at me but saw the funny side.

At first, Blanchflower had rejected my overtures to join, saying he did not need the stress at his age. His life was settled with his journalism and his passion for golf. Danny was 55 but seemed more shop-worn than the other managers. If I had not been so preoccupied with keeping Chelsea afloat, I would have seen the poignant situation he was in.

Danny's first match was away to Middlesbrough, then managed by John Neal. I had been an admirer of his style for some time. Boro slaughtered us 7–2. Peter Osgood opened the scoring for Chelsea, strangely enough. He was back at the Bridge from America after signing from Philadelphia Fury. Osgood scored in the first two minutes but then the roof fell in. I never felt it was a good move for either party, him coming back. Too much water under the Stamford Bridge and all. Osgood was quite unfit. He could no longer lift so much as a thigh. To me, he disappointed on every conceivable level. Somewhere along the line, he had put down the wand.

Duncan McKenzie, another of the game's lost talents, played sixteen games for Chelsea and scored four goals. I found him an extraordinary character: in all my years in the game, I never saw a fitter player. Even Webb or Hutchinson, when they first came to the Bridge, did not compare with him. Duncan was an amazing athlete: he somersaulted over tackles in training and his party piece was jumping over Minis. In his time at Nottingham, he was famous for chucking golf balls over the River Trent. Wherever he played, the fans worshipped him. To the Shed, he was a direct link to the salad days of the early '70s. The tantalising youngsters of the current side were failing to deliver.

In November, we went up to his old side, Everton, and his mere presence added 10,000 to the gate – the same sort of effect Lawton and Gallacher had on the Merseyside crowds. Duncan had had a golden spell at Goodison but had left after a bust-up with the skinhead manager Gordon Lee. Lee placed great emphasis on work rate and team play, and McKenzie's laconic style didn't fit well with him. The Chelsea striker made his point, though, with a dazzling individual goal in the second half that brought Goodison to its feet. The reception he received was the loudest that I can ever remember for a Chelsea player from an away crowd. McKenzie was mythologised in that goal.

Blanchflower had dropped the phenomenon for the Middlesbrough debacle and he played only a few more games. One of them was a 3–2 win at Manchester City in which he scored another dazzling goal. Walker and Osgood scored the others. Still, we could never string enough results together to lift ourselves up the table.

McKenzie joined Blackburn following the tragic death of his 17-day-old son. His frequent moves had earned him a beautiful home near Haydock racecourse and he was reluctant to move to London. In many ways, he was the first modern mercenary player, a generation before the commodified stars. In just six months, Chelsea dropped a bundle on his transfer. Blanchflower demanded a meeting with our bankers Barclays to know how much he could spend. We knew the answer already – it was zilch. You didn't have to be Peter Kenyon to work that one out.

Danny had already made two excellent signings: midfielder Eamonn Bannon from Hearts and Petar Borota from Partizan Belgrade. Petar was at the time rated the number three keeper in Europe. He would command a spot in the Chelsea side today without any doubt. However, players were still leaving in droves. Gary Stanley went to Everton: he was on the brink of breaking into the England set-up when once again a potentially brilliant career was blighted by injury. Steve Wicks, another superb player, whom I am still in contact with today, left us for Derby.

Blanchflower later sold Ray Lewington to Vancouver Whitecaps. I was really sorry to see him leave. He and Butch Wilkins had both joined Chelsea as ten year olds when the Doc was in charge. Ray was another south London boy born in Clapham whose family were Chelsea mad. Wilkins and Lewington played for the famous Senrab Sunday League side based in Wanstead. They were basically Chelsea juniors in those days. Sexton gave him a contract but it was under McCreadie that his career really took off, as he formed a useful midfield partnership with his buddy Wilkins.

Ray had a long career in management at Fulham and Watford, who gave Chelsea a fright in the third round of the FA Cup in January 2004. He was one of the players at Chelsea who was bewildered by the manager's training sessions. At first, Blanchflower tried to teach the youngsters an advanced push-and-run style that his previous side, Tottenham, had perfected back in the '50s. It was a complex system and required a high level of concentration and technical ability. The modern-day Chelsea, with a much more sophisticated training ethos, would even have found it hard to absorb. At the time, I travelled to the old training ground in East Molesey and sat in on some of the sessions. Under McCreadie, Chelsea largely prepared for matches on a diet of five-a-side games. With Danny in charge, it was all about repetition. The Irishman wanted the same routine day in, day out, like Stephen Hendry practising the same shot hour after hour.

The Chelsea players just ambled around. The youngsters looked bewildered, whilst older hands, like Harris, seemed bored. A dangerous brew. Sometimes Danny would wheel out a huge blackboard and lecture on some complex tactical theory by means of little diagrams and symbols. To the Chelsea team, he might as well have been explaining the repercussions of the assassination of the Archduke Franz Ferdinand in 1914. I wondered what Venables would have made of it all. I used to have a mental picture of him there, eyebrows rolling, his shoulders shaking with mirth.

Poor old Danny. It was like an episode from *Father Ted*. Another of Danny's stunts was to have the whole squad playing on the rugby pitch at the end of the playing fields. There would be teams of about 20-a-side hacking around with four balls that he threw onto the pitch. A complete shambles. I wonder what Mourinho would have thought.

The nightmare continued. Forest butchered us 6–0 under a frozen-mackerel sky at the end of March, the imposing Martin O'Neill, nearly as good a player as he is a manager, scoring three of them. The maniacal Clough ignored me in the tunnel, a look of disdain on his face. He always hated Chelsea, and cockneys in particular. Anyone who played for Chelsea was, in his eyes, a cockney. Even Borota. Danny's strained face looked like a pink balloon that was about to burst. The Irishman spoke about how well we had played for 15 minutes.

'What about the other 75 and the half-dozen goals?' Ray Wilkins asked in an uncharacteristically truculent manner.

At that time, Chelsea needed a manager who was a cross between Captain Bligh and Saint Francis of Assisi. Instead, we had Terry Wogan. Danny had this lovely Irish thing about him, as if everything that happened was all part of his fantastic plan. His marvellous humour was ironic and most of it went completely over the heads of his team. By chance, Forest came back to the Bridge the following week. Danny spent ages telling the team that he wanted their passing to be much faster so the game would be over more quickly. We only lost 1–3 that day and Danny seemed pleased with it all.

NEW YORK, NEW YORK

The only game I enjoyed that season was a friendly against the mighty New York Cosmos during their tour of Europe. A massive crowd of 39,659 attended the drawn match. (Only a stodgy 0–0 with Liverpool drew a bigger crowd that season.) The Cosmos side included the guesting Johan Cruyff, who had played for a North American Soccer League team before his surprise move to Los Angles. That night, I saw the most beautiful long pass ever played at the Bridge. Johan commenced the move with a classic one-two on the edge of his area with Franz Beckenbauer. In my view, the man known as 'The Kaiser' was Germany's greatest-ever player. The Dutchman (European Footballer of the Year three times) controlled the ball on the run, took it on ten yards or so then unexpectedly adjusted his stance to hit a superbly weighted forty-five-yard pass. It flew over the midfield and landed just in front of another legend, Giorgio Chinaglia. The Italian ace left Chelsea defender David Stride for dead and would have scored the winner if he hadn't been cut down by Bob Iles. Amazingly, no penalty was awarded. Even in that wretched season, I still had some wonderful memories and laughs. The reality, though, was that Chelsea were the poorest team in the division and went down with a meagre twenty points and just five wins all season. Twenty-seven League defeats is a record that still stands. Butch Wilkins subsequently joined Manchester United. He was out of contract. In later Bosman times, he could have walked and Barclays would have been due even more. Ray might have been a bit functional for the Stretford End but his career was blue chip all the way. From United, he went to AC Milan – he trod the same path as Greaves. Wilkins stayed longer than Jimmy and lasted five seasons, one of the few English players to make it out there. That is where he picked up the 'Armani For All Seasons' headlines and became an ardent customer of Brioni.

Ron Harris was more upset over the sale of Wilkins than most and took me to task about it. I had made a quote, often revived, about 'jumping off the roof of the new stand before selling Wilkins'. The bellicose Ron came up to me and barked, 'We're still waiting.'

I asked him what for and he said, 'You to jump off the roof.'

The rest of the team laughed along nervously but the point was not lost on me. I felt like something had snapped in my head. Butch was so popular he was a devastating loss to the club. The residual consequences were higher than even I thought. Then Blanchflower appointed Geoff Hurst as coach. An extraordinary decision in my view. Hurst is an icon. Let's be fair, guys, is another Englishman going to score a hat-trick in a World Cup final? Dinosaurs will walk the earth before such an event happens again.

Hurst joined us from non-League Telford, where he had been working in an attempt to carve out a fresh career in management. It had been 13 years since his World Cup fusillade and his sculpted features were heavier. The class of '66 were not yet the stuff of legend. I was worried that he lacked the experience in management at the highest level. To me, he always had that preening sense of self-admiration, like a Siamese cat licking its paws.

Hurst soon clashed with Osgood over training methods and his level of fitness. Osgood found Stamford Bridge a vastly different place from the one he had left. I think he expected it to be some mental opiate at the end of his career but instead it became an incinerator. To the younger players, he was the elder statesman: faddish and ephemeral. Always soberly dressed, he was shocked at how scruffy his teammates were. Most of them were dressed in jeans and trainers, eschewing the designer suits and subtly contrasting shirts and ties worn by Cole and his pals today. Punk rock had started on the Kings Road about then and some of the Blanchflower team were disciples of the movement. Chelsea Dreaming.

That season, as we boarded the coach for a trip to Old Trafford for a Cup tie, I remember a dapper Osgood being heckled by his teammates. 'Going to a wedding, Os?', 'Looking for a transfer?'

The old conquistador took it all in his stride but a meaningful glance in my direction told me he found it tiresome. We lost 0–3 that night but it had not been too many years since his wonderful diving header had helped bring the Cup home. Time in a bottle. Hurst and Osgood were soon to find out that yesterday's goals, no matter how superb, were to count for little in today's hooplah. You see, in football, the contest is never over.

LOVE IN A TIME OF CHOLERA

Blanchflower knew the time was up for him as season 1979–80 opened. The Irishman could no longer get his ideas across. The first match was a grim 0–0 home fixture with Sunderland, who were to haunt us throughout that frantic season. In the next match, Chelsea grabbed a 0–1 win at West Ham thanks to a goal from young prospect Gary Johnson. Petar Borota never played better than he did that night. One save from Frank Lampard Senior still lingers in my mind, a lifetime later. Get your dad to tell you about it one day, young Frankie.

Lampard Senior, who follows all his son's matches today, was in those days a real claret-and-blue harlequin, famed for his ferocious shooting. (Do you recall his goal at the Bridge on Boxing Day 1973 which triggered the Rat Pack transfers?) As the Hammers pushed up on Chelsea, Frank volleyed in from 25 yards and Borota somehow dived across to it and turned it over the bar. The West Ham crowd were not used to improbable continental goalkeepers and some jackals taunted him with racist remarks during the game. Borota treated them with the contempt they deserved and entertained the fans with some tricks from his huge repertoire, which included dribbling up field with the ball and squatting in his own six-yard box reading the match programme.

Unfortunately, such humour was at a premium that season. The bank was putting us under a great deal of pressure to get back to the big time asap. Danny told me we were going to win promotion the Irish way, by drawing all our home games and winning the away ones. Over two legs, Plymouth knocked us out of the League Cup. Osgood walked out of the club about then. The Windsor-born dissident asked me for his cards and never kicked another ball for the club. His flamboyant talent was matched only by his skill at squandering it.

Newcastle beat us at St James' and then we lost at home to Birmingham. The Brummies were the class side of the division and included Alan Curbishley, Colin Todd, Frank Worthington and the fiery Mark Dennis. They were like a school of hammerhead sharks, shredding our defence into blue thread. The Monday morning after, Danny resigned. He told me he could no longer relate to the escalating transfer fees and hated the rising racism and hooliganism in the game. He went back to his writing and golf. I would like to say our story had a happy ending but it didn't. Danny died at Christmas in 1993, a virtual recluse, forgotten by the game to which he had brought such style and vision. I recall that Spurs were asked a few years ago to help keep up the maintenance on his all but pauper's grave.

THEY THINK IT'S ALL OVER

When Geoff Hurst first arrived at Chelsea, he told me he could scarcely believe what he saw. He noted things at West Ham were laid back but that this was bordering on the absurd. At the first Blanchflower training session he attended, bemused players ran into one another in pantomime fashion. Michael Crawford was a great fan of Sexton's team and I used to see him with some of the chaps. So many of Danny's boys looked like Frank Spencers as the shambles continued. Morale was very low and discipline poor. The only motivation that characterised the team was greed. When Danny quit, Hurst was given the job of caretaker manager for a trial period. To my way of thinking, he was so irrevocably associated with the Hammers, I doubted if he could ever have the same passion for Chelsea. (In the same way, George Graham suffered at Spurs because of his links with Arsenal.)

I was keen to lure Venables from Crystal Palace where he had built a side of almost Diamonds potential. Palace blocked any move for him. Who knows how it would have worked out? Instead, Hurst clinched the job by winning the next five games. Chelsea glided on gilded wings above the financial abyss. Something told me not to appoint Hurst – the same voice that told me it would have been a good idea to quit when McCreadie's side had won promotion. Once again, I chose to ignore it. I had been in the field too long and was fatigued. All I could see was the next battle.

Hurst was grilled in front of the board at our next meeting and faced a torrent of questions. With no bad vibes or pregnant pauses, Geoff passed the audition with flying colours. On the basis of that interview, more than anything else, he was given the job. Attenborough, the knighted thespian, was as keen for him to land it as he was to dump the Rat Pack. Needless to say, we lost our next two games: at home to Fulham (managed by Bobby Campbell) and away to Sunderland.

For the next game, we went to Orient without Tommy Langley, our star striker. His place was taken by Lee Frost, who had scored the winner down at Cardiff on his debut a few weeks before. Frost was a real character, with cheekbones like wing mirrors and long bleached hair. He always wore a pork-pie hat, cocked over one eye. That afternoon, he scored a hat-trick as Chelsea whipped Orient 3–7. Four days later, Frost scored the winner against West Ham at the Bridge. Five goals in his first three matches – some going. He looked set for a golden future but, like Trevor Aylott, he didn't score for Chelsea again and drifted away to Brentford. I recall he was involved in a very bad car crash whilst driving over, or was it through,

Chiswick roundabout. He very nearly broke his neck. Another '70s casualty. Chelsea had a few like him: amused spectators at the dissolution of their own talents. Beautiful losers were always fascinating to the Chelsea crowd.

THE TALENTED MR FILLERY

Another player who did much to define certain aspects of that era was Mike Fillery, the ready-made replacement for Wilkins. Another youth product, he was a strong midfield player who should have found much greater fame and glory than that which his confusing career granted him. Born in Mitcham, he played eight times for England Schoolboys and signed on schoolboy forms for the Blues. Like Hollins and Wilkins, he was part of a football family. David, his father, was part of the tasty Tooting and Mitcham team that dominated the amateur game for a period. In Mike's breakthrough season, 1979–80, he played in 40 games and scored 11 goals.

I can still see in sepia tints the effortlessly photogenic Fillery flicking passes with the outside of his foot. He was always bankable: another class player that was unlucky to be playing in a shambolic side. He would often appear lackadaisical, which hindered his progress. If he was around today, he would be modelling for Gap and Joe Cole would still be in the Nationwide.

Hurst took one look at Bannon and was not impressed. Soon after he took over as manager, the former World Cup final hero told the multi-talented Scot he had no future at Chelsea. Eamon was Blanchflower's man: his elegant passing and thoughtful manner reminded me of Danny in his glory days at Spurs. Hurst sold him first chance he got for £40,000 less than Chelsea had paid Hearts a year before. Dundee United swooped to bring him back from west London. In a short while, Bannon, who did not relish the thought of being labelled a flop, had picked up two League Cup winner's medals and was chosen for Scotland.

The '80s started with Chelsea leading the division but eventually they had to settle for fourth spot and missed out on promotion. A Fillery goal on Boxing Day against Leicester had put us in pole position. It was a sad day for the club, though, because of news that Tommy Langley's mother, Freda, had died from cancer. Tommy had a little chat with me before the game, his voice barely a murmur, marked with pain. We decided that he should play, feeling that it was what his mother would have wanted. We were a real family club then but that was about to change.

Tellingly, Wigan knocked us out of the Cup on a freezing Monday night in a rearranged third-round tie. The warning signs were there.

Shrewsbury bulldozed us 2–4 at home and the adventurous John Bumstead (after Fillery, our most influential player) was badly injured. I saw our hopes receding as our confidence waned.

Our form was patchy. Below par, we won 2–3 at Watford in a breathtaking match. Clive Walker ran from the halfway line with the best part of the Hornets team chasing him to shoot home the winner. Then Watford missed a penalty in the dying seconds. It was a real firefight. That old Saturday afternoon favourite 'We are the famous CFC' was sung for the first time that day.

Bristol Rovers crushed us 3–0 as the travelling Chelsea fans rioted. It was a nightmare. A wall was kicked down, fans were stomped on and police horses charged the mob. Luckily, nobody was killed. Hammers, knives and hooks were seized from the arrested 'fans'.

Then we were crushed 5–1 by our main promotion rivals, Birmingham. We were just overrun. There was no fight whatsoever. It seemed to be a question of failed nerve, a criticism that could never be levelled against any side managed by Eddie McCreadie. We still clung to the top spot but inside I knew we had blown it.

BIG MOUTH STRIKES AGAIN

Ironically, the man who finally sabotaged our promotion hopes was none other than Tommy Docherty. The Doc now had his surgery at QPR and Ken Shellito was his assistant. When we played them one chilly April evening, it had been 13 years since Tommy had left. Only Ron Harris remained from the Diamonds: how fitting that it was the roughest of the diamonds that had survived. QPR won 2–0 as we froze like ice lollies. Steve Wicks was playing at centre-back for the Hoops and devoured everything. That is all you really need to know about that evening. The Doc made a point of looking me up at the end of the match: Tommy is nothing if not an agile talker. That night he had taken to dressing like Jack Nicholson's detective Gittes from Polanski's movie *Chinatown*. In a loud check jacket and with a huge self-assured grin on his face, I always remember him bluntly saying to me: 'Them's the breaks.' If I could have turned back the clock, I would have reappointed him then and there.

Leicester beat us by a solitary goal on Easter Saturday. Only Borota saved us from utter humiliation. Two days later, Colin Lee, whom Hurst had just signed from Spurs, scored in the dying seconds to scramble a point against Luton. It put us back into second spot and should have been the final springboard for promotion. We only drew up at Preston in a game we dominated. The pitch was a disgrace. Fillery scored for us but in general the goals from the strikers had dried up and we were running on empty.

Defender Gary Chivers scored the winner at home to Notts County which set us up for a grandstand finish with two games left. We travelled to Swansea needing to win to have any chance at all of going up.

Tommy Langley shot us ahead early on with a goal of dogged persistence. Swansea quickly equalised and we froze, almost oblivious to the seriousness of the situation. Five minutes from time, we had a golden chance to win the game and, possibly, promotion. Langley sent Chivers bursting clear and he instantly crossed a ball of Houseman-like precision into the box. Fillery soared to meet it but his header was weak and indecisive. The ball scraped off his forehead and flew the wrong side of the upright, although an open goal lay less than ten yards in front of him.

That did it for us, really. The agony dragged on for a few more weeks, though. We won our last game against Oldham but for Sunderland to gain promotion and edge us out, they had to beat West Ham at home. The East Enders had a little matter of an FA Cup final against Arsenal before that. Some genius scheduled the Sunderland game 48 hours after Wembley. Thanks a lot.

The rest is history. Trevor Brooking headed the ball for the only time in his career to score the Wembley winner. Two nights later, the 'Happy Hammers' crept up to Sunderland. Of course, the PR machine cranked it up high. The Hammers were full of good intentions. They would do it for their favourite son, Hurst, and for the sake of London. In a testimonial atmosphere, Sunderland won 2–0 and walked back to the big time: revenge for the Doc's thug side robbing them of promotion in 1963. We stayed down. As Jim Bowen used to say, all we had was the bus fare home.

If it had been a boxing match, it would have stunk the place out. I was away on holiday. I couldn't bear to watch it, so convinced was I that we had no chance.

AND NOW THE END IS NEAR

That was about it. Season 1980–81 was my last in charge. We finished 12th, washed away by the waters of oblivion. The team had a tactical and almost spiritual poverty about it and the constant presence of hooliganism added to the fade-to-grey atmosphere. Luck and fate were conspiring to bring an end to the Mears Dynasty. Only Petar Borota gave any real value for money.

I became very close to him; he was a very proud, pensive individual and resented players whose only motivation was money. I wonder what he would have made of modern-day Chelsea and all these foreigners. Borota was a fine artist and had his own one-man exhibition of paintings. He lived in some splendour with his glamorous wife Biba in Putney. (If you want to know what she looked like, think of Timothy Spall's eastern European wife in the 2004 series of *Auf Wiedersehen, Pet.*) The keeper would spend hours poring over a book of statistics logging every match he played in his colourful career. I lost touch with him when things went sour for me at Chelsea. Things didn't work out too well for Petar, either. His father was an army colonel and was killed in the war in Bosnia. In the days I knew him, it was Yugoslavia. Last I heard of Petar, he was in prison for some smuggling scam. I imagine that is where most Chelsea fans would have wanted to see their management team.

As the whacked-out Blues struggled, Tommy Langley left Chelsea. (He had just got married and wanted to improve his circumstances.) Why he chose to go to QPR, I was never really sure. His departure was another blow to us all – not least Tommy, whose once-promising career eventually fizzled out after a few strange transfers. Needless to say, he came back to the Bridge one drowsy afternoon a few weeks after his departure to score for Rangers. Out of respect for the chaps, he never celebrated his goal and just trotted back to the halfway line, his hair flopping like Hugh Grant's. Langley was another major personality within the Chelsea iconography. If my claims for Langley's importance seem overstated, I would remind you of the famous 'Tommy Langley Collection' badges worn around the ground: the Shed's unique take on the designer age we had entered at the time and have yet to leave. José Mourinho was the designer manager, Frank Lampard the designer footballer and Roman Abramovich the designer owner.

Stalin was a failed writer, Hitler was a failed painter, Langley was a failed superstar, Hurst was a failed manager. Was Mears a failed chairman?

TAMING OF THE SHREWD

> You have to be 100 per cent behind someone, before you can stab them in the back.
> **Ricky Gervais as David Brent in *The Office***

The press leaked a story about the Chelsea board having talks with Johan Cruyff about him possibly joining the club. Johan had played for DS 79 Dordrecht in a friendly against us. Also playing for them was Rob Rensenbrink, the Dutch superstar winger. Rob had almost knocked Chelsea out of the Cup-Winners' Cup when he played for Bruges the year we lifted it. In 1978, in the dying seconds of normal time, he was close to winning the World Cup for Holland when he hit the post against Argentina. People had forgotten how good a player he was. My dream was to sign the pair through an outside sponsorship deal but it fell through at the last moment. In my heart, though, I knew that the chances of players of that calibre joining Chelsea were as likely as Liz Hurley drinking in the Shed Bar. Hurst was furious he had not been privy to the deal and in an impassioned mood told the press he that had decided 'not to take the matter any further'.

Hurst had signed a player called Alan Mayes from Swindon for an inordinate price. The maladroit Mayes was a disaster. It encapsulated Hurst's time at Chelsea. It's incredible, really, when you watch the endless re-runs of Hurst's World Cup goals. Under his guidance, Chelsea had the driest period of goalscoring in their history. They completed their last nine League fixtures without scoring a goal. Since that November, they had only won three games and finished twelfth.

With two games left, I sacked him. How could I have a man managing Chelsea that preferred Alan Mayes in his attack to Cruyff? Hurst took it badly. He thought I was asking him for a drink when I called him into the boardroom. Geoff sat motionless in the chair and then the skin at the corner of his mouth ticked slightly. I remember his eyes misting and his upper lip filming with moisture, as though my office had suddenly become hot. I think I should have sacked Bobby Gould at the same time but I left him as caretaker. In hindsight, my opinion is I would have been better off asking the caretaker in the flats opposite to take charge.

Hurst whinged to the press about how badly the board had let him down. The papers wrote it up that in twenty games he had only won three and failed to score in the other seventeen. Yeah, that would be about right. Hurst never took another big job in the game. His legend grew but the unhappy spell at Chelsea haunted him. Too much had happened between us and, in truth, we did not like each other.

Like my hero John McEnroe always says, 'the older they get, the better they get', and nobody can ever top Geoff's World Cup achievement. They will be putting up statues to Hurst when Beckham and his ilk are forgotten.

I lined up John Neal as the next Chelsea manager. The last game of the season was at home to Notts County. It turned out to be my last game in charge. Tommy Lawton was not playing that day for County – the oldest team in the League with traditional names like Rachid Harkouk, Pedro Richards, Tristram Benjamin and Raddy Avramovic. The game was already changing.

We lost 0–2. The defence looked like they had nipped out for 20 Super Kings and the attack worked hard at destroying any forward movement. The cancer had spread to every level. Stamford Bridge would have gone down brick by brick if the 13,324 crowd had been any angrier. Every Chelsea fan had a morally impregnable defence to justifiably demolish the stadium. I came under a huge barrage of personal abuse from the fans. Magnificent in its awfulness, I always think of that Kenneth Williams line from *Carry on Cleo*: 'Infamy! Infamy! They've all got it in for me.'

Take heed, Mr Abramovich. It happens to all of us if we stick around long enough. My team of 1970 were better than anything your money could buy.

Ask not for whom the bell tolls . . . events have a way of conspiring to make you realise that it's all over. Looking back, I can see now that there was an orchestrated campaign to get me out. Agent provocateurs whipped up the crowd (and I don't mean the underwear you buy the girlfriend at Christmas). Leaflets were circulated. 'Shed no tears, it's the end for Mears.' Something poetic.

SAY HELLO, WAVE GOODBYE

I had decided to walk away anyway but with my usual sense of timing I left it too late. I was concerned about getting John Neal's feet under the table. The man was years ahead of his time. He wanted us to sign Bosco Jancovic from his old club Middlesbrough. Bosco was a dazzling centre-forward, John kept telling me. (Didn't he know all these foreign stars would never make it in London?)

John was my legacy to Chelsea. Bates could bathe in the glory John brought to the club with his wonderful signings of Pat Nevin, Kerry Dixon, David Speedie and Mickey Thomas, to name just a few. It was Brian Mears who gave John the job, though. After Blanchflower and Hurst, I had to find a winner.

Nearly 25 years after my departure, I still find it hard to talk about it. Attenborough told me that there had been a meeting and they thought I should stand down as chairman. They also wanted me off the board. I could not believe someone like him would have pushed me out so coldly. That day, he was as heartless as Pinkie, the murderous psycho he played in John Boulting's adaptation of *Brighton Rock*.

When I left the meeting, I saw John Neal sitting outside waiting to go in.

I tried the old gag on him. 'Do you want the good news or the bad news first?'

Leave them laughing.

That was it, really. You have to retain your dignity and step away. When Abramovich bought Chelsea, Bates clung on for a while. I never went back.

PART TWO
DALLAS

Never underestimate the other guy's greed.

Frank Lopez in *Scarface*

ELEVEN

PAUL X

I'll never forgive. I'll never forget and if I am guilty of
anything, it is of not leaning on them hard enough.
George Jackson, *Soledad Brother: The Prison Letters of*
George Jackson

It was season 1981–82 and Chelsea had finished 12th, exactly where they
finished the season before. The high spot of the season was the FA Cup
run to the quarter-finals. After two successive goalless draws at home in
the third and fourth rounds, Chelsea had beaten Hull and Wrexham after
replays. In the fifth round, Chelsea drew Liverpool on their way to a
European Cup win. In one of the biggest upsets of the decade, John Neal's
side, a mediocre Second Division team, beat a Scouse outfit, which
included Hansen, Lawrenson, Dalglish and Rush, 2–0. The first goal was
scored in the eighth minute by the splendidly named Peter Rhoades-
Brown who sounded and looked like he had just stepped off the set of
Brideshead Revisited. Rhoades-Brown actually got a Blue at Cambridge
(Peter would have got a pink too, if the cue ball hadn't cannoned off the
black).

Six minutes from the end, after almost constant pressure from
Liverpool, Walker broke away. Liverpool keeper Bruce Grobbelaar collided
with Phil Neal and Colin Lee rolled in the second.

In the quarter-final, a classy Tottenham came to the Bridge. In a
cracking tie, Chelsea lost by the odd goal in five. Chelsea were hit by
injuries which deprived them of Colin Lee and Mickey Droy. Mike Fillery
gave Chelsea the lead just on the break with the best goal he ever scored

189

for the club – a thundering free kick from 35 yards that flew past Ray Clemence; a real peach of a goal. For a short while, Wembley beckoned. Spurs were a fine side in those days and in the second half turned on a coruscating display. They tore into Chelsea straight from the whistle. Ossie Ardiles' free kick was slipped to Hoddle who smashed in a shot that Francis could not hold. The ball ran loose for Archibald, an early badge kisser, to slip home. He received terrible abuse from the Shed all game. His strike partner, Garth Crooks (another BBC pundit), was also on the receiving end of some harsh words.

The wonderful Ardiles ('on his way to Wembley' according to Chas and Dave) started to run the midfield. His World Cup credentials were put on view. Hoddle put Spurs in front with one of his specials as the Chelsea defence crumbled. The celebrating Hoddle did his famous knee skid across the terra firma in front of the massed Chelsea legions on the West Stand benches. During the following decade, he played an important part in helping to revolutionise the club but I don't think the fundamentalists at the Bridge ever forgave him for knocking Chelsea out of the Cup that day.

Mickey Hazard, a future Chelsea hero, made it three with a cracking drive. The creative Hazard was to be nicknamed 'the Duke' by the adoring Shed in homage to the popular television show *The Dukes of Hazard*. It featured the good ol' boys from Alabama – Bo and Luke Duke – who roared around in that '69 Dodge Charger. Their cousin Daisy was a bit useful, too, if I recall. Mickey, or 'the Duke', was a throwback to the '60s, one of the last English footballers to learn their basics by playing street football. He was another player that would have been a legend if he had played in Sexton's side. Today, he would earn a fortune and own a ride as tasty as the Dodge. Last I heard, he was driving a cab.

Hurst's chum Mayes pulled one back but Spurs held out to win the game and eventually retain the Cup, showing it was no fluke. That was the first time the infamous Auschwitz song was sung on the terraces.

It was a schizoid season for Chelsea. Bates was no Abramovich and there was no spate of cherry-picked signings to rejuvenate the club. Chelsea were just plankton swimming in someone else's sea. Rotherham beat Chelsea by a 10–1 aggregate over two games. It was 6–0 up there (Borota only played once more for Chelsea after that game) and 1–4 at the Bridge. Attendances plummeted like Buddy Holly. Only 6,009 fans attended a rainy night game with Orient – another legendary low point that tens of thousands of glory-hunting 'loyalists' have since claimed to have witnessed.

FAME! (I'M GONNA LIVE FOR EVER)

On Easter Monday 1982, Chelsea travelled to Crystal Palace. It was a non-event match between two mid-table teams. Palace were managed by Steve Kember in one of his stints at Selhurst. Johnny Brooks's son Shaun was in the Palace line-up. The only goal of the game was a thumping first-half header from Clive Walker. Near the end, he was substituted and a young player called Paul Canoville made his debut. A crowd of 17,189 attended the match and at least half of them were Chelsea fans. The young winger was greeted with an absolute wall of hate from the Chelsea supporters. Paul was black and just over 20 years ago that was a problem to a large percentage of the people who paid their money at the gate. The power of the mob – *Homo sapiens* with hate in their hearts – seems unbelievable nowadays. Where were the politicians, pop stars and celebs then as the Nuremberg Rally of bigotry spewed its venom?

Years later, on the same ground, a famous Frenchman encountered his own piece of race hate and reacted with a kung-fu kick. Canoville made no fuss, though. He simply got on with playing for his team. It was what he always did. Paul was amazingly resilient, as much a Chelsea soldier as Harris or Wise, perhaps more so because they had the crowd with them.

To put Canoville in a cultural context is not easy. He does not rank amongst the all-time greats of the club but is as big a part of the folklore of CFC as Greaves or Zola. Born in March 1962, he joined the club from Hillingdon Borough. In all, he played just 67 games (plus 36 subs) and notched 15 goals.

If you look in the record books, you will see him credited with scoring the fastest-recorded goal in Chelsea history: a mere 11 seconds at the start of the second half against Sheffield Wednesday at Hillsborough in January 1985. Canoville scored twice that night in an amazing 4–4 draw. It was a seminal moment in the history of Chelsea. The fifth-round replay was part of the notorious Milk Cup run that ended in a riot with Sunderland. Chelsea were 3–0 down when Neal pushed Paul into the fray. That was his greatest performance. He destroyed their rearguard with an unrelenting assault on the Sheffield goal. It was one of the stand-out games of the decade. Inspired by Canoville, Chelsea clawed back to lead 3–4, only to concede a penalty in the last minute of extra time. Only Chelsea, eh?

Canoville was a piece of work by anybody's standards. In his too-brief career, he was dogged by uncertainty, racism and misjudgement. Paul, in my view, was the most underused and underestimated player of his generation. So few players can improvise. On his day, the loose-limbed Canoville was a brilliant player. Today, he would be very valuable: he had wooshka, a dramatic change of pace; he was handsome, with doleful eyes. The vibrant Canoville was one of the first black players to shave his head. He looked like a cross between Leroy Johnson, the electric dancer from *Fame*, and the fighter Marvin Hagler. Always immaculate, he drove a black BMW with tinted windows and a baby-calf interior. Paul was football's first hip-hop hardman.

I draw a comparison between Canoville and the famous black leader Malcolm X. Both were martyrs for a cause. Canoville's career in the top flight was short-lived but he opened the door for a stream of young, gifted black talent. If there was no Canoville, there would have been no Paul Elliott, no Gullit, no Makélélé. He was the black man that would not act the white man. Canoville came from a tough part of London, Malcolm X from a similar environment across the Atlantic: both products of the ghetto with the kind of street gravitas that could not be bought. 'Trouble' was the middle name of both men when they were young. Paul was fined £150 with £50 costs at Old Street Court after admitting having a spring-loaded cosh as an offensive weapon. His lawyers told the Bench that he bought the weapon for self-defence after he had been attacked. Later, he was held for the alleged misuse of a pension book. Further reports of paternity suits made it to the tabloids, which gave Dr Shipman better press.

I note that Beckham tries to draw the accoutrements of black culture into his image. I wonder if he knew about Canoville. A player like Glen Johnson, the first player signed by Abramovich, probably hasn't a clue who Paul Canoville is. Johnson has pace and two good feet. It is for people like him I am writing this. When Ruud Gullit became the first black manager to win the FA Cup, I wanted people to know it wasn't always like that. Paul played in a climate when there was no black cultural back-up at all in the game. Paul was severely abused when he made his home debut against Luton, who were going up as champs. Nowadays, you have the madness that inevitably attends football celebrity: then, you just had plain lunacy and a descent into ugliness. Their manager, David Pleat was sickened by the treatment given to Canoville and said of the 'fans': 'I don't know why they come.'

GATE 13 (THE GANGS OF WEST LONDON)

Gate 13 was situated in the lower tier of the East Stand. For a few years during the '80s, it housed the most violent and racist of the multitude of hooligan gangs that had sprung up. In the early '80s, the Shed was little more than a tourist attraction.

Mick Greenaway led the Chelsea fans. He had founded the Shed in the

'60s but later decamped to the old West Stand where, during quiet spells in the match (and there were a few of them in those days), the plaintive cry of his famous 'Zigger Zagger' chant could be heard. An echo from happier, innocent times. By then, Chelsea were a clapped-out team playing in a clapped-out ground. The sociopath hooligans went to the seats, which were becoming increasingly popular. Their logic was simple: the area accessed through Gate 13 was the nearest point that they could get to the away fans who were located under the old North Stand. It was also close to the pitch and protected from the elements. Unless you were perched up high in the Shed, you were always at the mercy of the English winter. Plus, there was the added kudos of sitting in the best stand in the game, the blue haze of cigarettes wreathing the blue seats, away from the hoi polloi. Most of them should have had the word 'moron' tattooed on their foreheads. The hooligans distanced themselves from the civilians who came to cheer and chant. The designer age was upon us; designer violence the buzzword.

When I went to the Moscow Dynamo game in 1945 the crowd were Lowry-type figures dressed in grey two-piece suits. They may have been Burton, possibly demob, worn as a badge of proletarian honour. In the '80s, the terraces had became catwalks where the latest Armani, Stone Island and Boss fashions were worn. 'Dressed to kill' took on a new meaning. Toby Young wrote in style magazine *The Face* that the better you dressed, the harder you were. What we were seeing was a glint in the eye of the lad culture that was to develop later in the century. Julie Burchill described Young as 'a middle-class ponce'. In the twenty-first century, nobody dresses up to go to football. No Burberry, no Hackett, very drab, very disappointing, just rows of replica shirts and cheap sportswear.

BLACK-SKINNED BLUE-EYED BOYS

David Mellor, described by Patrick Collins as Bates' 'licensed jester', was quoted in 1983 as saying: 'I tried to give Fulham as much priority as work.' Mellor was a self-confessed Fulham fan; now he is a self-appointed Chelsea pundit unable to give up the limelight.

He has made comments in his putrid *Evening Standard* column about the racism that was prevalent during my era as chairman. It was a ridiculous thing to say because racism didn't begin in my time at the club any more than it did during Bates'. But then, how would he know?

Chelsea flirted with danger all season and almost took the unthinkable drop into the old Third Division. In the end, they missed relegation by two points. Canoville made sixteen appearances and notched three goals. The goals came in the final few matches as Chelsea hovered over the abyss. Paul scored two in a 4–2 home win over Carlisle, then hit a vital goal in a

1–1 draw at Fulham. Mellor's team were in the running for promotion and just missed out on the run-in.

The game that kept Chelsea up was a 0–1 win at Bolton, who were relegated as a result. Clive Walker struck a superb late goal after fine work from Canoville. The game was played out in torrential rain with 4,000 Chelsea fans making the perilous trip. They gave Chelsea fanatical support throughout the match. Abramovich should get a list of their names and pay off their mortgages. Walker and Canoville should get pensions for life, because if Chelsea had lost that day, the book would end here.

The second black player to make his debut that wretched season was 18-year-old Keith Jones, nicknamed 'Jonah'. Keith was still an apprentice when he came on as sub at home against Barnsley, who crushed Chelsea 0–3. Welcome to the wonderful world of pro football, Jonah. Chelsea were drained of all confidence and John Neal was keen to blood the youngster. Jones was a black Cliss. He had a brilliant career as a schoolboy, starring for Wandsworth District and London Schoolboys, and looked set for the very top. When he came onto the pitch, Keith recalls: 'There was a bit of jeering. When I made a mistake you could feel things were being said. It would have been bad to make it visible that it affected me and so you just have to shut your mind to what is being said.'

At the time, the levels of racism increased as the National Front (NF) and renegade skinhead gangs became extremely prominent. The Headhunters were the Gestapo of the hooligan army that followed Chelsea. The NF boneheads were outside the Bridge selling their newspaper *Bulldog*, which featured a soccer column usually mentioning who were the top racist fans. Badges, T-shirts and other merchandise were also on sale: fascist designer wear. It made the 'Tommy Langley Collection' look like Armani primo gear. Chelsea fans were named top fascist supporters by the Centre of Contemporary Studies, set up by Eric Moonman, a former Labour MP. In second place were West Ham, with Millwall a close third. There was a special mention for Leeds.

In December 1987, Mickey Droy lamented that Chelsea were no longer a London side; there were no longer home-grown stars in the side. 'Chelsea seems to have all Scots or Irish. There was even an Aussie and a South African.' An Aussie and a South African! Good Heavens. Little did he know what was around the corner.

In January 2004, the 'Let's Kick Racism Out of Football' campaign was celebrating its tenth anniversary, and while it was accepted that much still needed to be done, it gave credit to the fact that great strides had been made. Lord Herman Ouseley, chairman of Kick it Out, said: 'Before 1993, my experience of trying to get anyone in authority to back a campaign to rid football of racism was met with ridicule and rejection.'

Gordon Taylor of the Professional Footballers Association added: 'Pioneering black players such as Clyde Best, Cyrille Regis, Viv Anderson and many others had to endure horrific levels of racial abuse from the terraces. It will always remain a testament to their strength of character that they were able to silence many of those racists with skill and composure.' Canoville's name deserves to be mentioned alongside those black role models.

His life should have been the subject of one of those Hollywood biopics. Paul stayed at Chelsea for two more seasons and won an Under-21 cap. John Barnes blocked his way into the full side at that time. Barnes was the most talented player in the game since a young George Best had exploded across the scene. Ironically, Barnes had made his debut for Watford at Stamford Bridge in the autumn of 1981. The Gate 13 section had derided and hooted the young Jamaican but, after a hesitant start, he recovered his composure to mastermind a 3–1 victory. John never forgot the treatment dished out at Chelsea and repeatedly reserved his best displays and goals for them.

Niggling injuries hindered Paul's progress considerably. The internal discord of the Hollins era added to his problems and he was surprisingly sold to Brentford. Paul's lifestyle and enigmatic bad-boy persona were at odds with the establishment image of the Chelsea management. By that time, he was a firm crowd favourite; even the rascist hardcore had grudging respect for him.

I went to Fulham one afternoon to see a pulsating 3–5 Chelsea victory. Canoville was being closely marked by Paul Parker, who ended up at Chelsea and was in the Cup final squad against Middlesbrough. Parker went in hard on the Chelsea winger and decked him. Two Chelsea skinheads were sitting in front of me and could take no more of this, urging Canoville to kick the 'black b******'.

Another incident towards the end of his Chelsea career was when he was put on as sub at Tottenham with the Blues trailing 4–1. Hoddle was in wonderful form for Spurs, laying on all the goals. Skipper Pates had been sent off and Chelsea were taking a bad beating. Spurs back Danny Thomas (whose career was also sadly terminated by injury) was giving out some stick and Neal sent Paul on to remedy the situation. Within a few minutes, he slamdunked the Tottenham man. Thomas fell over backwards and Canoville stood over him taunting. It was like the famous picture of Ali standing over the fallen Sonny Liston in their second fight.

Canoville moved to Reading. It was there he rediscovered flashes of the form that pushed him to the fringes of the England squad. The top clubs were looking at him again. Tragedy struck, though, when he sustained a terrible knee injury in a game at Sunderland which finished his League career. He drifted down to Enfield and monitored the progress of his nephew Lee. The youngster, like Keith Jones, had a wonderful schoolboy career and was a product of the FA National School at Lilleshall. Last I heard, Lee was on Millwall's books. I do not know what Paul is doing.

After Chelsea's defeat against Monaco, Ron Atkinson was forced to resign as a football pundit for ITV, the result of racist remarks he was overheard making about Chelsea centre-half Marcel Desailly. I wonder what Paul made of it, after all these years.

TWELVE

WHAT'S THE FREQUENCY, KENNETH?

My prayer to God is a very short one, 'Oh Lord, make my enemies ridiculous.' God has granted it.

Voltaire, *Lettres sur Oedipe*

Bates cast himself first as Caesar and then as Christ, when the truth is the historical character he most resembles is Captain Mainwaring of the Home Guard; insufferably pompous and terminally deluded.

Patrick Collins, *Mail on Sunday*

I'd get rid of Ken Bates. I don't like him. Chelsea Village. It's a bit of a ghost town, really. If the man had taste it might have worked, but it lacks it completely.

Phil Daniels, actor and Chelsea fan

The Romans didn't build a great empire by organising meetings. They did it by killing anyone who got in their way.

Ken Bates

I am glad he said Romans and not Roman; it might have caused some unpleasantness.

Dynasty became *Dallas* as the house of Mears fell and, in April 1982, Ken Bates bought the club for £1. Bates' partner was a South African called Stanley Tollman, who also became a director of the club.

NIL BY MOUTH

When Abramovich bought the club as an executive toy, Bates ended his reign with huge debts. It was by far Chelsea's biggest ever loss. It was the third biggest loss ever sustained by a British club, only beaten by Fayed's Fulham and our friends in the north, Leeds.

Although there was some success during Bates' flabbergasting reign, the few victorious teams, which played under no less than nine different managers, won only what I would call Mickey Mouse cup finals against inferior opposition. The behaviour of some of the club's star names brought disgrace to the club.

The team once known as the 'Pensioners' went from being the harmless, eccentric fall-guys to the most hated team in the League. Abramovich's money has done little to redress the situation.

The first time I ever saw Ken Bates was in the boardroom at Manchester City in the mid-'70s. He spotted my glamorous wife June and asked the brilliantly innovative City manager Malcolm Allison who she was. A friendship developed between Bates and his then-wife Pam, and June and I. In 1978, Bates invited us to spend a holiday with him and his wife in the Virgin Islands. He had possession of a 90-foot boat with crew that was either lent to or chartered by him.

My friendship with Bates continued and the following summer I took my family to Monte Carlo where he had the use of a flat. To my mind, the holiday was a bit of a disaster. I remember us encountering some problems over who would pick up the tab for meals and drinks.

I used to see Bates occasionally at the Bridge with Stanley Tollman. He was no longer my guest as he had been in the past. At one match, however, he was involved as a sponsor because of his position in a firm called Trafalgar Travel. They were based in Buckingham Palace Road and had been bought by Tollman with loans from an Irish Trust Bank.

The hard drive of my memory has some golden Chelsea moments embedded in it and I have tried to convey many of them to you in this book – Lawton's header in the Moscow game, Osgood's goals in the '70s Cup finals, the Eddie McCreadie promotion side of that same decade and the old-fashioned genius of Gianfranco Zola. Unfortunately, none of them include Ken Bates.

I monitored for years his battles with the newspapers. The bitterest was surely the shellacking he had with the *Daily Mirror*. They once ran a poll posing the question, 'Is Bates the most odious man in football?' His response: 'Most newspapers end up as fish and chip paper; with the *Mirror* it is lavatory paper.'

The last time I had dealings with him was in March 1982 when we met at the Mayfair Hotel after I had left the club. I wished to dispose of my shares in SB Property Ltd, who at that time owned the ground. I told Bates that I would sell them for a set price without any haggling. Bates offered me exactly half. Consequently, no deal was struck.

The Mears family finally sold the freehold of the stadium and surrounding land to Marler Estates. Marler subsequently gave Chelsea notice to quit when the lease expired at the end of the '80s. The situation was saved by the insolvencies of Marler and Cobra Estates, the subsequent purchaser of the freehold. The Royal Bank of Scotland then assumed the freehold and gave Bates a 21-year lease. Then, he created the Chelsea Village complex, once described by the *Mail on Sunday* as 'rampant naffness'. An area of restaurants, shops and a hotel, who can tell how long it will remain part of the landscape?

Bates was given a two-year contract at the time of the Russian entrepreneur's takeover which was due to end in the centenary season. At that point, he was to become a life president. Kenyon's arrival, however, spelt the end of Bates' time at the Bridge. The writing was on the wall when American lawyer Bruce Buck came in to replace him as chairman of the Chelsea Village parent company in the spring of 2004. Bates' programmes notes, in which the Mears family used to feature, were axed. He was never one to sound the retreat bugle, but after his alleged comments over Abramovich's close friend, Pini Zahavi, Bates quit the job (but not Stamford Bridge – he retained his penthouse suite in the Village). I never went back when I made my exit; I found it too emotional.

> But you play the hand you're dealt,
> Or stop gambling,
> Throw in the deck,
> Cash in your chips.
> **Julia Phillips,** *You'll Never Eat Lunch In This Town Again*

After his departure, Bates wore a slightly grizzled, capsized expression. I almost felt sorry for him. It was reported he had made £17 million from the deal with Abramovich. It sounded even better than Mrs Parlour's divorce settlement. Bates then sued Chelsea Football Club for a further £2 million for an alleged breach of contract. I wondered where he was to go from there. Leeds seemed a strange choice.

On the anniversary of the storming of the Bridge by the Red Army, he was asked for his comments on events; on the year of living dangerously. Bates seemed subdued, by his old standards anyway, limiting himself to:

'All I'll say is what I said to [club director] Mr Tenenbaum last August, that Manchester United must be laughing. He asked why and I pointed out they'd sold Verón and Kenyon to Chelsea, that's two lemons in three weeks.'

What would he have made of Ranieri's successor José Mourinho? In his first few days, Mourinho had put his demands to the players in writing and had reorganised the training sessions. I bet they were more organised than in the far-off days of Danny Blanchflower. José slimmed-down the squad to more manageable proportions.

Bates and Mourinho: I wonder if the Village would have been big enough for both of them.

THIRTEEN

THE GODLIKE GENIUS OF PAT NEVIN

> Celebrity is like ice cream; it melts.
>
> David Soul

> I'm looking at two pictures which just about sum up everything that's right and everything that's wrong with football. One is of Pat Nevin, the other is of Bates.
>
> Mike Ticher, *When Saturday Comes*, March 1986

The elfin-featured Pat Nevin was the last romantic player to turn out for Chelsea. Zola was a different species altogether but I have hopes for Robben. Pat was the last tanna ball player to come down from Scotland.

Shortly before Nevin came south, Julian Cope, the ex-Teardrop Explodes singer, issued a timeless, grey-jacketed compilation album long since off the presses called *Fire Escape in the Sky*. There were no photographs, just the subtitle: 'The godlike genius of Scott Walker'. Scott was an American singer who issued four unsurpassed solo albums which matched his consummate musical talent with a voice powerful enough to affect the emotions, a singer who got lost in a wilderness of neglect and wasted opportunity. Watching Nevin play was like listening to Scott Engel Walker sing . . .

In the summer of '83, John Neal went shopping with a list provided by his assistant, Ian McNeill. If Neal was Clough, then McNeil was Peter Taylor. Ian had a wellspring of knowledge about players in the lower leagues and Scotland which he drew on. To me, the acid test of any manager is who he buys and who he sells. Sexton sold Hudson and bought

Kember. Hurst could have bought Cruyff and ended up with Mayes. Ranieri bought Geremi yet ignored Forsell. Neal bought Kerry Dixon, Pat Nevin and David Speedie. I rest my case. Nigel Spackman, Eddie Niedzwiecki and Joe McLaughlin also joined the club. They were not in the class of the big three but were solid pros who never let the side down. The total cost was under £500,000, most of it recouped with the sale of the talented Mr Fillery who went to the elephant's graveyard at QPR. Those players had more instant impact than any of the influx of talent Abramovich's megabucks purchased 20 years later. What the Russian can never buy is the camaraderie that Neal built up in that side.

Patrick Kevin Francis Michael Nevin was the jewel in the crown, signed for a bargain £95,000 from Clyde in 1983. The 'Wee Man' (5ft 6in.), as he was nicknamed, was a student in commerce and played football part-time. Nevin was a massive Celtic fan and spent four years playing for their Boys' Club. In one season, he scored 180 goals at schoolboy level but was eventually rejected by the Parkhead management. After a spell with junior side Gartosch United, he joined Clyde, who were managed by future Scotland boss, Craig Brown. During Pat's first season, he scored 12 goals and helped them win the Scottish Second Division title.

One of six children, he was born on 6 September 1963 and brought up in the tough Glasgow area of Easterhouse. Pat was the only one not to get a degree. The urchinlike Nevin was en route to his BA when he was called up by the Scotland Under-19 team to play in Mexico. Scotland won the tournament and 110,000 watched the final in the Aztec Stadium. Nevin was man of the match as a riot broke out. Chelsea came in for him and he never resumed his studies.

The young winger moved to London the same day that Charlie Nicholas joined Arsenal. Charlie came to guzzle champagne and chase Page 3 girls; Pat came to read Gogol. His first appearance was in a Blues v. Yellows practice match before the start of the season. Nevin was playing in yellow along with the other new boys. It was little more than an exhibition game. Alan Hudson had boomeranged from America and was back in Chelsea Blue. By now, though, he was largely irrelevant and never played in the first team. Johnny Hollins was back as well, signed from Arsenal as player–coach. Terry Neill had bought Johnny from QPR a day before his 33rd birthday, just as he was on the point of signing for Norwich. Four years and nearly two hundred games later, he went back to the Bridge. Hollins finished up at Highbury as Arsenal captain; his playing career was unblemished.

About 2,000 fans were in the ground; the sun was flame grillin' their skin as they gathered to witness the genesis of another Chelsea icon. Hard man and folk hero Joey Jones was playing for the Blues. In the opening minute, Nevin sold the ex-Liverpool defender a delicious lollipop that left him on his sorry ass. The only nutmeg that compares to it was the one that Zola used on Julian Dicks in his first season at Chelsea. The little guy put on a breathtaking masterclass of football that day and his piece of outrageous skill did grievous damage to Dicks' defensive reputation. The fans blinked in disbelief at Nevin – they had not seen wing play like that since Charlie Cooke used the flanks as his personal amusement arcade.

The new-look Chelsea instantly hit it off and started season 1983–84 with a 5–0 drubbing of former League champions Derby. Dixon opened his Chelsea account by scoring twice and was to add 191 more by the time he left. Walker, the hero of Bolton, was on one wing, with Canoville on the other. Walker was in a dispute over his contract and soon left for Sunderland. It was a shabby end for a player that had saved the club from possible extinction. Nevin's first goal for Chelsea was in a stunning 3–5 win at Fulham and he ended the season with fourteen: the highest figure by a winger since Bert Murray scored seventeen in 1964–65.

The best piece of football demolition that Nevin produced that season was a run against Keegan's Newcastle in a 4–0 thrashing. Just before the interval, he set off on a run that took him past five defenders with no Chelsea player able to contact the pass that he played across the open goal. The pitch was strewn with the bodies of defenders trying desperately to stop him.

The Blues never looked like missing out on promotion and Neal was the first to admit he was surprised at just how quickly his team knitted together; they eventually went up as champions just pipping Sheffield Wednesday on goal difference. They only lost four games all season. Neal was a shrewd old fox: when Chelsea started showing a few jitters around Christmas he went out and bought the experienced Mickey Thomas. The talented Welsh international had a great sense of style and humour. Thomas was another maverick character, moving like a hired gunslinger from club to club. In six years, he had made five moves from Wrexham (where Neal, as the club's manager, had spotted his potential) to Manchester United, Everton, Brighton and Stoke. The boggly-eyed winger scored twice on his debut against Wednesday in a 3–2 win that was to go a long way in securing the title. Nevin had charioted through to score the winner.

Thomas soon fell out with the club and left the Bridge after a brief but successful spell.

That first season was a golden period for Nevin; no other player was so private or perplexing. The *NME* ran their famous 'Post Punk Footballer' interview by Adrian Thrills (which sells for a fortune on eBay). Pat was the only Chelsea player to write for the music weeklies, put together an exhibition of paintings for the Arts Council and be made an official member of the Cocteau Twins.

The tabloids never really understood him; his early interviews were studded with references to visits to the Tate or parliamentary debates. As his mystique grew, he put on shades, wore long overcoats and barely spoke to his teammates, who regarded him as some type of a kook.

Chelsea never built on the solid foundation that the Second Division championship gave them. They had a marvellous strike force with the trinity of Dixon, Speedie and Nevin. Where they needed strengthening was in defence: Joe McLaughlin was solid but the overrated Pates always looked fallible. Doug Rougvie, bought from Aberdeen as a back, was dour and lacked pace.

Canoville's star continued to rise. A thigh strain hampered his fitness but a hat-trick against Swansea and a fine goal against Leeds in a late season demolition were the high spots.

Dixon clinched the title with his 28th goal of the season away to Grimsby. Nevin made it with a perfect chip from the byline, a classic move that brought them so many goals at that time. Things looked encouraging but in early summer, John Neal had a five-hour operation for by-pass surgery.

Season 1984–85 marked Chelsea's return to the big league after five years' absence. They finished sixth – a promising enough start but the ever-present spectre of hooliganism cast a giant shadow over the season. Nevin was the star turn in the run to the Milk Cup semi-final. Dixon scored a hat-trick in the 4–1 win over Manchester City in the fourth round. What most fans remember, though, was Nevin's fluffed penalty, caught by the BBC cameras. Pat recalled:

> I tried a technique used by Altobelli, the Italian, in training the previous week and it worked a treat. I took just one step before shooting and by doing so, stopped the goalkeeper moving before the ball was kicked.
>
> Niedzwiecki could not get near any of my efforts on the training pitch but I didn't connect properly against City and messed it up completely. As the match was being televised, I knew the camera would be showing a close-up and although I knew I should have been disappointed, I couldn't help laughing because it was such a feeble effort.

Nevin played his part in the epic trilogy of matches in the quarter-final against Sheffield Wednesday. He cleverly set up Speedie to score at the Bridge in the second replay with a cheeky free kick. Thomas eventually settled it, threading an 89th-minute header from Canoville's surgical corner through a packed goalmouth. It gave Chelsea a 2–1 win, 7–6 on aggregate. The next week, Chelsea went up to Sunderland to play the first leg of the semi-final. It was a bad night for Neal's lads. The game was played on a frozen pitch, in temperatures that Abramovich's countrymen would have found uncomfortable. Big Joe McLaughlin dislocated his right elbow in the ninth minute and midfield prospect Dale Jasper was switched to the centre of defence. Jasper was seen as the coming force: the new Fillery with a smattering of Hudson and Butch. When Nevin was asked what player he would buy for Chelsea, he replied a combination of Dale's right foot, Dale's left foot, Dixon's head and Thomas's heart.

Dale was no defender, though, and gave away two penalties, ruthlessly dispatched by the Sunderland striker Colin West. Jasper was unable to overcome the stigma of that night and sadly never established himself in the top flight.

A week later, Chelsea entertained Sunderland in the second leg, 0–2 down but determined to get to their first Wembley final in a dozen years.

WILD BOYS

Chelsea got the perfect start they needed. Speedie, later sent off, smashed in a goal after Nevin had subtly developed a free kick from Jones. It was 1–2 and Chelsea threw themselves forward like Tommies at the Somme. They needed an older head in the team to steady them down. (Hudson had returned to Stoke, though, and was already winning rave reviews for his performances.)

Sunderland coolly weathered the bombardment and, eight minutes before the break, Clive Walker did what he had done so often before – scored a killer breakaway goal. David Hodgson, one of Neal's old Boro boys and soon to join Liverpool, fooled the Chelsea defence with a clever decoy run. Walker burst past Rougvie to slam a shot under Niedzwiecki. It was 1–3. Walker turned to the benches, who had been cursing him all game, and gave the Russell Crowe salute.

The second half was one of the blackest in Chelsea's history. The ground became a battlefield on and off the pitch. Walker went past Joey Jones throughout the game. It was as easy for him as it had been seven seasons previously in the 4–2 victory over Liverpool. Now, though, it was some *X-Files* parallel universe deal: Walker was in the Red and Jones in the Blue. In the 70th minute, Clive scored again with another goal he had the patent on. Colin West crossed, Jones failed to clear and the uncatchable Walker made it a watertight 1–4 on aggregate. It was perhaps the biggest mistake of Neal's career to put Joey up against Walker, knowing what every Chelsea fan in the ground knew. It was as suicidal as pitting Frank Sinclair against Anelka in more contemporary times.

All hell broke lose. The fans on the benches broke them up and chucked the splintered wood at the players or at the police horses that had galloped onto the pitch. Coins, bottles, bricks and cans rained down from all sides. One idiot, later christened the 'fat man' by the media, ran onto the pitch to get at two-goal Walker. The 'fat man' was pursued by four policemen. By now, Walker had worked his way out to the byline in front of Gate 13 and lobbed high into the penalty box. There were more police in the six-yard area than Chelsea defenders and the unchallenged West headed home. It was Sunderland's third goal of the match, West's third goal of the semis, which made it 1–5 (as if anyone was counting by now). I had heard about the Thin Blue Line and police protection but this was ridiculous. 'Previously on CFCPD . . .'

The 'fat man' is still around it would appear. In February 2004, Walker was waiting in Stuttgart Airport for a flight home after covering Chelsea's 1–0 victory in the Champions League. A 'Fatty' Foulke figure approached him and apologised for attempting to whack him back in 1985. Walker stated the assailant was even bigger than he was 19 years earlier.

In a surreal atmosphere, Nevin scored a bizarre goal, intercepting Gary Bennett's back pass to lob gently over Sunderland keeper Turner. There is a famous picture of the ball hitting the back of the net, watched by a disinterested policeman on a horse who also happens to be inside the penalty area.

The game ended in pandemonium but the trouble spilled over onto the streets as Chelsea fans bricked the Sunderland coaches. In the players' bar, Walker was attacked by Speedie. They had history going back to when the fiery little Scot had joined Chelsea from Darlington. Mickey Droy pulled them apart as the chairs flew and glasses were smashed. Years on, Walker has returned to the fold and does the guided 'Legends' tour of the Bridge – only £49 per person ending in lunch; what value. I wonder if he points out where he went past Joey Jones on a motorbike, or the bar where Speedie threw a punch at him? Legends, every one of them.

Chelsea were vilified in the media. The hooliganism had gotten worse over the years. Bates had put out his 'Don't be a mug, don't be a thug' appeals when he took over. It was about as apposite to the social plague as a sticky plaster on first-degree burns. Shortly afterwards the mugs/thugs ambushed Leeds fans at Piccadilly Tube station and 153 arrests were made.

Later in the season, when Kevin Wilson (later to join the club) scored twice for Derby to knock Chelsea out of the Cup, a riot ensued and hooligans ripped out seats and threw them on the pitch. Bates tried to quell the riot but they started chucking the seats at him.

In the promotion season, there were two bad riots. One at Brighton, when four policemen were hospitalised, and one at Portsmouth, when five hundred seats were ripped out. After the Sunderland debacle, the usual headlines were trotted out. They could have covered any game over a 20-year period: 'Bates: I will kick out the yobs' *Evening Standard*; 'Mindless!' *The Sun*; 'Chelsea Mayhem' *Daily Mail*; 'Bridge of Shame' *Daily Express*; 'Riot Act' *Daily Star*; 'Bridge Too Far' *Today*; 'Riot at the Bridge' *Daily Mirror*; 'Fans Rampage as Chelsea go out' *The Guardian*.

Bates' reaction to the extreme hooliganism was to apply to the council to erect an electric fence in front of the benches. Bates seemed to disregard the continuing public protests, unapologetic for suggesting the idea. The application was rejected by the local authority.

THE RETURN OF JOHNNY ENGLISH

It was by now season 1985–86 and Chelsea finished sixth again. At one time, though, they were challenging for the title. There was a change in management: John Hollins stepping up from player–coach to replace Neal, whose health was giving cause for concern. Hollins was given a contract with a three-year notice period.

Neal recalls his relationship with Bates: 'We had a bit of a love–hate relationship. He'd ring down and invite me to lunch. I'd tell him I'd brought sandwiches and to take someone else. But he thought John Hollins was better than he was and that was a mistake.'

Nevin scored ten goals that season in the League and the Cup and won the first of his twenty-eight caps for Scotland. In the space of three days at the end of January, Chelsea lost vital cup games at home to Liverpool (FA Cup, 1–2) and QPR (League Cup, 0–2). Key players, Dixon and Niedzwiecki, picked up bad injuries in those games which hampered their long-term careers. Dixon never seemed quite as dynamic after that (although, like Osgood, he still scored prolifically), whilst Eddie eventually had to quit the game.

At Easter, Chelsea were still in the hunt for the title but two staggering defeats at home to West Ham (0–4) and away to QPR (6–0) blew their chances. One-time teenage goalkeeping sensation Steve Francis was recalled from the wilderness but had a torrid time and never featured again.

Chelsea looked out of contention but a great win at Old Trafford put them back in the frame. Dixon scored both Chelsea's goals that night, the second after an unforgettable breakaway set up by Jerry Murphy. Hollins was tinkering with the midfield and had bought Hazard from Spurs and the underrated Murphy from Palace. Both were superb footballers, far superior in my opinion to, say, Scott Parker, but neither could translate their massive skill into any cohesive form. Murphy had the sweetest left foot I ever saw, his corners and free kicks made Beckham's efforts look like Mickey Droy toe punts.

One Tuesday night in April, Chelsea went to West Ham still smarting from their four-goal beating. The Hammers were riding high and the whole of the East End thought they had a real chance at the title. Nevin was carrying a very bad bruise that he had picked up after a clash with Stuart Pearce of Forest the previous Saturday. Chelsea had drawn 0–0 at Forest and the thuggish defender, who called himself 'Psycho', had cruelly fouled him. I always found it strange that such attention was given to Pearce. His mistakes put us out of two World Cups and skilful players like Nevin always had the beating of him, providing they had the courage to stand up to his bully-boy tactics. Pearce was always a sucker for Nevin's *pedaloes* or step-overs.

Shortly before the kick-off at West Ham, Nevin declared himself fit. Hollins played him up front alongside Dixon in the absence of the suspended Speedie, and the manager anxiously packed the midfield with Bumstead, Murphy, Hazard and Spackman. After a tense, hectic first half, the Hammers scored soon after the break, Frankie 'Boots of Gold' McAvennie setting up Cottee to blast home. Chelsea quickly hit back, though, and Spackman fired an equaliser home from Murphy's corner.

With 12 minutes left, Dixon burst to the byline leaving England centre-half Martin trailing in the dirt. The blond pin-up boy chipped over a perfect cross and there was Nevin flying in to nod past Parkes. Chelsea supporters packed that whole end and let out a mighty roar. It was a tense night – they were heavily outnumbered by the ICF (Inter City Firm): the elite of the West Ham hooligan army and a particularly nasty gang. I think they killed a fan one year. They got their nickname from the trains they would use to travel to away games. They liked to leave a calling card on their victims: 'Congratulations, you have just met the ICF'. Something poetic. I think they ripped off the idea from the demented Colonel Kilgore (played by Robert Duvall) in *Apocalypse Now*, who leaves playing cards on his dead Vietcong victims. The Wee Man danced a jig in the back of the net. The perfect Nevin–Dixon gag had been reworked and West Ham were the fall-guys.

That win wrecked the Hammers' bid for the League. I honestly think if they had beaten Chelsea that night they would have gone on to take the title. Their momentum was broken and they eventually finished third, four points behind Liverpool who stole the title from long-term leaders Everton.

The Upton Park result put Chelsea third, only three points behind Liverpool with five games left. Typically, Chelsea did the hard bit, winning at United and West Ham, but they only took one more point that season.

Season 1986–87 was a disappointment as Chelsea tumbled to 14th place. Neal left the club, sacked for disloyalty, whatever that may mean. It was a sad end for a man that had rescued Chelsea from the Third Division and provided them with the nucleus of a Championship-winning side. Neal had found himself increasingly isolated from the players he had moulded into honours-winning material. Neal once said: 'I was called consultant director but Hollins didn't consult me. Things turned sour. I was deeply hurt and disappointed that my team was dismantled. They had the ability to win trophies.'

That season, Nevin played in thirty-six games and scored five goals. Gordon Durie joined the club from Hibs; he was popular with the fans (till he defected to Spurs) but never really justified the hype. A 'Hollywood' player, as Docherty would say. A better acquisition was Roy Wegerle, signed from Tampa. The youngster was never given a chance to show what he could do.

In the early autumn, Forest slaughtered Chelsea 2–6 at the Bridge. Winger Franz Carr ran amok as he set up goal after goal for hat-trick scorers Birtles and Webb. A Luther Blissett goal dumped them out of the Cup. The 'Crazy Gang' side of Wimbledon, including Vinnie Jones and the people's dwarf Wise, came to the Bridge and trimmed us 0–4. The warning signs were all there as the cracks appeared.

BEYOND THE SUN

That season, a player called John McNaught, a £75,000 buy from Hamilton, made his debut for Chelsea. John starred in the 3–1 win over QPR on New Year's Day, 1987. The young Scot would not have played but for an injury to John Bumstead. McNaught scored with his first touch of the ball, a sweet, curling left-foot shot that completely deceived the Hoops keeper David Seaman (*sans* ponytail). He scored again with a terrific strike into the roof of the net with a set-up from Dixon. In all, he made eight appearances in the League in that troubled season.

It should have been the start of something big but as we have seen so often it does not always work out like that. John had a wild streak in him: as an amateur in Scotland he once served a nine-month suspension. He only played one more game for Chelsea, against Manchester United, scoring in a 3–1 defeat at Old Trafford in that weird season of 1987–88: three goals in nine games for a midfield player looked a pretty good return to me. I recall that he was arrested for the possession of an offensive weapon before drifting back to Scotland. I heard Nevin was a pal of his. They were both fans of the singer Billy McKenzie, who ended up committing suicide. A few years later, I read that he had bought the farm. The circumstances in which the stricken star died were never fully explained.

DEAD SOULS

> He is the classic NCO who didn't make an officer.
> **Brian Glanville on John Hollins, *Sunday Times***

Chelsea were relegated at the end of season 1987–88. At the end of September, they were second but as their confidence drained away they crashed and burned. Bates could do nothing to avert the situation; he was loyal to Hollins till the end of March but then it was too late. Chelsea went down after losing in the play-offs to Middlesbrough. They actually finished fourth from bottom with the same number of points as Charlton and West Ham but their inferior goal difference sucked them down.

Nevin played thirty-six games and scored six goals. Another Scottish winger, Kevin McAllister, was on the books at the time and Hollins had briefly flirted with the idea of using him as a replacement. There was only one Nevin, though, and he was still the most popular player with the fans. Before each game, he would give an exhibition of ball juggling that would transfix the thousands of Chelsea fans who arrived early at the ground specifically to see him.

Rows, transfer requests and scandals blighted the whole season as the team internally combusted. Speedie and Spackman left the club after bust-ups. Kerry Dixon was lined up to go to Arsenal after the clubs had agreed terms but Bates blocked it. Ernie Walley was sacked as coach in February. Hollins lacked the experience and nous to defuse the tension and was eventually sacked in March. Bobby Campbell, formerly manager of Fulham, was put in charge. I heard that it was some Masonic arrangement – he had originally been brought in to replace Walley.

A 1–1 home draw with Charlton condemned Chelsea to the play-offs. Ex-Tottenham defender Paul Miller scored Charlton's equaliser and was later involved in some ugly confrontations with the Chelsea strike force. In later years, he was to be seen in the hospitality suites telling everybody what a Chelsea/City boy he was. Miller was another product of the Senrab Sunday team in Wanstead.

The team rallied briefly with a 0–2 win at Blackburn in the first of the play-off games. A support of 5,000 made the trip and Nevin rifled home a great goal to clinch victory. It was his last goal for the Blues.

On a stormy night at the end of May, Chelsea lost the first leg of the play-off final at Middlesbrough 2–0. Durie missed a great chance when the score was 0–0. The same player scored the only goal of the game in the return match but an insipid Chelsea slid out of the division. Like the Sunderland nightmare, the game ended in a riot as Chelsea fans tried to invade the pitch. The same headlines littered the sports pages. The FA closed the Stamford Bridge terraces for the first six games of the new season.

Nevin left the club a few weeks later. The party line was that he quit but I have a letter from him stating, 'If you are not wanted . . .' Everton offered a meagre £300,000 for him – a figure which fell short of Chelsea's valuation by £1.4m. The Football League's independent transfer tribunal set the fee at a record £925,000.

Pat never really settled at Goodison, although he played in the FA Cup final defeat to Liverpool. His ball-playing style was no longer fashionable and Tranmere signed him. Always the entertainer, he played over 200 games for them, scoring 30 goals. I used to try to see him play whenever they came to London. Still mazy after all those years.

FOURTEEN

THE WICKER MAN

Matthew Charles Harding, businessman, born Haywards
Heath, Sussex, 26 December 1953, vice-chairman Chelsea
Football Club 1995–96, died 22 October 1996

To the living one owes consideration. To the dead only the
truth.

Voltaire, *Lettres Sur Oedipe*

If there was ever a story to rival the complex plot of *The
Wicker Man*, it is the tale of the troubled post-production and
afterlife of the film. Director Robin Hardy's film, starring
Christopher Lee, Edward Woodward and Britt Ekland, would
be woefully mishandled and overlooked, only to be belatedly
recognised as a brilliantly original, audacious debut.
Grudges, rampant paranoia, fractious egos, heartaches and
bad timing have all contributed to the movie's martyrdom.
And, like many cult films, *The Wicker Man* has been kept alive
only by the eternal diligence of its fans. It's tempting to
ascribe some sort of evil spirit to its initial failure.

Ali Catterall and Simon Wells, *Your Face Here*

Matthew Harding was the prototype Chelsea boy – when he died, he
owned the Stamford Bridge stadium and had sunk £26m into the club. If
he had lived, Chelsea would have won the Premier before Abramovich
rode into town. If Harding had lived, Abramovich would be superfluous,

just another Russian oligarch trying to join the London self-preservation society. Gullit would still have been manager and the team would have been a dazzling mixture of the cream of Europe and an influx of young English talent. Abramovich has this as an agenda but Harding was working towards it years before. Harding drafted the Blues-print of global domination. If only he had lived . . .

One autumn night in 1996, the helicopter carrying him back from a Coca-Cola Cup tie at Bolton crashed in flames. It was suggested that it hit power lines but later this was disproved. In *The Wicker Man*, the anti-hero is sacrificed – burned alive – in an immense wicker structure resembling a man.

It was the golden autumn that Frankie Dettori rode seven winners at Ascot. David Beckham's wife continued the domination of the world with the Spice Girls. The most popular television show was the *X-Files*, a programme dealing in cases without solutions.

Harding died an iconic figure for the cause of Chelsea Football Club, some going so far as to see his helicopter sacrifice as an ironic martyrdom echoing Christ's crucifixion. Did he die in vain? It's a question that begs an answer.

We have a magnificent stand that bears his name but already he is being airbrushed out of the history of the club. His memory was being erased with the absoluteness of Soviet regimes banishing dissidents from the historical record (ironically, before a Soviet regime took control) in the same manner that Lady Diana Spencer, once the most famous woman in the world, is now a vague figure on the edge of reality. Soon, to a new generation of fans, Harding's name will be as obscure as that of Hudson's. A Chelsea legend, yes, but your father could tell you why.

Where were you when Matthew died? When you heard the news? Just like the old stories about people who could tell you exactly what they were doing at the time of President Kennedy's assassination.

I was at home as the morning of 23 October 1996 dawned, recovering from a heart attack I had suffered a few weeks before which had all but done for me. I had lost three stone and as I lay stricken, I wondered if I would ever get off the canvas. Harding had rung me a few days before to see how I was progressing. His voice sounded strange, hesitant and even nervous. Harding wanted to meet me as there was something he wanted to tell me. I told him that we should meet at the Howard, our usual, as soon as I was up and about again. Harding had said that it was too crowded.

On our last visit, Harding sounded anxious. He said he would send a driver for me. We chatted briefly about Chelsea. Harding thought that the future was bright for his beloved Blues. The Ruud boy was in charge, Glenn had the England gig. Harding had been very disappointed at the former England star leaving but Glenn hadn't been an easy man to know. Things hadn't happened quickly enough for Hoddle at the Bridge, Matthew said; that was why he had left. Harding really thought it was Chelsea's year for the Cup and fancied them to go all the way. One of his most cherished dreams was to see the Blues win the Cup at Wembley.

'Be well' were the last words he ever spoke to me.

I was still in pain and slept badly. That night, the wind had blown constantly but it suddenly subsided and the sky became as white as Leeds' shirts the night of the Old Trafford replay. I got up, made black coffee, fixed a bowl of Weetabix and flipped on Wogan. A news item on Radio 2 told me about a helicopter crash in Cheshire. Some Blue scarves were found in the wreckage. That reminded me about Chelsea playing the previous night at Bolton. I had not heard the final score as I had dozed off at about nine o'clock with the scores locked at 1–1. Scott Minto had initially given the Blues the lead – the last goal Matthew ever saw Chelsea score. I went back to bed exhausted, dreaming about Baldwin's hat-trick on the same ground, a lifetime ago.

About 9.30, my wife June came into the room. 'I have some bad news. Your friend Matthew . . .' she said.

'I know,' I replied. I had known the moment I had heard about the scarves; my brain just hadn't processed it. My words were like wet glass inside my throat.

SUCCESS CAN'T FAIL ME NOW

> People forget, but what's happened at Chelsea is what Matthew Harding used to dream about. That's what he wanted for the club. He was a Chelsea man through and through.
>
> Glenn Hoddle, September 2003

The first time I met Matthew was in the Howard Hotel, his salubriously located base. Vaguely expensive, vaguely exclusive. Harding had slurred my family in the press and I had taken great exception to his comments. It was wrist-slashingly unfunny and probably made me feel more insulted than I'd been for a long time. Well, maybe a couple of weeks. Like with Osgood, I put it down to yet another case of success going to someone's mouth. I phoned him in his Fenchurch Street office. I was surprised that he took my call; so few people did. His response dignified him and we chatted cordially for more than half an hour. At the end of the conversation, he invited me for a drink at the Howard.

Now, the satellite TV deals meant the game was awash with money and transfer fees, and wages were escalating. Clubs like Chelsea walked into the trap modern capitalism had made for them. Football was a game in transition: old money was being challenged or inveigled by the nouveaux riches. Football had become the biggest distraction in the world but it was emotionally stunted. I wasn't sure if I still loved the game; I even hated the kits – those red diamonds Chelsea wore away in the early '90s were hideous. Another vile combination was the orange and slate-grey.

Harding was smaller than I had imagined but, then, who wasn't? I recall being introduced to Steve McQueen by Attenborough when they were filming *The Great Escape* and thinking the same thing. Harding was better looking than in his photographs but, again, who wasn't? Even at 4 p.m., in a distinctly soggy London, Harding was immaculately turned out. He was wearing a plain-blue Boss single-breasted suit, a plain virgin-white shirt and a perfectly knotted tie with a swirly Paisley motif which might have been Versace. As for the black, highly polished brogues, they might well have been Church's. The whole ensemble was downplayed with a gold-link bracelet and gold watch, possibly Jaeger-LeCoultre (contrast this with the plastic Swatch I see on Abramovich's wrist).

I had expected an edgy *arriviste*, an upstart mixture of Headhunter and *Wall Street*'s Gordon Gecko in a Huntsman suit. Harding had dark, collar-length hair clipped around his ears with just a graze of silver. He stared straight ahead when I entered the bar; he had been reclining on a leather sofa with languid English grace. Somewhere in the background, a record was playing, a woman's voice telling us it was too late. I noticed a slight distortion of his pupils and between his eyes a deep indentation suggested a lifelong sense of perplexity. I got on with him right away. I liked him. That was how it was with Matthew – if he liked you, he talked to you. If he didn't like you, bye bye. You see, we were both fans of Chelsea and that was the key. The irony of us meeting and becoming friends was very profound. Like the number one Shed boy, Mick Greenaway, we had a common knowledge, a shared love of the same fickle woman. No matter what barriers of class, money, race or background separated us, it was our love for the Blues that surmounted it all. There was a bonding. That is what Chelsea was about in my time.

Abramovich appropriated that culture when he bought Chelsea: the Russian turned it into a richman's playground. A Russian billionaire bought the world's greatest private collection of Fabergé imperial Easter eggs the week Scott Parker joined Chelsea. What was the difference? They were both just commodities.

When Lampard's penalty beat Manchester United 1–0 in November 2003, the richest man in the world (under 40) had flown 500 of his closest friends from Moscow to see the game. Lord Rothschild, 'a keen Chelsea supporter', has been a VIP guest of Abramovich. He should read Petronius's *Satyricon*. In it, a vulgar social upstart, Trimalchio, gives a banquet of unimaginable luxury. Over the table hangs a large clock and during the meal guests are reminded that time has elapsed by a uniformed trumpeter who appears to blow his horn. Nothing good lasts for ever.

Harding's money gave him the kind of confidence that overrides everything. In a hundred photos, he refused the questioning lens; through a thousand media articles he resisted definition. The Chelsea shirt with Vialli's name emblazoned on it, the Thomas Pink linen, sky-blue business shirt with the cutaway collar, worn with the TM Lewin floral tie; the stance at once confiding, yet distant. Everybody who followed Chelsea knew Harding, but what was it we knew?

The fans always saw him as reverent and perceptive; the man behind the image and the image behind the man. How could he inspire all that warmth and devotion in a manner Abramovich attempts to emulate? Both seem distant and yet comfortingly close. Both migrating in life from controversy to celebrity. Abramovich let slip his ignorance of football matters when it was revealed that John Terry was his favourite player. Harding's was Greaves, or was it Hudson or Ossie? Terry would not have been Matthew's favourite today, had he lived. It was like the gulf between Audrey Hepburn and Jordan; John Lennon and Liam Gallagher.

What did he do to earn his eternal Chelsea glory? Score Cup-winning goals like Di Matteo? Dribble past people like Nevin? Manage world-famous teams like Ranieri? No. He made mountains of money and spent mountains of money; Abramovich does the same in his quest for self-esteem and respectability.

This only served to enhance his radiance: Matthew was rich and he wanted to be richer. Others, like Crespo and Wenger, may strive and perform; Harding only had to be.

THE BURNING SKY

Then we'll all be happy and we'll all be wise and together and
we will all bow down to the burning sky.

The Jam, 'Burning Sky'

My first meeting with Matthew was in the late spring of 1995. The years
had flown by – it was almost a decade and a half since I had left Chelsea.
As chairman of the club, I had lived a life of so much stress, trying to
sustain their unstable empire, that it had almost killed me. So I moved to
America and tried to deconstruct myself. Wandering in the wilderness,
backlashed by apostates, a pariah of the media. I found myself being
treated like some Orwellian 'unperson' as I tried to appraise the new
situation. I had got off light – all it had cost me was my career, my health,
my family's estate and a lifetime of insults from certain parties.

What I found particularly abhorrent was that the 'Baron of the Bridge'
called my family 'lepers'. It was a distraction and a gift to the tabloids.
Unfortunately in football, when the press turns against you, so does
everyone else. Ask David Beckham.

Chelsea bounced back at their first attempt in season 1988–89. Bobby
Campbell grafted an iron spine into the side with the purchase of hard
men Graham Roberts and Peter Nicholas. They literally ran away with the
League: in September, they were 20th, then they started playing. It was a
record-breaking season: the 99 points they accumulated have never been
beaten and neither has the total of 29 wins. That included a straight run
of 27 matches without defeat and 7 straight away wins (a 0–7 romp at
Walsall was the high spot). It only emphasised the point that a side
including players like Dixon (who finished top scorer with 25 goals) and
Australian defender Tony Dorigo should never have been relegated. The
cliché, 'too good to go down', is often used but that Chelsea side would
never have been relegated if Hollins had been given some proper
managerial guidance.

The following season, Chelsea finished fifth in the First Division.
Another successful return to the big time. The type of player needed
most in the twenty-first-century Chelsea was a leader in the mould of
Graham Roberts to drive them on. Roberts had a great season but the
Cup competitions were not so successful. Scarborough (who gave

Chelsea such a hard game in the fourth round of the FA Cup in 2004) knocked them out of the League Cup. Bristol City dumped them out of the FA Cup 3–1 after an appalling defensive performance let Chelsea down. Graeme Le Saux made his full debut against Crystal Palace and scored a late equaliser in a thrilling 2–2 draw. This was the season that Chelsea made their second Wembley appearance in the Full Members Cup final. Bates had been instrumental in setting up the competition – in my view, it should have been Walt Disney: the theme was strictly Mickey Mouse.

Chelsea's finances had failed to improve but Dennis Wise and Andy Townsend (who sported a feather cut then) joined the club in the summer of 1990 for huge fees. Both found it hard to settle and Chelsea finished 11th in a mediocre 1990–91 season. The best result was a fantastic 0–3 win at Tottenham in the Milk Cup. Terry Venables was managing a Spurs side that included a young, fit Gazza and über-star Gary Lineker. He and Terry Venables can be seen now in crisps ads on a television near you. Wembley dreams were dashed, though, by a dour Sheffield Wednesday who beat Chelsea 5–1 over two legs in the semi-final. Forest slaughtered Chelsea 7–0 in one of Frank Sinclair's first League matches. He never could avoid trouble.

In May 1991, Bobby Campbell became Bates' assistant and Ian Porterfield took over as manager. The club was fined a record £105,000 after being found guilty of irregular payments. Chelsea seemed stuck in mid-table, though, finishing 14th in the 1991–92 season, the last year of the old First Division. Clive Allen, the nomad serial goalscorer, had a brief tour of duty with the club that his father Les had played for in the '50s. Clive's nine goals in nineteen games helped them to the quarter-final of the FA Cup where once again Sunderland were to crush their hopes. Clive gave them an early lead at the Bridge but a careless defensive error let John Byrne in to equalise. In the replay, Chelsea put up a tremendous display, and a late goal from Wise to equalise looked like taking the game into extra time. Another defensive lapse, this time by Townsend, let Armstrong up for a last-minute winner, though.

THE BEANO KIDS

Vinnie Jones had come to Chelsea from Sheffield United in August 1991 to join up with Wise, his brother-in-arms from the Crazy Gang at Wimbledon. Dave Beasant, the penalty-saving hero of the Wombles Cup final win over Liverpool, had been signed by Chelsea after an unhappy time at Newcastle. In the Cup victory over his old side Sheffield United, Vinnie was booked after only three seconds. Jones had clashed with Dane

Whitehouse straight from the kick-off and cheekily stated that his tackle could hardly have been late!

Dennis and Vinnie were cartoon characters, indulging in Tom-and-Jerry-like violence, wearing comic-cut clothes and looking like they stepped straight off the pages of *The Beano* circa 1975. Jones only spent a brief spell at the Bridge but, like everywhere he went, he soon won the respect of the fans. Jones knew how to work the crowd, and still does as he carves out a career in the movies. Like Gallacher and the chaps, trouble was never far away, though, and he was fined £1,500 by the FA for making obscene gestures to fans prior to Chelsea's clash at Highbury. Vinnie claimed that he had seen his sister's boyfriend in the crowd and greeted him with a hand movement, mouthing 'w*****r' at him. Those sensitive Gooner chaps were deeply offended and lodged complaints. Chelsea lost 3–2. I suppose it must have been funny for all of 27 seconds.

Season 1992–93 saw the inception of the Premier. Chelsea's first-ever game in it was a 1–1 home draw with Oldham – Bates' old club, now fallen on somewhat harder times. Mick Harford, an old-fashioned gunslinger of a striker in the mould of Lawton and Hutchinson, scored Chelsea's goal.

Paul Elliott had joined Chelsea the year before from Celtic for £1.3m and looked set for a glorious career. Elliott was an extraordinary player, on a par with Desailly at his peak. He would walk into the twenty-first-century Chelsea side. He had the aggression of Terry but was 50 per cent quicker and more dependable. Terry was always a boy trying to do a man's job. Elliot was a man in every sense of the word: he had the legs of a kick boxer with a head like an Easter Island statue. A dreadful clash with Liverpool's Dean Saunders at Anfield ended his career in the September of that year. Paul took Saunders to the High Court but did not have so much as a Mars bar to show for it at the end. It was called the soccer trial of the century. Eventually, Mr Justice Drake, in a voice like a melting Werthers Original, ruled that Saunders' tackle, which ended Elliott's career, was not reckless. Elliott carries his reminders of that incident to this day in the form of two vivid eight-inch scars either side of his knee. Saunders' stud marks gouged his thigh and left scars there also. Paul's knee was effectively moved two-and-a-half inches around his leg by the impact. The pain must have been excruciating. He needed three major operations. Wise used to call him Big Jamaica – he had a heart as big as the island.

Porterfield signed Robert Fleck at the start of the season for £2.1m. The Glasgow-born Fleck was another wild-boy jock in the mould of Gallacher. The ex-Rangers striker scored 29 goals for them in 85 games before joining Norwich. The Scottish international had scored two fine goals at the Bridge the previous November for the Canaries. On the strength of that performance alone, he was signed. 'Lethal Weapon' the headlines screamed when he joined but in forty-three games for Chelsea he only scored four goals. The consequences and knock-on effect to Porterfield's managerial career were obvious.

Porterfield lacked the dominant personality to subdue strong characters like Wise or Jones and was sacked in February 1993. His last game was a 0–1 home defeat to Aston Villa. Mark Bosnich, before his problems with cocaine, was in goal for Villa and Ray Houghton scored the only goal of an appalling game. David Webb (remember him?) was put in charge temporarily. Webb, always the fighter, halted the slide and Chelsea finished in a comfortable 11th spot. Porterfield was last heard of managing a K-league side in South Korea – a good career move for him.

The accounts for Chelsea Football and Athletic Club in March 1992 showed an accumulated deficit of £1.5m. Two new companies were formed: Chelsea Village and CFAC. Maybanks (no relation to Teddy Maybank – thirty-two games, six goals – who briefly shone during the McCreadie era), the programme printers, issued a formal winding-up order for unpaid debts. In May 1993, CFAC was placed into receivership.

When Matthew Charles Harding arrived on the Chelsea scene waving his chequebook he must have been as welcome a sight as Abramovich. Harding was born two years before Bentley lifted the title in 1955. He didn't live long enough to see Chelsea gain the title under José Mourinho. Like Abramovich, he had a modest childhood. The television on which he watched *The Lone Ranger* after the Chelsea score on *Grandstand* was rented. Matthew was privately educated at the public school of Abingdon. It was a rugby-playing, football-banning, academically inclined environment and he left at seventeen with ten O levels and one A level. Matthew's father Paul, a huge Chelsea fan (whose favourite player was McCreadie), was a cargo underwriter at Lloyd's and secured his son a job as a teaboy with the re-insurance brokers Benfield. The deal was struck in the Lamb Tavern in Leadenhall Market which stands in the shadow of the Lloyd's building. The teaboy's starting pay was £17 per week, £3 less than Greaves' wage when he left to join Milan. That was in 1973, the year that Hudson was the epitome of cool in crushed velvet with a bouffant haircut. Matthew told me that his all-time favourite shirt was a Paisley design with a Henry Hill collar. It was a copy of one he saw Alan wear on the late Brian Moore's *Big Match* television show, purchased in Take 6 on the Kings Road.

Matthew said it took him five years to find his feet in the convoluted business of re-insurance. In 1982, Ted Benfield took him onto the board and when Ted retired two years later, Matthew assumed total command. Seeing the money to be made, he led a management buy-out of the company. It grew massively as a result of a string of disasters in the late '80s which forced insurance companies to re-insure themselves with organisations like Benfield. It was his involvement in football, the most venal industry in the world, that raised his profile, as it did Abramovich's. Both just showed up at the pleasure dome that was Stamford Bridge on match days and the place went crazy. Harding's alter-ego had a life of his own, obeying the laws of comic books. Harding, like the ex-Wombles Jones and Wise, could have stepped from the pages of a comic. The *Wizard* – no that would be Ossie or Cooke; the *Hotspur* – no, wrong name altogether. Maybe the *Lion*. In the famous strip, Roy of 'Roy of the Rovers' loses his leg in a helicopter crash.

Despite the media overkill at the time of his death, Harding resisted language. I recall a fulsome tribute at the funeral from the then Chelsea manager Glenn Hoddle (Porterfield's replacement), standing under a tree in his Chelsea blazer. Rudd Gullit stood behind him in a beautifully cut leather jacket. The world had suddenly become a colder place without their friend and advocate. Johnny Prescott turned up. I do not know if he had a Jag with him.

Hoddle took over Chelsea for 1993–94. In his first season, the club finished fourteenth but Hoddle took them to their first FA Cup final in twenty-four years. The problem was they played a Manchester United side on their way to the Double. The United of a decade ago were a more formidable side than the 2003–04 'Beckhamless' model. Only two players remain from that side: Keane and Giggs. Ferguson's class of '94 included Mark Hughes (who was soon to join Chelsea for a last hurrah), Andrei Kanchelskis and the incomparable Cantona. Looking at their line-up and that of the Chelsea squad, which included Sinclair, Newton and Kjeldbjerg, I think Chelsea did well to only lose 4–0.

Season 1994–95 was hardly an improvement. Chelsea finished 11th (there's something about that number). Millwall knocked them out of the Cup at the Bridge 4–5 on penalties – Millwall were the last team other than Manchester United, Newcastle or Arsenal to beat them in the FA Cup. Chelsea figured in the European Cup-Winners' Cup that season for the first time since 1972–73. By virtue of United landing the Double, Chelsea were handed a passport to Europe. At that time, only three foreign players were allowed to play per team in the competition, which caused some selection problems. Graham Rix became the oldest player in the history of Chelsea when he made his debut as a sub in the home leg of the 4–2 victory over Viktoria Zizkov. Graham was 37 years and 11 months old at the time. They went out in the semi-final 3–4 to a powerful Real Zaragoza side that included Gus Poyet.

IN MY TIME OF DYING

Unspeakable nostalgias were triggered by Harding's death. It was difficult to read anything not written in the suspect, maudlin tones that the tabloids used to describe the ambiguous power of Matthew's passing. He dominated the media at the moment of his death more than ever. Their coverage was conformist and bland. Indeed, the press collaborated on a revisionist rehabilitation of the complex relationship that Matthew had with Ken Bates with Old Money v. Les Arrivistes.

Harding was quickly elevated to sainthood. His role as a model father was clearly emphasised. Matthew nicknamed his son Luke 'Greavsie', after the greatest Chelsea icon of them all. The first time I saw Matthew on television was on a late-night sports show with Greaves a guest on the panel. Matthew made a crack about the Chelsea goal machine not being successful when he left the Bridge for Italy. Jimmy corrected him with a cold comment quoting his ratio of goals to appearances.

Some people said of Harding that he knew many people but that he did not have many friends, a reference to the pub full of adoring young Chelsea boys in the Imperial. To the majority of them, the sums that Harding dealt in and Abramovich deals in today are abstract, surreal. I think Bates was always shrewder than Harding: less emotional, more detatched. He survived the madness of CFC but deep down he was not a Chelsea boy. That's why the fans never chanted his name. Going home one night, shortly after the funeral, I saw a huge poster at Hammersmith Broadway advertising the latest Bruce Willis action movie of the day, *Last Man Standing*. Soon after, Hoddle was to jump ship for the England job. Then Ruud came and went in a blaze of glory. For a while, Bates was the last man standing. But the ship was going down.

Harding's life was played out in the flash-lit world of the paparazzi's cameras. He invoked two types of politics: the then-trendy Blair, Paul Weller, Pat Nevin-type of the '90s; and the politics of style: Wildean wit and aristocratic hedonism. Osgood, one-time 'King of the Kings Road', became a close friend.

Shortly before he died, Matthew made a huge contribution to the Labour Party. The helicopter owned by Aeromega had ferried Tony Blair to the Blackpool Party Conference just a few weeks before. I think he would have gone into active politics. He had abstained from 'serious' politics because he knew the time it would take to start a political career would cut deep into his Chelsea time. Who knows what the future would have held for him or Chelsea? A goal like Mutu's effort in the Watford third-round Cup replay in 2004 was his holy grail. Harding loved football

– like all the true fans, just when you think you have seen it all, your senses reel from a devastatingly magical act.

We can replace heroes with scenarios of how different Harding's life might have been, if the gods, for a moment, had countenanced a betrayal of the already carefully scripted sequence of events. If Matthew had lived . . .? Chelsea Football Club was always tinged by tragedy. Chelsea fans were always gorging on the improbable, tossing out the evidence. Who would have thought that Abramovich would have arrived seven short years after the death of Harding? At the time of his death, the Chelsea team included a plethora of world-class players, a delight to watch and a subversion of fact. To a generation of fans who cut their teeth on Matalan strikers like Joe Allon and defenders like Pates, it seemed inconceivable that Gullit graced the field alongside Zola. They were the first generation of foreign superstars before Crespo, Mutu and Robben.

Most people carry a belief that a certain charmed instant in every life is possible but after that time has elapsed, one's fate is sealed for ever. Those were the days my friend, I thought they'd never end. That was a brief golden period for Harding: Gullit leading from the front, Vialli plundering goals. Matthew was assembling a collection of superstars. Then fate moved its giant hand and a Eurocopter Twin Squirrel helicopter carrying a father of five and his pals smashed into a meadow near Middlewich, Cheshire. The Hardings seemed cursed: 'Greavsie' Luke Harding was devastated by his father's death. He was convicted of hurling a beer can at an Asian woman and narrowly escaped jail. Ruth Harding remarried but her second husband died of cancer.

HARDING, VIALLI AND THE JUVENTUS CONNECTION

> So let a prince set about the task of conquering and maintaining his state, his methods will always be judged honourable and will be universally praised. The common people are always impressed by appearances and results . . .
> A certain contemporary ruler, whom it is better not to name, never preaches anything except peace and good faith, and he is an enemy of both one and the other, and if he had ever honoured either of them he would have lost either his standing or his state many times over.
>
> Niccolo Machiavelli, *The Prince*

Shortly after Matthew's death, I bought a well-thumbed paperback in

Oxfam at the World's End that dealt with the life of Gianni Angelli, Europe's most glamorous businessman and the uncrowned 'King of Italy'. From the blurb on the back of the book, it seemed to tell the story of a remarkable Italian dynasty of intrigue and alleged improprieties at the pinnacles of international finance, politics and sport. Above all, though, it was the story of a relentless drive to expand and crush the opposition. 'What's past is prologue.'

Gianni Angelli was a playboy-turned-industrialist who made Fiat Europe's leading conglomerate. They own Juventus. Gianluca Vialli was captain of Juventus that sumptuous Roman night in the last spring of Harding's life when they beat Ajax on penalties to win the European Cup. Vialli regarded the victory as their first win of the Cup.

Eleven springs earlier, Platini, Rossi, Tardelli and co. returned from the hell of Heysel with black ribbons of mourning on the handles of the European Cup. 'We do not talk about 1985 in terms of victory,' Vialli was quoted as saying at the time. Juventus is tinged by tragedy like Chelsea; both teams have torment and death in their histories. As the Juventus fans celebrated winning the Cup, the Stadio Olimpico assumed a surreal, apocalyptic aspect. Red flares like in the movie *Platoon*, fireworks and rockets glowing through the swirling smoke. The noise was overpowering; all it needed was the sound of a Huey helicopter whirring overhead. In the midst of it all stood Vialli, tears streaming down his face. Vialli, Vialli, Vialli.

It was said that Vialli wore sunglasses when training in Turin, firing in his armour-piercing volleys. James Dean wore sunglasses because, like Hudson, he was disaffected. Matthew Harding wore them because he wanted to look like Bob Dylan circa 1969. Vialli's Juventus were put in the limelight by Gianni Angelli's father Edoardo. Remarkably, he was also killed in an air crash. Edoardo was a revolutionary: it was said that 'his jackets were more interesting than his thoughts'. He accomplished the feat of taking Juventus from provincial anonymity to being one of most powerful teams in the world. Like Harding, and now Abramovich, making a team into the best was done by bestowing money, truck loads of it, into a club. The success of Juventus was a very early example of the power of money to develop the star system. Angelli simply outbid everyone to buy the best players of his day. He raided South America to buy two Argentinian stars, Raimondo Orsi and Luisito Monti – the Verón and Crespo of their day, gauchos to a man.

Apart from football, Angelli's abbreviated life was dedicated to socialising; his untimely death came because of his hedonistic streak. On the morning of 14 July 1935, he was preparing to leave the family villa situated in a Tuscan seaside enclave favoured by the rich and famous.

Angelli was scheduled to take a train to Turin but decided to stay on a few more hours to enjoy the beach and its delights. Edoardo then arranged to fly by private seaplane as far as Genoa. The plane crashed during an attempted landing and Edoardo was killed.

Harding's death over 60 years later had remarkable parallels to that of Angelli but I always thought of that last phone call he made to me. In the Oliver Stone movie *JFK*, Donald Sutherland told the investigative Kevin Costner to forget about all the baffling clues and concentrate on who stood to gain by Kennedy's death. Years later, I still try to make some sense of my friend's tragic death but it is too complicated.

FIFTEEN

BOBBY DI MATTEO'S BLUES

Sometimes I feel guilty, because I have had the fortune to do what I want to do, to earn a lot of money, to be famous and other things that my sister does not have because she is blind.

Roberto Di Matteo

'Macche!' said Campello. 'It was the Scots who invented football. They brought it to the world.'

'No,' said Mengalvio, one finger primly raised, 'there I take issue with you. In Italy, it was the English. Dr John Kiplin.' He stressed the words with a certain, narcissistic pleasure. 'Of the old Genoa, with his knee breeches, and his little white cap. They wouldn't let the Italians play for them – and they were right! Football should be an English game, a game for gentlemen, in knee breeches.'

Brian Glanville, *The Rise Of Gerry Logan*

Bobby Di Matteo, wearing Chelsea blue, racing through the Middlesbrough defence in 43 seconds to hammer in a record-breaking goal in the 1997 FA Cup final.

Bobby Di Matteo, wearing Chelsea blue, firing home the only goal of the game in the 2000 Cup final against Villa after David James had dropped the ball.

I read recently of the reformation of the Harlem Globetrotters, the wonderful exhibition basketball team of the 1970s. Chelsea fans will no doubt weep when they recall an era when a team made up of highly paid clowns, fooling about on the ball without any intention of winning the match, was considered a novelty.

Roberto Di Matteo and his fellow Euro-blues changed all that – he was already a natural phenomenon and a Chelsea legend; the club's only player to score in two Wembley finals. The least famous of the Serie A imports, Bobby was not as glitzy as Zola or Vialli but he was an unsung hero and an integral part of Chelsea's renaissance.

Bobby Di Matteo, wearing a salmon-pink jacket by Martin Margiela from the Harvey Nichols collection, watching Chelsea beat an ineffective, slothful Liverpool 2–1 in the final game of the 2002–03 season. They clinched a place in the Champions League by finishing fourth. The game was awful. Marcel Desailly dominated the proceedings, scoring a fine goal and 'old manning' Michael Owen out of any attempts on goal. The crowd were in a holiday mood, kidding themselves that fourth place in a Mickey Mouse league of only two class teams was some kind of achievement. It seemed confirmation that the Premier League was being crushed to death by its own stupidity. Bates gazed down on the Chelsea hordes. The Chelsea PR machine had milked the dull occasion for everything it was worth. Sitting next to him that warm, late-spring afternoon was Bobby Di Matteo. The biggest cheers of the afternoon (even greater than those announcing the relegation of West Ham United) were reserved for him. Bates was clever – the man on his right-hand side was the equivalent of arm candy at a premiere.

The young man looked embarrassed by it all, as if gripped with Victorian melancholia. While the crowd chanted his name, he imagined another warm English afternoon six springs before, when his savagely struck shot whistled into the Middlesbrough net as most of the crowd were still finding their seats. Roberto Di Matteo – how Chelsea could have used him that day. Their lightweight midfield struggled to contain the Red axis of Steven Gerrard and Danny Murphy with his Hoxton fin haircut. Di Matteo gave Chelsea another dimension: he possessed that liberating lack of self-consciousness necessary for genuine stardom. He was a marauder, capable of turning a game with his ferocious shooting power or his eye for a chance. Gus Poyet scored vital goals in his spell at Chelsea but his contribution to the engine room was negligible and his tackling non-existent. The Uruguayan had a heroic but fragile talent. Di Matteo was the powerhouse, playing mainly on the left side of midfield, the problem area of modern football. His darting runs and first-time incisive through balls lit up games. Gullit used him to gallop from deep, to punch holes in the defence. Lampard plays a similar role today to great effect. I notice he plays further infield for England than where Ranieri employed him to play. The Chelsea role fitted Frank like a pair of battered old Church's brogues.

IMMIGRANT SONG

The Italian-born Bobby was someone who had known adversity and fought hard to overcome it. He had experienced racial abuse as he was growing up in the German-speaking area of Switzerland, where he spent the first 23 years of his life. His immigrant father worked in a steel factory, going to Italy only for family holidays, to a place near Pescara. Roberto learnt German as well as Italian but he grew up with Italian culture; an Italian mentality was soon ingrained in him.

Times were hard for the Di Matteo family. To make things worse, Bobby's sister Concetta was blind. The olive-skinned boy started playing for Schaffhausen, a country side, where he encountered similar racism to that experienced by the young black Chelsea players Canoville and Keith Jones in the early '80s. Roberto played for two seasons at Schaffhausen before a serious ankle injury wrecked his third. FC Zurich took a gamble with him and he repaid their faith in him by scoring six goals from midfield in thirty-odd games. He was soon transferred to SC Aarau and then a dream move took him to Italy to play for Lazio.

His family longed to move back to Italy, but when they arrived, Di Matteo's troubles began. The Czech disciplinarian Zdenek Zeman ran the Stadio Olimpico in Rome like a legionnaire's bootcamp. Zeman was a cross between Alex Ferguson and Ronnie Kray, and was famous for his psychotic rages. He was certainly a different character from Sven, who was later to manage Lazio. Zeman's game plan was based on strength and stamina. Roberto's natural attacking instincts were curbed and he was encouraged to play deeper and not to venture forward.

The then Italian manager, Arrigo Sacchi, noticed the swashbuckling style of the young Di Matteo, though, and rewarded him with his first cap for the Azzurri in his debut season for Lazio. (Zola rated the obsessive Sacchi as the best manager he ever played for.)

Bobby was soon on a collision course with Zeman after missing training at Lazio following an international. Zeman openly criticised his midfielder in the Italian newspaper *Corriere dello Sport* and the volatile Lazio fans took umbrage.

Certain elements of the Lazio support made the Headhunters look like a bunch of daisies. They are probably best remembered for displaying a banner in memory of the indicted war criminal Arkan (whose real name was Zeljko Raznatovic) in a home game against Bari. The banner –

reading 'Honour to the Tiger Arkan' – was displayed soon after he had been machine-gunned down in a Belgrade hotel.

Lazio star Sinisa Mihajlovic, who once scored a superb free kick at Stamford Bridge during the Champions League, wrote an obituary in a Belgrade newspaper for the 'Tiger'. Patrick Viera complained that Mihajlovic had called him a 'black monkey' during the Champions League game against Arsenal. When Chelsea crushed Lazio 4–0 in the Champions League, Sinisa was sent off for two bookable offences: stamping on Mutu as he lay on the turf and later spitting into his ear. After the match, Lazio supremo Roberto Mancini described him as 'a nice man who doesn't normally do that sort of thing'. Mutu's form dipped around then.

Di Matteo's home was attacked by Lazio Ultras and his entry phone and postbox were smashed by the mob. Soon he became the victim of the 'boo boys' and their hazy allegiance to right-wing politics. Rumours were rife in the Milanese press of spats in nightclubs and a long-running feud with Billy Costacurta (who picked up another winners' medal for AC Milan when they beat Juventus at Old Trafford). The Italian men's fashion magazine *L'Uomo Mondo* sang Di Matteo's praises, featuring him as one of the best-dressed footballers in Serie A. Bobby was surrounded by fauxmosexuals and young models whenever he ventured out to sample the nightlife in Rome.

The pressure on Di Matteo was immense. He was looking for a way out of the straitjacket of his light blue Lazio shirt. At the time, no playing Italian international had ever left the country. There was simply no reason for an Italian to leave home: the money was much better, the football more intelligent, in addition the weather, the food, the clothes, the cars and the women were all immeasurably superior. The Italians, we hear and read so often, have everything we don't. For a superstar player like Roberto, a transfer to rainy London was an allegorical punishment from Dante: 'Thou shalt forsake the land of the olive, the cappuccino and the Armani for the unknown' – the rain, the dirty pavements, fat yobs in Burberry baseball caps. Bobby Di Matteo was determined to leave his mark, though.

Di Matteo's first goal for Chelsea was strangely enough scored against Bryan Robson's Middlesbrough in a Premier League game on a hot August night in 1996. It came near the end of a dull match only enlivened by Bobby's low 25-yard drive. His first game had been a few days earlier in a tedious 0–0 draw with Southampton. Di Matteo had made the tabloids for the wrong reasons that game, by scrawling an obscenity on a young Southampton fan's hat.

JOHNNY FOREIGNERS

The Italian invasion of London was initiated by Ruud Gullit, who was enticed to Chelsea from Sampdoria, where internal politics and a nagging injury were bringing his stupendous career to a premature end.

Within a year, he was player–manager of Chelsea – a replacement for Glenn Hoddle, who left the Bridge after his spell of seagull management to coach England. Spraying 50-yard passes around and generally eliciting a brand of football not seen at the Bridge since the Rat Pack were in their prime, the Surinamese superman was soon able to lure Gianluca Vialli from Juventus. Vialli was the first Italian player of any real standing to succumb to London. At that stage, Vialli had seemed to abandon himself to his own self-image. Another player on Ruud's shopping list was Parma's Gianfranco Zola but first he purchased the stylish Di Matteo. Roberto was looking for a new start both personally and professionally, and joined the Blues for £4.9m in the summer of '96.

The previous season, Chelsea had reached the FA Cup semi-final before bowing out to Manchester United (having beaten Newcastle in the third round, albeit on penalties, they beat QPR, Grimsby and Wimbledon on their way to Villa Park, always a graveyard for Chelsea's Cup hopes). During the game, Gullit headed Chelsea in front and that is how it stayed till the second half. Beckham, who had a normal hairstyle then, was just starting to get noticed for United. The future England captain had been contained by the Chelsea back Terry Phelan, another former Wimbledon player. However, Phelan tore a muscle and Beckham took full advantage to set up an equaliser for Andy Cole. Four minutes later, Craig Burley inexplicably tried to turn the ball back to the Chelsea keeper Hitchcock (why exactly he did this remains a mystery) and like the unfortunate Dale Jasper after the Sunderland debacle, his career never really recovered from it. Beckham intercepted and raced through to score the winner.

A year later, Chelsea were back at Wembley with the *carabineri* of Di Matteo, Zola and Vialli against Middlesbrough. The Smoggies also included two Italians in their line-up: Ravanelli and Festa.

Chelsea's passage to Wembley had been relatively smooth. Wimbledon had been crushed 3–0 in the semi-final with Zola scoring a memorable goal. In the fourth round, Chelsea appeared to be going out being 0–2 down at half-time to Liverpool. This was only a few months after the death of Harding and the crowd were feeling brittle. Frank Sinclair gifted the Reds their first goal. He completely mistimed his jump to clear a cross and Robbie Fowler side-footed home his 21st goal of the season.

Fowler was at his peak around then. Stan Collymore doubled

Liverpool's lead after a ball from Zola, of all people, was miscontrolled by Eddie Newton in one of his idiosyncratic moments. Stan 'the Man' dispossessed him before racing through to score. (The week I wrote this both Sinclair and Collymore were front-page news for different reasons.) McManaman and Fowler both missed further clear-cut chances which would have put the game beyond redemption. The Chelsea players were listless but Gullit made a match-winning decision to bring Mark Hughes on and switch Di Matteo to mark John Barnes. Barnes was coming to the end of his career but was still a hugely influential player. He had run the first half with a textbook display of midfield play, Scott Minto allowing him far too much room. In the second half, Bobby operated in a similar position to that of Claude Makélélé after he joined Chelsea from Real. Roberto was not an eye-catching player like Hudson or Hoddle – running deep from midfield, spraying passes and supporting everyone was his forte – he just had that priceless knack of finding space and doing the simple thing, efficiently and quickly. Hughes was Liverpool's nemesis – the Scouse defence was nervous of the Welsh Genghis Khan and dropped deeper to regroup. The great Liverpool side of the Shankly days always made a point of holding the edge of the box but against a team with the firepower and midfield energy of Chelsea, it proved suicidal. Hughes had sustained an ankle injury in a 1–0 League victory over Liverpool a few weeks before. The match-winning goal on a bitter afternoon had been slotted home by Bobby Di Matteo.

Within seconds of being on the field, Hughes caught Liverpool defender Mark Wright with a shuddering challenge. The late Ian Hutchinson could not have made a more dramatic impact. A bell ringer, I think they call it in rugby league. Hughes always played for the shirt; now it was blue with a logo for Coors. Within a further three minutes, Hughes scored a fabulous goal, pulling down a cross from Steve Clarke and swivelling to bullet past David James. The Bridge caught alight; it was a classic Mark Hughes goal. The fans in the stand named after their recently deceased hero were on their feet. They did not sit down again for the rest of the game.

On the hour, Hughes brushed Barnes aside to feed Zola. The softly spoken Sardinian scored instantly with a glorious dipping volley. With that goal, Zola claimed his place amongst the all-time Chelsea elite. He scored 80 goals but that was the best of a wonderful lot. What Abramovich should really be doing with his billions is building a time machine for Zola and Hughes. Some *Back to the Future* deal.

The third goal was the Azzurri in full force: Zola again to Dan Petrescu, whose raking pass picked out Vialli running alongside Di Matteo. Before the square Liverpool defence could recover, Vialli was in. He neatly skipped forward to fire low past James. Vialli plundered another goal, scoring with a downward header off his Mussolini head from Zola's impeccable free kick. The fans could not have taken any more power or poetry from the Italians. Even the hardened hacks in the press-box were speechless. Chelsea ran out 4–2 winners. Was there a better game in the '90s? Zola recalled: 'That night, I could not sleep. It was just unbelievable.'

In the next round, Gullit's men played Leicester, who gave them a fright. In between, Zola had scored the only goal at Wembley as Italy beat Glenn Hoddle's England. It was another vintage Zola goal: Sol Campbell, who tried to tackle him at the crucial moment, looked at his footwork like a dog watching a card trick. If the dummy Zola sold him was any better, Campbell would have been outside the stadium. Deary me, what a player. The Cromwellite puritans at Leicester did not take to the idea of an Italian, particularly as he wore a Chelsea shirt, scoring a winning goal against St George and spent the whole game booing the little guy.

Bobby Di Matteo, wearing Chelsea's away strip of lemon and turquoise, a confection bright enough to strip wallpaper. The yoke-style shoulder pattern was superfluous and the whole thing resembled a washing-up liquid container. Even Bobby struggled to lend it any fashionability. He then put Chelsea ahead when he raced through the left-hand channel to fire past the American keeper Kasey Keller. Bobby Di Matteo had a hand in Chelsea's second goal, carving out a chance with Petrescu for Hughes to smash home. Hughes had discovered the fountain of youth somewhere in the car park at Stamford Bridge and splashed around in it all season. In a game marred by crowd trouble (rare in those times), Chelsea looked to be in an unbeatable position but Leicester, managed by the rising force of Martin O'Neill, scored twice in the second half to force a replay. Leicester's equaliser in the dying minutes was a bizarre own goal by Eddie Newton, who, under no pressure, steered a Garry Parker free kick into the Chelsea net. A controversial Frank Leboeuf penalty, given by referee Mike Reed, settled the replay but Chelsea were lucky to sneak through. Leboeuf was to spend most of his Chelsea career babbling about something but he could strike the ball wonderfully.

Portsmouth was the next stop on the run to Wembley – another hazy Sunday afternoon game. Terry Fenwick managed them but Terry Venables was the supremo. My old friend came up with a bold zonal-marking plan to try to halt Hughes' and Maradona's one-time understudy. Hughes wrecked Venables' plan with an early goal. Wise made it two and then Di Matteo set his fellow countryman Zola up for the third with a powerful run and a beautiful, mathematical pass. Pompey pulled a goal back but

Wise silenced the 'Pompey Chimes' when Hughes made his second and Chelsea's fourth.

Around this time, Gullit was keen to bring the Italian captain, Paolo Maldini, from AC Milan to the Bridge to link up with his compatriots Zola, Vialli and Di Matteo. AC Milan had just bought the Dutch international Winston Bogarde, of whom great things were expected. The impossibly good-looking Paolo would have been a sensation – instead, Chelsea had to make do with Sinclair and eventually ended up with Bogarde.

THE RUUD BOY: THE GULLIT YEARS

> They have told me that I was getting too much attention at Chelsea Football Club. Chelsea were becoming Gullit – that's what people have told me. It was the same situation with Matthew Harding: the scenario developed and people have told me that Harding became too popular; even after his death they would sing his name.
>
> Ruud Gullit

Gullit's short spell at Chelsea coincided with Bates' most successful period as chairman. Ruud, like Norma Desmond in *Sunset Boulevard*, grew too big for his epic drama and was unceremoniously sacked in February 1998. At that time, Chelsea were second in the Premiership and favourites to win the European Cup-Winners' Cup. Gullit had been runner-up to Cantona as Player of the Year in 1995–96, his first season in England. It was a platinum era compared to the decades of failure that had preceded it.

I was never clear why he was sacked. Bates stated that it was over his wage demands and later called him 'a part-time playboy manager'. Then we had all that nonsense about 'netto' trotted out by Mellor and his ilk. It was the beginning of the end for Bates, in my view, when he aced Gullit. If he had stayed, Chelsea would have won the big prizes and maybe their finances would have improved. Mr Abramovich's euros would not have been required.

Gullit was more than a footballer: his appeal was massive. Intelligent, articulate and stylish, his glowing white teeth and beefcake physique belied the fact that at his peak he was one of the greatest players of all time. His greatness came from the fact that he was never sated. No victory was too small; no victory, whether it be Euro championship or European Cup, was large enough to satisfy him.

Born in September 1962, he was registered with the name Rudi Dili, his mother's surname. Ruud was brought up in the Jordaan, the Jewish district of Amsterdam and one of its oldest areas. It's not named after our favourite celebrity model but is a Dutch version of the French word *jardin*. It was a colourful, pleasant environment, home to many artists, actors and musicians, not unlike Chelsea in the '20s. An only child, Ruud grew up kicking a ball with his childhood friend, Frank Rijkaard, who became another legend and ended up managing Barca. Ruud was signed as an amateur by DWS Amsterdam (who were last heard knocking Sexton's Blues out of Europe) and later joined FC Haarlem. It was for them he made his debut at centre-half just ten days short of his seventeenth birthday. Ruud was the youngest player to kick a ball in first-class football in Holland. Within a year, he was switched up front and scored 14 goals as Haarlem romped to the Second Division title. The Surinam superman was by now sporting his world-famous dreadlocks and was voted player of the division. It was the first of a truckload of honours that made him the Audie Murphy of football (Murphy was America's most-decorated soldier in the Second World War). By this time, he was a transfer target for Arsenal and John Neal wanted to sign him for Boro. In one of our first meetings prior to his acceptance of the Chelsea job, John Neal told me that young Ruud was one of the players he wanted to bring to London. The other board members dumbly stared at him. It was just unheard of to try to sign foreign teenagers. Before anything could develop, Johan Cruyff snapped him up for Feyenoord. Johan prepared Ruud for the hardships that came with the terrority of being the world's greatest player.

In 1985, Gullit left Feynoord to join the gritty PSV Eindhoven – not before he helped Cruyff's team win the League and Cup Double. In Ruud's first season, they won the League. Despite playing as sweeper, he managed to score 24 goals. He was that good. The next season, he joined AC Milan for 17 million guilders – don't ask me how many euros that is. The transfer was arranged personally by Silvio Berlusconi, the president and owner of the club. Silvio, also known as Il Cavaliere, has risen to become Prime Minister of Italy and President of the European Union. He gets to hang out with Tony Blair and the gang. As an entrepreneur, he made all the other movers and shakers in the Premier look like *EastEnders'* Ian Beale. Silvio had made the leap from cruiseship singer to billionaire around the time Ruud was starting out in Holland, launching his career with property development before branching out into television, advertising, publishing, supermarkets and football. Like Bates and Abramovich, the Berlusconi phenomenon always attracted controversy. Conflicts of interest, an aborted corruption trial and several political gaffes have left him with as many enemies as friends. There was no doubting his love of football, though, and he immediately set up a famous, enduring team with Gullit at the hub. Milan were almost bankrupt and hadn't won a major honour for 14 years but Berlusconi quickly assembled a tremendous side. In an Abramovich-style operation, he signed Ruud's boyhood pal Frank Rijkaard and perhaps the greatest striker to walk the earth, Marco Van Basten. It was a confection made in heaven. The exuberant Milan side dominated Europe; they were literally years ahead of their time. The Italian side could be best described as a fusion of the Dutch tactical all-out attack and the Italian pressing game. Claudio Ranieri tried to refine the pressing game at Stamford Bridge with mixed results.

Marcel Desailly was another stalwart of the Milan side. In those times, he was a midfield player. As his career wound down at Chelsea, some of his latter performances attracted criticism. Marcel gave Chelsea some great service and made other lesser talents (like Terry) look better than they were. The Desailly of a decade before, though, was just superb; he was on a different level.

In Ruud's first season at Milan, he helped them take the title, clinching it with a famous win in Naples over Diego Maradona's team. Diego scored with one of his special free kicks (the knack of which he passed on to his little friend Zola). Ruud's winning goal clinched the title, though. The last time I saw Maradona was on an Italian cable show. He was wearing an Osama Bin Laden T-shirt and smiling a great deal. His health then deteriorated.

Gullit was voted the World and European Player of the Year in 1988. In the next season, he scored nine goals in twenty-nine Serie A games and the following season he scored eleven in twenty-eight games. The icing on the cake, though, was a 4–0 European Cup final win over Steaua Bucharest, Ruud and Van Basten notching two goals apiece. A terrible knee injury nearly wrecked his career the following season. He only managed two starts in Serie A, scoring once. He did play in the European Cup final in Vienna against Benfica, though. His boyhood pal, Frank Rijkaard, scored the only goal of the game as AC retained the Cup.

They crashed out of Europe the next season to a Chris Waddle goal, scored in Marseille. Soon, Waddle's old singing partner from the 'Diamond Lights' tour, Glenn Hoddle, was to come into Ruud's life as Chelsea rescued him from Italy. Things had started to go sour for him quickly. He enjoyed the support of Berlusconi but fell out with the new coach, Fabio Capello. The pouty Capello, once seriously linked to the Chelsea job, had replaced Arrigo Sacchi, who, like Hoddle, was off to manage the national side. Worries over fitness and rumours about his crumbling second marriage added to the Rasta man's woes.

2FAST 2FURIOUS

Ruud eventually quit the bustle of grimy Milan for the sanctuary of Genoa and joined Sampdoria. Away from the intrigue and wearisome politics of Capello's side, his health and fitness slowly returned. Ruud had a great season at Sampdoria, the high spot being a 3–2 victory over Milan. Ruud shot the winner with an acrobatic volley, one of the most viciously struck drives ever seen anywhere. They used to run it a lot on Channel 4's much lamented *Football Italia*. Gorgeous.

Milan, realising they had got it wrong, tempted Ruud back for a few months. The old adage of 'never go back' is never truer than in football. Like the unhappy return of Hudson and Osgood to Chelsea, some things are best left. Go, before you break my heart.

Ruud returned to the tranquillity of Sampdoria. His knee trouble flared up again and he quit international football. The tragic death of Sampdoria's chairman Paolo Mantovani hit him very hard – another strange parallel to Harding's death a short while later. I remember Ruud talking about the double grief he was feeling at Matthew's funeral.

Ruud's love affair with Italy ended under the hideous combination of continual media pressure, a failed marriage and his serious injuries. When Hoddle asked him to come to Chelsea, he saw it as a way out of the emotional, mental and physical turmoil.

THE CLOSEST THING TO CRAZY: THE VIALLI YEARS

> His situation is like driving a Formula One car without a licence.
>
> Fabio Capello, the Milan coach at the time of Vialli's appointment

Bobby Di Matteo, wearing a chocolate-brown overcoat and cashmere black scarf, heading for the exit as Arsenal celebrate their 1–2 League victory at Chelsea on a bitter February afternoon in 2004 – a victory that put Arsenal nine points ahead of Ranieri's side. How Chelsea could have done with Bobby in midfield that day, as Arsenal, with Viera dominating, recorded another victory over them.

It reminds me of a Russian called Grigory Potemkin, a favoured minister of Catherine the Great. In 1787, he prepared for her visit to the Crimea by building a group of model villages where the new residents, press-ganged in by Potemkin, could be shown as jolly peasants. When Catherine went walkabout, the peasants made a great fuss about how happy they were. That's where we get the phrase 'Potemkin villages', used to describe something that is not what it seems.

So, now Chelsea Village becomes Potemkin's village – the players just another bunch of misfits like the Russian serfs. The phonelines for Talksport Radio and Radio 5 Live were jammed that evening by worried Chelsea fans calling for Ranieri's head. Vialli's name kept being mentioned as a replacement or as the benchmark against which future Chelsea managers were to be judged.

When Gullit was sacked, Vialli was allowed in to scoop the glory. Five trophies were won but how many of them can people recall? The European Super Cup against Madrid in Monaco, the League Cup against Middlesbrough, the European Cup-Winners' Cup and the Charity Shield along with the only trophy of any significance, the FA Cup against Aston Villa. In statistical terms, Vialli's spell at Chelsea was highly successful but a valid comparison with Gullit indicates to me that Chelsea failed to build on the incredible start he had given them. The appointment of the fifth son of a multimillionaire industrialist reminded me of the political puppets who are put in charge of a banana republic following a revolution. The military junta had ousted the leader and replaced him with a mouthpiece, a token figure, a stooge. Vialli knew his Armani from his elbow, though, and within three months of being appointed manager, lifted two trophies: first a 2–0 victory over Middlesbrough (again) in the Coca-Cola Cup, then a 1–0 win in the European Cup-Winners' Cup final. In the Coca-Cola Cup, Middlesbrough took Chelsea to extra time. Bobby Di Matteo scored a goal to maintain his Greaves-type Wembley record. The unpalatable truth was that the Middlesbrough finals were poor by anybody's standards. Ironically, their first-ever victory in a final came courtesy of a goal from on-loan Chelsea winger Zenden.

The opposition was equally weak in Europe for the Cup-Winners' Cup, Chelsea meeting Slovan Bratislava (Di Matteo opening Chelsea's account), Tromso, Real Betis and Vicenza on the way to the final – all of them minor powers in Europe. It took a superb goal from Hughes in the semi-finals to overcome Vicenza.

Zola came off the subs bench to score the only goal of the game against Stuttgart in Stockholm. It was a goal as special as the man himself. The tiny Sardinian had only been on the field for 22 seconds when he ran on to Wise's through ball to instantly smash a shot past the Stuttgart keeper Wohlfahrt.

It was amazing that Zola played at all. Eighteen days before, he had torn a muscle in his groin in a match against Liverpool. It was the sort of injury that puts a player out for anything up to six weeks. Zola bounced back, though, and Vialli gambled by putting him on the bench. On such decisions, cups are won and lost.

Vialli was born in 1964 and made his debut aged 16 for Cremona. At 20, he was signed by Sampdoria for £1.8m. Italy called him up at the age of 22. In 1991, Sampdoria won the Championship and Vialli was the top scorer in Serie A. The following season, Juventus bought him for a world-record £12.5m. Today, he would go for four times that. When he was appointed manager, I recall him saying: 'I was born to win.'

Season 1998–99 was the nearest Chelsea came to winning the title since 1955. That championship season, Tony Bennett topped the charts with a song called 'Stranger in Paradise'. Chelsea were strangers to the paradise of topping the Premier. Just before Christmas, they led briefly – the first time in nine years.

In the summer, Vialli signed Marcel Desailly, Albert Ferrer, and the ill-fated pair, Pierluigi Casiraghi and Brian Laudrup. Compare this to Gullit's acquisitions at the end of his first season: Celestine Babayaro, the Nigerian wing-back, was signed from Anderlecht along with Poyet on a free transfer, and Tore André Flo from SK Brann. Flo was snatched from under the nose of Everton for half a million. In 2000, Chelsea received £12m from Glasgow Rangers for him. It is still a record fee received by Chelsea for a player and with Abramovich's billions I cannot see anybody raiding the club for talent, as has been the case in the past. One of the criticisms levelled against Ruud was his transfer dealings.

Brian Laudrup was a fantastic player but he never settled at Chelsea and failed to sprinkle any stardust from his tiny boots. It was against FC Copenhagen in the Cup-Winners' Cup that Laudrup scored his only Chelsea goal against the side that eventually bought him. In one cameo from the game, I recall him strolling past defenders like they weren't there. Instead of cutting over a cross for Flo, he tried a delicate pass to Zola with the outside of his left foot. Zola, himself boxed in by two exhausted but desperate defenders, controlled it instantly. His cut-back centre was narrowly headed over by Flo. His passing around the edge of the area was a sheer delight. In September, a scotched Laudrup walked out of Chelsea and returned to a happy prosaic life in Denmark. He had a talent nobody was able to tame and was a tremendous loss to Chelsea at that stage.

Lazio tried to buy Di Matteo back. The season for Chelsea started badly, losing 2–1 to Coventry (they didn't lose another Premier game till the following January). For the first time in their history, Chelsea fielded a team of internationals. The team was almost completely European and had cost nearly £35m to build – the wage bill was over a million a month. Desailly had a nightmare debut and gifted Coventry both their goals, scored by Dion Dublin and Huckerby. No matter who puts on that blue shirt and defends for Chelsea, they all at some point look weak and vulnerable. Desailly was the defender of the World Cup but at Highfield Road he had a mare. He played the ball long when he needed to keep it short, he tried to make fine touches but ended up hitting the ball too hard. He pushed hard when he needed to play slow.

Chelsea beat Real Madrid in the Super Cup held in Monaco. Plenty of caviar munchies. When Osgood and the lads lifted the Cup-Winners' Cup in 1971 against the same team, the competition was unheard of. In that Super Cup, though, played on a Friday night in August 1998, 20 of the players involved in the match had just played in the World Cup (won by Mr Leboeuf's fellow countrymen). It was, however, a profoundly terrible match. The only high spot was some brilliant footwork by Zola that set up a goal from Poyet. Madrid treated the game as an exhibition match and a weekend away in a playboys' playground. A long-range free kick effort from Roberto Carlos was their only decent attempt on goal. The press and propagandists built up the three trophies in less than six months but in essence the Super Cup was as meaningless as the Members Cup finals at Wembley.

The Dutch maestro replaced the sacked Dalglish as manager of Newcastle. The only reason he took the job was to get some revenge over Chelsea but it didn't work out for him. The man born Rudi Dili lived his entire life on the outside, like a Richard Rogers building. Gullit brought some good players to Newcastle, though – Dietmar Hamann and Kieron Dyer. I always figured that a campaign was orchestrated by sections of the media to drag his name through the mud and boost Vialli's profile even higher. Clearly, Ruud would not have lost the contract talks unless he was betrayed by his own soldiers. Chelsea said Gullit was sacked because he asked for £2m netto. Looking at the pool of eastern European money that Abramovich squandered in his first few months on has-been players, crocks, misfits and ludicrous wages, it looks like the bargain of the century.

I only ever met him once. It was at the flower stall in Sloane Square on Christmas Eve 1997, shortly before he was sacked. He was experimenting with different haircuts then but he was still the most recognisable man on the Kings Road, casually dressed in a leather coat, grey shirt and dark trousers. I introduced myself to him as the former chairman of Chelsea and a member of the Mears family who had formed the club.

'There was a chairman before Bates?' he said. He cracked a joke about the age of his employer. I don't think he had a clue who I was but he was very affable. We chatted briefly. I congratulated him on winning the Cup and told him about my 1970 team. We were interrupted by his girlfriend,

Estelle Cruyff, the great man's niece, stunningly beautiful and laden with Harrods bags.

'Nice to meet you,' he beamed, as they disappeared into the crush outside the Tube station.

RIX'S TRIX

Pierluigi Casiraghi sustained his career-ending injury through a collision with West Ham's keeper at their home ground. Graeme Le Saux, one of Chelsea's toughest players, despite his leftie, rather fey image, was in tears when he saw the extent of the Italian's injury. Razor Ruddock, the Hammers hard man central-defender (before he became a jungle celebrity), turned away in horror. The 'Razor' scored West Ham's goal. Casiraghi never played top-class football again. He was the 'nearly man' of Italian football, always threatening but not quite fulfilling. The Jack Kerouac of Chelsea. They have a word in Italy for it: *domani*. Tomorrow, you have to wait until tomorrow. The talent of Casiraghi smouldered then died. Given the right breaks, he would have been another legend. Vialli was pinning a lot on him and Laudrup but within a few months his dream partnership had evaporated. Typical Chelsea. Then he lost his coach.

Graham Rix was charged with indecently assaulting a 15-year-old girl and drew 12 months. He ended up spending 184 days in Wandsworth prison. Rix was always a loser. He had looks, northern savoir-faire but no really outstanding talent as a player or coach. What he did have was a good reading of the game and an ability to deploy his personality in order to ingratiate himself within the football world. Nevertheless, fate rewarded him with money, fame, England caps and stature. For a time, he floated on a big bubble and could do no wrong, then one evening he met a young girl and it all went sour. Rix became a laughing stock, in a farce worthy of his namesake, Brian. Fortune granted Rix more than he dared hope for, then revenged with such perversity even his most envious enemies must have pitied him. I used to wonder what Gullit made of it all – Rix was critical of Ruud after he was kicked in the gullet.

Rix served as coach under four managers at the Bridge but had worked his way up to be the Rasta man's first lieutenant. The youth talent around at the time included Mark Nicholls, Jon Harley, Nick Crittenden, Leon Knight, Jody Morris and John Terry. Only Terry ever really established himself. Rix exuded the corporate image and I thought at one time he would get the manager's job but the poisoned chalice had already been passed to Vialli, who was swigging long and hard.

F·R·I·E·N·D·S

Bobby Di Matteo, wearing a black Armani suit, pausing to sip the last of a long line of Diet Cokes. It is the opening of his new restaurant, 'Friends', on Hollywood Road, just off the Fulham Road. A sea of Dolce & Gabbana shirts, designer jeans and hair gel. The 'friends' are clattering back the hooches. Among those present, in the ensuing palaver and feast of risotto Milanese, were Wise, Le Saux and Roberto's special pal, Lombardo. Rumours were rife that Bobby wanted to go home to try to win back his place in the Italian team. Just like Scotland, in the days of Gallacher, Italy had put an embargo on players plying their trade away from the mother country. (Zola ended up with a scant 35 Italian caps.)

In the previous season, the restaurant owner had scored ten goals from midfield, the best of which was the astonishing trajectory he put on the left-foot strike at Tottenham in Chelsea's 1–2 victory. A Sol Campbell own goal had put Chelsea in front. That year, Vialli had Bobby playing deeper in a more defensive role. It seemed a waste to me; he was most effective advancing on retreating defenders.

Friends was a good name for the restaurant. It was perhaps named after the most popular programme in the world. It was said Vialli had a collection of *Friends* DVDs in his luxury Eaton Square flat. I expect Bobby watched Aniston and co. on the expensive television set that dominated his three-bedroomed apartment on the fourth floor of the mansion block in Hyde Park. Today, football is sold like the characters in *Friends*. Lampard is the Joey Tribiani of football. The slightly dim guy with a limited range, thrust into the big time. Good looking, media friendly, always blinking at the glare of the spotlight, almost disbelieving the position he has found himself in. Joey even plays fussball with his roommate Chandler on their table soccer game. Planet football. Now, Joey's got his own spin-off show and Euro hero Frank is doing ads with Jamie Oliver.

Vialli's side was more functional than Gullit's 'lovely boys' but less exciting. Gullit was a very emotional person – when he was voted European Footballer of the Year he dedicated the award to Nelson Mandela, who was in jail at the time. I couldn't imagine Vialli doing such a thing.

Chelsea beat Spurs a few days before Christmas to go top of the Premiership for the first time ever. Late goals from Poyet and Flo were enough to overcome George Graham's side. The last time Chelsea had been top of the pile was under Bobby Campbell back in the First Division in November 1989, when the only Italian name in the line-up was Dorigo.

On the last day of January 1998, Arsenal (who else?) knocked Chelsea off the top of the Premiership. Bergkamp scored the only goal of the game from a wonderful pass from Petit, Arsenal's best player that day. The Double holders were not relinquishing their title without a fight and their mean defence gave Chelsea's attack no clear-cut chances. It was only their second defeat in thirty-three games.

Bobby Di Matteo, sporting a platinum blond haircut at Sheffield Wednesday in the fifth round of the Cup. He came on as sub and headed the only goal of the game five minutes from time. Perhaps the defenders were still in shock after seeing the colour of his hair.

Di Matteo, wearing soft-blue boots and looking like Billy Idol circa 1985. Billy Idol once formed a band called Chelsea. I used to see him on the Kings Road when he lived near the Pheasantry. Nobody else had hair like that till Di Matteo copied him.

Di Matteo was sent off at Old Trafford in the 0–0 draw in the sixth round of the Cup. He had been booked earlier for an innocuous tackle on Beckham and during injury time in the first half, he walked after a lunge on Scholes.

Dwight Yorke, the father of Jordan's first son, was at that time probably the quickest striker in the game. He scored twice in the replay to dump Chelsea out of the Cup. Beckham incensed the Chelsea fans by his sniggering celebrations of Yorke's second goal. The cult of Beckham was already going into overdrive with a deluge of publicity. I recall Yorke made some risible comment that the celebration was for Beckham's recently born son Brooklyn. Brooklyn Bridge. Wayne Bridge.

Throughout the game, Beckham and his wife were vilified by the Chelsea enthusiasts in the Matthew Harding Stand. The orthodoxy of their sex life and the parentage of Brooklyn were amongst their insinuations. Ferguson had a drink with Vialli after the game. Around that time, Bates was allegedly in a dispute with then United flexecutive Peter Kenyon over television money.

Chelsea had little punch up-front and were very reliant on Di Matteo to chip in with vital goals. If Hasselbaink had been on the books, Chelsea might well have won the title. Four days after Chelsea's Cup exit, West Ham came to the Bridge and wrecked Chelsea's chances of winning the Premier. Zola had threatened to have a similar Billy Idol haircut if Chelsea won the title. The hairdressers of Knightsbridge could relax, though. A quarter of an hour from time, the late Marc-Vivien Foe's powerful header was blocked by De Goey but Paul Kitson clipped home. Flo overelaborated a couple of chances and as Alan Hansen later commented on television: 'Chelsea passed the ball to death.' West Ham had a useful side with Rio Ferdinand, Di Canio (injured that day) and the impressive Frank Lampard, in his earlier incarnation in blue and pink, who subdued

Bobby Di Matteo all match. It was a shattering blow, though, to Vialli – as devastating to the Blues as Nevin's goal back in April '86 had been to West Ham's title challenge.

The season slowly faded out. Di Matteo scrambled the winner at Charlton to keep their hopes flickering but too many games were drawn. Leicester City was a classic example. With Zola (then the most fluent striker in the Premier) in magical form, Chelsea were cruising 2–0 up with only eight minutes left. Martin O'Neill gambled big time. He pushed on the burly Ian Marshall and went for route one. Le Saux had been left on the bench at the start of the game as Vialli went for three at the back, his thinking that Leicester would go for a passing game. Albert Ferrer, who had an excellent match, was replaced by central defender Duberry. Vialli hoped to counter the threat of Marshall. It backfired badly as Duberry conceded an own goal under the pressure. Then Leicester's Guppy cut in from the left to strike an extraordinary equaliser. Chelsea's last chance of the title in the twentieth century disappeared as the ball flew high into the net. Both Leicester goals came from the wide area Ferrer had defended so well earlier in the game. Vialli later admitted he had made the wrong substitution.

Worse was to follow, with Real Mallorca putting them out of the European Cup-Winners' Cup. It was the last one ever and Chelsea wanted to retain it. Danni had put Mallorca ahead at the Bridge before substitute Flo levelled. Wise was involved in a flare-up with Marcelino and was accused of biting him. In the return, Wise was baited by the Mallorca fans who barked like a dog every time he had the ball. Chelsea lost 1–0; they were little more than an unruly rabble. They conceded an early goal after a criminal defensive lapse and Wise's misery continued when, in the last minute, he headed wide of an open goal. It was a dreadful miss, the Chelsea skipper contriving to head wide when it looked easier to score. The only worse miss by a Chelsea player was Webb at Orient when Chelsea crashed out of the FA Cup in the '70s. Wise's miss summed up Chelsea's imploding season. He was quoted as saying that if he had scored, he would have run to the corner flag, got down on all fours, cocked his leg and pretended to urinate on it. That about sums up the mentality of the man. Wise had a disgraceful season, even by his standards, being sent off a record four times. In those days, he seemed entirely made of blue touch paper: once lit, stand back.

Chelsea ended the season with no silverware. Di Matteo was desperate for Chelsea to get to the Cup-Winners' Cup final as they would have played his old side Lazio. They broke some Chelsea records, though. To lose only three League games all season was a great performance. They also broke our record for best defensive performance over a season, conceding just 29 goals (previous bests were the 34 conceded in 1906–07 and the 42 conceded in 1970–71, the year we won the European Cup-Winners' Cup for the first time).

The great news was Chelsea were back in Europe, in the Champions League.

MILLENNIUM

Vialli started to lose the plot around then. In the summer, he purchased Chris Sutton for a staggering £10m. Didier Deschamps joined from Juventus for £3m and Carlo Cudicini joined from Serie C side Castel Di Sangro as a back-up keeper. Amongst the fans, there was justifiable brouhaha that this would finally be the season that the title came to Chelsea.

The 1999–2000 season started with Vialli in a subdued mood, restrained and intense, not the cut-throat that had lifted the European Cup a few years before. Now, he was mealy mouthed, still wearing that old grey jumper and a striped tie with a huge Duke of Windsor knot. I used to see him driving his green Merc down the Kings Road, Simply Red blaring, his huge forehead corrugated with worry lines.

Nelson Bunker Hunt, who cornered the world's supply of silver in the late '70s, once declared that, 'A billion dollars isn't what it used to be.' Way to go Bunker. Are you taking notes, Roman? When I watched Chris Sutton struggling to control the simplest of through balls in one of his early games in Blue, it crossed my mind that £10m isn't what it used to be.

A few days after Christmas and a few days before the end of the millennium, on 29 December 1999, Chelsea beat Sheffield Wednesday 3–0 on a freezing night. It had been a mediocre Christmas: an epidemic of flu had hit the country, on television there were four episodes of the *The Vicar of Dibley* and the cobbled-together tent that was the Millennium Dome was about to open to universally bad reviews. Words like overblown, intellectually feeble and overpriced were used – it could have applied to the state of Chelsea Football Club. Amongst the goalscorers was striker Tore André Flo. He had a lanky, loping style and looked like a member of the '80s band A-ha (not the good-looking one, though). He rode the same wheel of fortune that Gudjohnsen currently spins. They were both Nordic – great players but, in my opinion, somehow never quite achieving the success their talent warrants.

The high spot of the season was when Chelsea demolished United 5–0 at the Bridge. Didier Deschamps had his best game for Chelsea, masterminding the epic victory which was United's first defeat in twenty-nine Premiership games spanning ten months. Manchester never really recovered from Poyet's goal in the first thirty seconds and after fifteen minutes Sutton made it two. It was one of the few goals he scored for Chelsea but it was a vintage Lawtonesque header. He rose majestically between Neville and Jaap Stam to thump Albert Ferrer's cross home. With Neville fully occupied by Zola's box of tricks, the ex-Barca back was free to pepper the Reds' box with those crosses that the ex-Blackburn striker thrived on. Nicky Butt was sent off for lashing out at Wise after he had pinched him.

Second-half goals from Poyet and an own goal from Berg sent the crowd wild. Morris wrapped it up when he shot the fifth through the legs of the unfortunate Italian keeper Massimo Taibi. Mark Bosnich, who was to join Chelsea in January 2001, was then out of the United team. A few months before, he appeared to have it all: Bosnich was hailed as the natural successor to Peter Schmeichel. He had rejected Vialli's old side, Juventus, to join United. He fell foul of Ferguson, though, and eventually came to the Bridge. It seemed a great move for him. Chelsea were just like him – brash, ambitious and hungry to win things.

Bosnich found it hard to stay out of trouble. The Chelsea fans always had a soft spot for him after a controversial clash whilst playing for Villa against Tottenham striker Jurgen Klinsmann. Bosnich was fined £1,000 and found guilty of misconduct the following year after angering Spurs fans by *Sieg Heil*ing them at White Hart Lane.

Further controversy followed when a tabloid leaked stills of a sex video showing him and an unidentified woman. The tape was found in the rubbish bin of his former Villa teammate Dwight Yorke, last heard putting Chelsea out of the Cup.

Bosnich's second marriage broke up around the time he joined Chelsea. His first marriage to an English girl ended after two years. Rumours abounded that allegedly the marriage had been a sham as he needed a work permit.

Chelsea's nightlife proved too much for their new custodian. He became a serial celeb dater and had relationships with television presenter Danni Behr and the model/socialite Sophie Anderton.

Bosnich's war of words with Ferguson continued. On the eve of a 0–3 home defeat a few years ago, he delivered a scathing attack on the United boss: 'If you have a fantastic horse, the jockey doesn't have to be great.' A prophetic choice of words, in light of Sir Alex's subsequent difficulties in connection with the horse, Rock of Gibraltar.

Bosnich forced himself into the Chelsea team and starred in their ill-fated UEFA trip to Israel. Bosnich had this unshakeable confidence and was looking forward to a long run in the team before he got injured in a goalless draw at Everton. Cudicini grabbed his chance and never looked back. I always thought that at their peak there was very little to choose between the goalkeepers.

Bosnich was admitted to the Priory suffering from severe clinical depression after the *News of the World* revealed he had tested positive in an official FA drugs test. Chelsea sacked him and he is currently out of the game. Asked at his departure to name his worst buy, Bates named Bosnich. It must have taken a while for him to answer because he had a lot of names to choose from. For Mark Bosnich, his fine career was in tatters and his name was being so compromised that it would be hard for him to ever work again.

Speaking of tattered careers, Jody Morris had forced himself into the Chelsea team and was playing his best football in a blue shirt. Butch Wilkins had taken over Rix's duties at the Bridge. Ray had jumped at the chance of working in the big time again. After being sacked by Kevin Keegan from a similar role at Fulham and an excruciatingly embarrassing spell at QPR, he was attempting to deal with the thought that he may have shot his load.

Hindsight is a great thing but looking back you could say that Rix was the power behind Vialli's throne. Would Chelsea have won the title if Rix had stayed out of prison? His highly valued tactical skill was missed, that was for sure.

CHELSEA IN THE LEAGUE OF CHAMPIONS

The first match in the big time was a 3–0 home win over Skonto Riga which masqueraded as a qualifying group game. Sutton scored his first goal for the club and Cudicini made his debut for Chelsea in the scoreless return.

AC Milan visited the Bridge in the group stage. Flo kept Sutton out of the team. The nearest Chelsea came to scoring was when Zola hit the post. Desailly received a wonderful reception when he returned to the San Siro. Chelsea took 5,000 fans to the game and they were rewarded when Dennis Wise equalised with a fine goal which they still sing about. Bobby Di Matteo, fit after a long period off for injury, came on as sub to set up the chance.

The fine performance in Italy was marred by an awful performance in Berlin against Hertha. Sutton, who came on late in the game, won a penalty from which Leboeuf scored. Chelsea scraped home 2–0 in the second leg thanks to the highly valued Deschamps' first goal for the club; it was, curiously enough, his only goal in Europe despite his collection of honours. Albert Ferrer, another battle-scarred Euro veteran, shot the winner. Sutton was sent off in injury time to add pressure to his sticky start. It was Rix's first match following his release.

The matches against Galatasaray were both good wins. The home leg was very close and only a bold Petrescu goal separated the sides. Petrescu was probably the greatest attacking wing-back in the world around that time. Chelsea butchered the Turks 0–5 in the return game. It was the biggest humiliation that they ever suffered in Europe on their own ground. Flo, who seemed to reserve his best games for Europe, hit two and Zola chipped in with one of his specials. Wise, sporting that Keanu Reeves haircut, and substitute Ambrosetti wrapped it up. Great things were expected of Ambrosetti but he failed to establish himself in the team.

Chelsea drew Barca in the quarter-finals, then a more powerful side than they are today. In the first half of the first leg, Chelsea played their best football under Vialli and raced to a 3–0 lead. Flo, who terrorised the Spanish defence all night, scored twice. Chelsea looked booked for the semis but Barca, stung by the ferocity of the early Chelsea attacks, reorganised and came back strongly in the second half. Figo carved out a priceless away goal; Deschamps had an excellent game.

Chelsea conceded five goals at the Nou Camp, the same total they had let in when Docherty's side were bounced out of the Fairs Cup in '66. Vialli opted for a defensive approach, sending Di Matteo to play deep and surprisingly including Jody Morris at the expense of Gus Poyet. The midfielder had just scored twice in the FA Cup semi-finals to knock out Newcastle.

Chelsea bore the brunt of a tremendous opening barrage and were regrouping when Deschamps' late tackle on Rivaldo needlessly conceded a free kick. Rivaldo's shot glanced off Babayaro in the wall and flew past De Goey. Chelsea's tallest-ever keeper was stranded just on half-time when Figo jabbed home after Patrick Kluivert smashed a shot against the post.

On the hour, Flo put Chelsea back in front when Hepp, the Barca keeper, hit a poor clearance straight to him. Chelsea were seven minutes away from the semis when substitute Danni headed in Figo's precise centre. Blues defender Lambourde mistimed his clearance and it was 4–4. The closing seconds were as frenetic as any in the club's century of games. Kluivert, running amok, burst into the box and was scythed down by Leboeuf. The ball trickled into the net off De Goey's fingers but the referee had already blown for a penalty. How it could have been heard over the din was anybody's guess. Rivaldo blazed wide and the game went to extra time.

This time, he scored from the spot after Babayrao had been sent off for fouling Figo.

The term 'striping' would adequately cover the treatment Babayaro received from Figo that night. Kluivert completed the massacre when he headed in the fifth goal from Danni's excellent pass.

A few weeks later, Bobby Di Matteo scored the only goal of the game against Villa to win the FA Cup for Chelsea for the second time in three years. Ironic that the goal Roberto scored was to prematurely end his golden Chelsea career. It launched Chelsea into the UEFA Cup but in September 2000, a few months after his Wembley triumph, Roberto sustained a triple leg break against St Gallen, which was to cruelly force him to quit. Roberto's match winner was also to signify the end of the Vialli era.

Despite winning the Cup, Bates was unhappy at Chelsea's failure to qualify for the money-spinning Champions League. The youth system was only producing precocious talent. The beating Chelsea received at the hands of Barca convinced the regime at Chelsea that they were some way off superpower status in Europe. Following a catastrophic start to season 2001–02, Vialli was sacked and replaced by the fastidious Claudio Ranieri.

SIXTEEN

OUTRAGEOUS FORTUNE

'Father,' he asked. 'Are the rich people stronger than anyone else on earth?' I said, 'There are no people on earth stronger than the rich.'

Dostoevsky, *The Brothers Karamazov*

New wealth. How very, very common.

Bubble, *Absolutely Fabulous*

Zero was invented in the fourth century by the Babylonians. Mr Abramovich has nine of them in his bank balance or Abbey passbook. To the average Chelsea fan and tabloid hacks, Roman (pronounced Ro-Man) was a dream come true . . . Churchill said that Russia was a 'riddle inside an enigma wrapped in mystery'. An apt description of Chelsea in the last 100 years as well.

WHAT DID THE ROMAN EVER DO FOR US?

Apart from the sanitation, the medicine, education, wine, public order, irrigation, roads, a fresh water system and public health, what have the Romans ever done for us?

Life of Brian

Abramovich was brought up by an uncle in Komi, a Siberian province that housed the Stalinist gulags. He has always been coy about how he made so much money in such a short time. When he took over the gulag of Chelsea

Village, he got rid of Bates. Until Roman arrived, any hope of Chelsea becoming a superpower had gone into the ground with Matthew Harding. Better red than dead. If totalitarianism had not been created – and then collapsed into bread-queue chaos – the economy in Russia would not have thrown up the multitudinous oligarch. Roman cashed the old Soviet Union's state-owned assets into Premiership superstars. He:

- Spent £215 million (probably far more by the time you read this) on players in a Roman orgy of reckless rapacity.
- Saved the club from financial collapse.
- Made the future so bright you have to wear ski goggles.
- Gave Chelsea fans their pride back. (In the late '80s, comedian Harry Enfield invented a comedy character called Loadsamoney. A product of the Thatcher era, Enfield portrayed a gauche builder/wide-boy/jack-the-lad character flushed with success and black-market cash. Chelsea fans connected with the persona straight away and satirised the plight of their northern rivals (particularly Liverpool), many of whom were unemployed. He had a catchphrase: 'Shut your mouth and look at my wad.' With the Russian takeover, Chelsea fans started waving their cash at rival fans and asking them, 'Shall we buy a player for you?' (Against Fulham, who had decamped to QPR's ground, they changed it to 'Shall we buy a ground for you?')

Roman Abramovich, core shareholder of Sibneft, Russia's fastest-growing energy company, with his borderline peasant face, was at the top of the *Sunday Times* Rich List in 2004. It is said that his wealth is growing at £14 per second. The Chelsea owner was described as being worth £7.5 billion – the 22nd richest man in the whole world. Not bad for a guy who used to sell plastic ducks out of a Moscow apartment when he was a mogul-in-training. The other Romans knew something about financial excess: amongst his many depravities, Caligula would wallow in vast piles of gold coins; Nero, after Rome had burnt down, pillaged Europe to replace his lost treasures. The fiddler, as Nero was known, began building the Golden House – a folly of frescoed walls and colonnaded arcades studded with jewels, gold and ivory which was never finished. Nero committed suicide and the house was ransacked and built over. Why do I always think of Chelsea Village when I hear that story?

Why did the young man in faded jeans and a Burberry polo do all this? To find a bolthole from Putin's purge on those he deemed to have profited unduly from the collapse of Communism? To oversee more underachievement by Verón and his ilk . . .?

Abramovich's massive wealth changed the rules. It is highly possible now that Chelsea will be the biggest club in the world because they have such resources. When Chelsea were sold to 'the Man', everything changed. The game plan was to be the Coca-Cola of football. The conspicuous consumption of players angered the rest of the game; so many chairmen had malicious envy and sanctimonious comments. It was playing Monopoly with unlimited money – no matter how much you squandered, all you had to do was wait, keep playing and keep spending. How could you lose?

Something had gone, though; twenty-two years of Bates' rule had sucked the soul out of it. The joy of watching young players like the unquestioned genius Jimmy Greaves or the energetic Tommy Langley work their way up the well-trodden path from the South East Counties League to the first team and then on to success was pure. The snapshots are fading but the emotion felt when young Tommy Langley scored after coming on as sub against Birmingham in February 1975 was felt all around the 18,000 crowd. We were all family; Tom was our little brother making good. When the godlike genius of Scott Parker arrived in January 2004 – disturbingly attired in his torn jeans – it was just his first day at the office. He later joined Newcastle. The last junior of any real promise, Jody Morris, was sacked from Leeds the day I wrote this, allegedly released after turning up drunk for training. Rix's pocket playmaking prodigy was a celebrity and had long since ceased to be a starlet. The dismal glitter of fame and the pressure on a young player to succeed was never more intense; the problem was that the agenda was stardom, not Chelsea Football Club. The bloated secretariat of fame, the agents, managers, PRs, scouts, frienemies and middlemen cannot produce them fast enough. The immediate financial pressure at the club was removed but the pressure of expectation and the fear of failure was far greater than ever. Abramovich demanded trophies, *now*. Everybody in football wanted Chelsea to fail. Every player signed had to be a dud, not a stellar talent. Charlton fans jammed the phone-ins praying that Parker would languish on the Chelsea bench and his England career would stall. (He failed to make the Euro 2004 squad.) Parker not only drove Lady Penelope, he drove the south London side as well. At the end of season 2003–04, the Charlton boss, Alan Curbishley, was lamenting that the sale of Parker had cost them a Champions League slot.

THE HAPPY-ENDING MACHINE

We all like a happy ending: like in Frank Capra's *It's A Wonderful Life*. George Bailey's workplace, the Bailey Savings and Loan Company, is saved at the last moment as his friends rally round. The evil, greedy banker, Henry Potter, is denied the pleasure of bankrupting him. I could not have written a better ending to the book, or a more unbelievable scenario. Where's my hankie . . .

Of course, you can't please all the people: the Mayor of Moscow, Yuri Luzhkov, said that Abramovich 'spat on Russia by buying Chelsea'. He must have been a Spartak fan.

Bobby Di Matteo, wearing a Gieves & Hawkes business suit, Tods loafers and a Marks Autograph shirt with discreet Paisley lining on the cuffs and collar, sitting in his broker's office. The Italian restaurateur's story had a happy ending. Chelsea's pauperdom meant that they were unable to pay his £1.5 million compensation package when his career ended with a smashed leg. Bobby agreed to an issue of 7.5 million shares worth around 17p each at the time. Abramovich's takeover doubled their value and he trousered £2.6 million.

Abramovich, like Leon Trotsky, was of Jewish origin. Sad to relate but in the bad old days, the Shed's pogrom against Tottenham players and fans (because of their perceived Jewish connection) was as vicious as their early treatment of Paul Canoville. Twenty years before, a Jewish–Chelsea supremo was as unthinkable as Gullit as manager. The 'nu' Chelsea fans have now hijacked the Chelsea support. They comprise Abramovich's friends and upper-middle-class families whose sons wore the dark navy away strip and bought the Pro Evo Soccer game. The Chelsea fans were once condemned as racists but were then criticised in the media for welcoming too many overseas players into the club. Another allegation was that the common white-trash herberts who populated the terraces were now replaced by gutless, glory-seeking yuppies, who viewed an afternoon at the Bridge as the social equivalent of a visit to the Spearmint Rhino pole-dancing club – they go to the bar ten minutes before half-time or stay downstairs chatting with TV screens on in the background should Chelsea score. The club is a lifestyle accessory. To them, Chelsea is best experienced on DVD, or a download from a website . . . *Chelsea's 10 Best Goals: 2003–04*. In the '80s, the BNP did the same: they would go to Chelsea to boo the black players but they would play cards with their backs to the game.

The word 'Chelski' appeared on Alan Collis's Red Card website in early July 2003, a few hours after Abramovich and his henchmen had purchased the ground. If Alan had a royalty for every time the word was used in a headline about the club, he could probably afford his own millennium suite in the ground.

Roman Abramovich spent his match days in the upper tier, watching from his own enclosure. The only time I saw Bates and him together was when the deal was done, but even then Roman was staring ahead into the future.

Bates had cashed in his chips then and should have walked away. When the ex-United executive, Kenyon, arrived, he had his chips. When I fell on my sword after being relieved of the chairman's post, I deliberately walked away from the club. It broke my heart. You become *persona non grata* overnight whatever you do.

Bates was redundant the moment Abramovich first gazed down on the Bridge from his helicopter, like God looking down on the earth, or Zola as he looked at the ball before he took one of his effortlessly special free kicks. Bates hung around because the imbroglio of Chelsea Football Club was his life. The former owner had bestowed the mantle of saviour of the club on himself and continued to wear it. The prosaic truth was that for the patriarch, his time had come and passed. A classic case of hubris leading to nemesis.

THE RAIN (IERI) MAN

> He spent a lot of money and won nothing.
>
> Ron Harris, June 2004

Karl Marx, who lived in London for a while, said that history is men in pursuit of their own ends. The problem for Ranieri was Arsenal in pursuit of their own ends and one player in particular: Thierry Henry – the Frenchman who appeared to walk on Perrier water.

Bates fired Vialli four months after he had won the FA Cup. It was the 2000–01 season when Ranieri joined and Chelsea were lying tenth in the Premier. They ended up sixth and Arsenal knocked them out of the Cup 3–1 at Highbury. It was a pattern that was to continue for the next four seasons.

In his first two seasons, Ranieri lavished almost £42m on Emmanuel Petit, Boudewijn Zenden, Nikola Jokanovic, Jesper Gronkjaer, Frank Lampard and William the Gallas cowboy. Only the last two players have made any significant impact. (The unfortunate Mark Bosnich and Enrique De Lucas both joined on free transfers.)

Jesper Gronkjaer deserves a special mention, though. My favourite player after the departure of Le Saux was the underachieving Dane. He should be the best winger in the world. Very occasionally, he looked it, like in the epic Champions League win at Highbury. Ranieri introduced him at half-time and his ceaseless running at the yellow-carded Ashley Cole unhinged the Arsenal defence and set up Chelsea's hootenanny. Gronk was in the mould of Clive Walker; on his day, he was a match winner but only did it sporadically. Sometimes, his less-than-precision crosses would scatter the tourists on the Fulham Road. Jesper's goal against Liverpool on the last day of the 2002–03 season set up the Abramovich takeover.

A superb strike by the much maligned Dane against Monaco in the second leg gave Chelsea a lifeline they could not grasp. He received unfair criticism that night as the defence chucked away the chance of an appearance in the Champions League final. Three days later, he starred in a 1–1 draw against Manchester United at Old Trafford. If he did not intend the top corner effort in the Champions League semi, then he certainly meant the explosive volley that flew past Tim Howard in the Reds goal. I recall Kerry Dixon's goal up there in the '80s but Gronkjaer's effort was stunning. The United back four stood around like diplomats who had missed the last 'copter out of Saigon. Jesper left that summer; as Brando once said, he 'coulda bin a contender'.

I was a huge fan of the affable Claudio – I liked him from the start; a virtual unknown when he was Bates' hired help. By the time he became a victim of the politburo, he was a legend and the most popular manager in their history. The dignified Ranieri was also the most experienced manager Chelsea had ever had. Bates and his bean counter of the time, Colin Hutchinson, gave him a four-year contract at the start. At the beginning of his Chelsea career, Claudio reminded me of a character that the late comedian Andy Kaufman invented on his NBC *Saturday Night Live* show. The character was Confused Foreign Man, a befuddled, curiously accented *naif*.

I expected him to break into a version of Joe Dolce's 'Shaddap You Face' at any moment. His use of English became legendary the longer he was at the club. He enlisted the aid of Italian-speaking ex-steward Gary Staker to help with his translations. At his early press conferences, the results were often hilarious as Gary would spice up the Italian's responses. Gary was a deeply charismatic Shed Boy: Mick Greenaway reborn in the twenty-first century. It was a shrewd move by Ranieri because it gave him a direct line to the guys in the Matthew Harding Stand, the stalwart fans who hold the real power and can make or break a manager or player. By the end of his reign, the chant of 'There's only one Ranieri' had replaced the never ending dirge of 'Vialli, Vialli', featured in the earlier days. A large section of the crowd pleaded for the return of their favourite son. The ex-Juventus striker's comet had left scorch marks over the modern history of Chelsea.

Ranieri was a real renaissance man. Travelling and painting were his pleasures in life as he relaxed away from the white-hot crucible of Chelsea. His wife, Rosanna, owned two shops in his native Rome specialising in designer furniture and ornaments. In his spare time, they would trawl the antique markets in the Kings Road, Notting Hill and Portobello looking for stock as carefully as he assembled a galaxy of star players. Claudio soon fell in love with Londonium; the Ranieris moved into a luxury house in Parsons Green with a huge garden by London standards. When he wasn't relaxing in that, he was visiting the National Gallery to gaze at Van Gogh's *Sunflowers* or walking his dog, Shark.

My favourite expression of his, as he began to master the language, was his reference to 'champions'. A champion presumably was a star player. His plan was to 'do the best and mix young players with champions'.

Ranieri was brought up in the tough area of Testaccio, the son of a butcher. A staunch Roma fan, he was determined to play for his local side and at the age of 18 played for their first team as a central defender. When he quit playing (after a modest career without silverware), he started his coaching career at a regional level with Vigor Lamezia. Claudio's methodical style and watchful intelligence enabled him to quickly work his way through the divisions before arriving in Serie A with the Sardinian side Cagliari, now the home of Zola. He moved to Napoli in 1991 where he linked up with Zola and Diego Maradona. Then he took Fiorentina back into Serie A in 1993–94 and, two seasons later, he helped them win the Coppa Italia.

In 1997, he left Italy to move to Spain and take over Valencia. The Italian nurtured the young talents of Santiago Canizares, David Albelda and Gaizka Mendieta (now at Middlesbrough after an unsuccessful spell with Lazio). This was in much the same way as mediocre players like Lampard and Terry, chromosomes away from the big time, were turned into internationals and crowd favourites. The regime of behaviour and abstinence that he imposed was a lot to do with it. Claudio's success at Valencia (a Spanish Cup and Champions League qualification) laid the foundations for the two subsequent consecutive Champions League finals that the club appeared in. Valencia clinched the Spanish League in 2003–04, scooping the title from Beckham's Madrid. Ranieri rejoined them when he left Chelsea but was sacked after an unhappy spell.

Ranieri was then lured away to Atletico Madrid run by Jesus Gil, their ruthless president, who died just before Chelsea beat Leeds 1–0 in the last game of 2003–04 season. Gil was one of the most colourful characters in world football. Atletico had played second fiddle to Real since the Civil

War and Gil was determined to change that. Like Abramovich, he demanded instant success and bought some world-class players, like Paolo Future, Venables' pal Bernd Schuster and Christian Vieri (whom Chelsea almost signed). When they won a cup Double in 1996, he paraded through the streets on a white horse and bathed in champagne. Even Abramovich would find him a hard act to follow. Jesus simply could not tolerate failure and in his 15-year spell changed managers 40 times. In 1993, he used up six of them. Poor Ranieri struggled to find a blend and recapture the magic of his Valencia days, despite having the sharpshooter Jimmy Floyd Hasselbaink on the books. Jimmy joined the Blues for £15m in June 2000, a few months after Ranieri had quit the relegation-bound Madrid side. Claudio followed Jimmy into the Bridge in September.

In season 2001–02, Chelsea finished in sixth position. They won through to the FA Cup final but lost a disappointing match 0–2 to Arsenal in Cardiff. It was a match as flat and awful as the abomination that passed for the first cockney Cup final against Spurs in 1967.

> The strategy was to pick up the best players in the world but now the strategy is to reduce the salary bill and pick up good young players.
>
> Claudio Ranieri

The corporate debt was rising as the Roman manager fought to lower wages and ages. He released Frank Leboeuf and the dandy highwayman Gus Poyet. Company Sergeant-major Dennis Wise flounced out of Chelsea and joined Leicester City for £1.6m. His fractious personality led to a disastrous time and he was sacked after he broke teammate Callum Davidson's jaw. In 20 years playing, he collected 13 red cards.

Season 2002–03 saw Ranieri take Chelsea into the Champions League as they finished fourth. At last, Chelsea were trying to stabilise after nine managers in eighteen years. It was a remarkable achievement by Claudio because he hadn't spent a penny on players for 18 months, something that was to change dramatically when Abramovich's petro-dollars started pouring in. Enrique De Lucas was Ranieri's only close-season signing the year before the oligarch's arrival. The midfielder was signed from Espanyol in July 2002. He only played 20 games and at the end of the season he joined Spanish Second Division side Alaves. A legal row broke out following his departure and details of De Lucas's alleged contract were published in a writ he issued against Chelsea.

They make interesting reading, bearing in mind that this was before the 'Russian revolution' and that Chelsea's debts were mounting: an annual salary of £833,000 in the first season, rising to £875,000 for the next two years and a staggering £916,000 in the final year, plus performance-related bonuses; to this, add an appearance fee of £2,000 for every first-team game in which he played for more than 45 minutes; a housing allowance of £2,000 per month; a two-litre car provided by the club (Chelsea also picked up the tab for the running costs); and a 7.5 per cent cut of any transfer fee in any future deal. The contract went on listing private medical cover and English lessons. All this was for a player who was hardly a marquee name.

I made the point in the past that if Chelsea were to be successful, they had to replace the ageing talents of Zola and Marcel Desailly. Despite the millions spent by Abramovich in 2003–04, no player remotely near their class was signed. In the 2002–03 season both were the mainstays of Chelsea. It was Zola's last season at the Bridge. Already, he was hatching a plan to end his brilliant career on his island in the sun and play golf in the Cellino Country Club.

THE LITTLE FRIEND

Zola was nearly the best player that ever pulled on a blue shirt. Greaves would be tops, Ossie third. Hudson would figure in the top ten along with Cooke, Venables and Nevin. Any of today's heroes in it? Lampard for sure.

Zola left Chelsea at the top; his last appearance was 18 minutes against Liverpool in the match that sealed the Blues' place in the Champions League. Abramovich approached him three times to return but the little guy wanted to play for his own people and give something back. In 312 games for Chelsea, he created a unique place in the history of the club.

ABRAMOVICH'S DONKEY SANCTUARY

> Donkey Sanctuary, donkey sanctuary
> Hey, Mr Abramovich, will you buy one from me?
> Donkey sanctuary, donkey sanctuary
> They're overpriced, they're over here, they're playing for Chelsea.
>
> Attila the Stockbroker, 'Abramovich's Donkey Sanctuary'

Season 2003–04 was one of the most amazing in the club's history, and perhaps the most significant. In a few months, Abramovich took an iron grip on Stamford Bridge. In the glasnost, Chelsea's unwieldy corporate structure was gutted. The rock was pushed back to reveal the worms. Second banana, Trevor Birch, the chief executive, left for Leeds. He was quickly replaced by the Mancunian candidate Peter Kenyon – ruthless, efficient and intelligent. To lure Kenyon from Manchester United, Abramovich doubled his salary to £1.5m and gave him a £3m 'golden hallo'. One of his first quotes was about making Chelsea a sustainable success story and that how, for a club of their position and size, they had underachieved.

Bates was to quit the Bridge in the spring with journalist David Mellor's homilies ringing in his ears. Shortly afterwards, he issued a £2m writ against Chelsea, which was settled out of court. In *The Devils*, Stalin's favourite book, Dostoevsky explained why Marxism must inevitably lead to absolute dictatorship. This is what we have now – the Romanisation of football started the day he bought his first player, the naive Glen Johnson. The mechanics of Abramovich's power numbs my imagination. Vialli talked about how Abramovich would have to win the love of the people. The Russian had started his own personal 'Save the Bridge' fund.

For Signor Ranieri, it was his fourth trophy-less season. Chelsea finished second for the only time in their history. We had finished first just once and third twice but second never. Chelsea also won through to the semi-finals of the Champions League before crashing out to a fine Monaco side 3–5 on aggregate.

Looking back at Chelsea's endless, chaotic purchases of superstar flesh in those crazy days of that madcap summer, I feel that few were good value. Abramovich became an ATM as Chelsea welded on a phalanx of nomad talent to Ranieri's Champions League side.

The 29-year-old Verón signed for £15m from Manchester United with impassioned zeal. His brief was to take on the role of orchestrator of Chelsea's assault on Europe. The Argentinian midfielder's total transfer value was £77.2 million on wages of £100,000 a week. In his first League game at Liverpool, he scored and looked every inch a world-class player. Injuries limited him to only 14 appearances, which worked out at around £1 million per game. Ranieri's quixotic decision to introduce him at half-time in Monaco was the downfall of both of their careers. The difficulty with Verón is that like all genuinely creative players, he cannot entirely control what he does. Verón, like Hudson, and to a lesser extent Gazza, was an intuitive player who acted on instinct. Another problem was that he played about as often as Winston Bogarde (annual salary £2.1 million).

Claude Makélélé was billed as the 'final piece in the New Chelsea jigsaw' when he signed on the transfer deadline day from Real Madrid for £16.6m and £60k a week. The little midfielder had helped the Bernabeu club lift seven major trophies in four years. I recall his comments at the time about the fact that Beckham was earning five times as much as him in Madrid. In Monaco, though, he was involved in an unsavoury incident with their midfield dynamo Zikos. They both clashed for a ball and Zikos tamely touched the Congo-born Chelsea player on the back of the head. Makélélé went down as if hit by a baton from the riot police that infested the touchline of Stade Louis II. The merry whistle blower fell for it and Zikos walked; it was a shameless piece of play acting.

Roy Bentley commented: 'When players dive, it makes me sick. They're cheats. Makélélé's dive was pretty blatant. Zikos tickled him under the chin and he went down straight away. We had one or two players who tried it on in my day but if one of my teammates cheated to win a penalty, I felt very rough about it.'

Makélélé admitted that he found it hard to settle in London. He was quoted as saying that there was 'no comparison' between Chelsea's squad and the Real set-up.

Mutu could have been a contender, signed for £15.8m, to slide into the kaleidoscope. I do not remember a player making such an instant impact with the fans. A huge hit in Italy the previous season, he scored 18 goals for Parma in Serie A. The scandal that hit the Parmalat Group also hit the Italian club and they were forced to sell their star player. Adrian embodies the broiling energies and contradictions of the nation that produced him. An eccentric verging on genius, his father was a mathematician and his mother was a computer operator. In his early games, he kick-started the Russian revolution as he dispatched the ball with arrogant shimmies, notching four goals in his first three games. In one of his first interviews, he was on record as saying: 'Abramovich is a bit crazy as president but I don't mind that. I like such crazy people a lot.'

Mutu had the transcontinental allure of Ginola, the chiselled cheekbones of Fillery and that reckless look in his eyes that I used to see in Attenborough's stunt men. His strong physique was packed into a lean frame. Mutu was a man so in thrall of his own image that he hardly took off his Ray-Bans. The Romanian was quicker than the Aston Martin Vanquish he drove. He had a tattoo on his arm in Italian that read 'One day without a smile is one day lost'.

Right.

What was it Morrissey sang about the last of the international playboys? Mutu by anybody's standards was a playboy, knowingly pretentious and dressed to the nines, almost blinded by the flashbulbs monitoring his movement from nightclub to VIP enclosure. The exclusive No. 5 nightclub in Cavendish Square was his base. He only had an occasional glass of red wine but he smoked. Within a few weeks of his arrival, the tabloids were splashing stories of his divorce from his wife. At the height of their romance, they had been called the Posh and Becks of Romania.

Right.

Soon, he had replaced Frank Leboeuf as Chelsea's most arrogant foreigner and rumours were rife of his unpopularity with the other players. The fans loved him, though, and were soon chanting his name in a strange falsetto. Mutu played with an unusual theatrical spirit that nothing at that time could quench. He was a mixture of David Speedie, the swaggering rogue of the '80s, and the late Keith Weller of the Sexton era. Vialli was quick to compare him to Zola: 'He's a really complete player. He scores, fights, runs. He does everything.'

In essence, he was like a Russian doll – as the season grew, he got smaller and smaller and his impact diminished. No player better represented the cardboard cut-out waste of modern celebrity. They could have done with him in the home leg against Monaco as the game slipped away. To me, he was never the same player after Sinisa Mihajlovic spat on him in Rome. Perhaps it was a curse.

At the end of the season, his relationship with Chelsea had deteriorated to such an extent that he had been frozen out of Chelsea's first-team squad and was ordered to train with the youth team as a result of going AWOL. It reminded me of Sexton banishing Osgood and Hudson from training with their teammates just before it all went so terribly wrong. With soaring fees, team spirit died. McCreadie's young promotion side of the late '70s have been unfairly disregarded by posterity but no Chelsea side had greater spirit.

Joe Cole was another player who failed to deliver. When he was spinning wide onto Lampard's passes, the East End little guy looked a better player. Always on the periphery, he had to wait until mid-October for his first Premiership start. Another Hammer that took the sickle up. His early asymmetrical haircuts amused me greatly, as did the strange clothes. His website looked like a cartoon.

Popular with a crowd electrified by his skill, he was a throwback to the Hudson/Fillery/Hazard school but lacked the devilment of those three refuseniks. A romantic player in many ways, he was a statement against the corralling of football talent but was never harnessed by the Ranieri system. Sven liked him wearing the badge of St George and Little Joe was a regular – up until the Euros where he may have shoné but was ignored by Sven.

It was a schizoid season. The air was so thick with bumptious self-celebration it made my stomach churn. True Blues would say it was a success but to me it was hollow. I kept my record of being the only chairman to win a major honour in his first season in charge, something Bates and Roman failed to do. Chelsea never had a better chance of winning the Champions League. The superpowers Real Madrid (with Beckham's form collapsing as the pressure internal and external grew), AC

Milan and Juventus had all taken early baths. All that lay between Chelsea and the final was Monaco, 125–1 outsiders at the start of the competition.

In the previous round, Chelsea had knocked Arsenal out of the Champions League. It was probably the most satisfying result since Chelsea had beaten Leeds in the 1970 FA Cup final. I wondered how many of the Rat Pack would have flourished that night. One report called it ice hockey masquerading as football. Arsenal were the great tribal enemy now. In the first leg, for long periods of the game, they gave Chelsea a football lesson, stringing together immaculate triangular passes and darting runs. Hey, Bobby, what's French for sheer class? Gudjohnsen, his blond hair highlighted like some surfer dude, put Chelsea in front after an error by Jens Lehmann. Pires headed a quick equaliser after an elementary error by Terry let him in.

At Highbury, the magical Henry was subdued and carrying a back injury; Reyes (whose two goals had put Chelsea out of the FA Cup) gave them the lead just on half-time. Lampard equalised early in the second half and got stronger as the game wore on. Bridge scored near the end after a wonderful pass by Eidur.

It was Monte Carlo or bust. The first leg was disastrous. The Blues lost 3–1, the shambolic dilettante side of Chelsea was to the fore. My take on it was that the pressure that Ranieri had been under for so long finally got to him. Didier Deschamps was managing a barnstorming Monaco and shrewdly plotted Chelsea's downfall. Abramovich left his yacht parked rakishly on a meter outside. I read that the players who visited it were impressed by the miniature submarine that patrolled its hull. After the match when Chelsea were mesmerisingly bad, tears filled his eyes as he walked around the track. That is how it affects you. I was always upset when we lost a vital game, and I lost a few. I was always reminded of the great Casey Stengel who managed the hopeless New York Mets in the '60s and used to enquire of them, 'Can't anyone play this game?' I thought I had labelled that box and shut the lid but sometimes it gets to you still.

When I used to go on the trips up north as chairman, I used to hear Greenaway and the chaps sing a little ditty about northern slums. Questioning whether we should be playing (and invariably losing to) Liverpool, it went:

> In your Liverpool slums,
> You look in the dustbin for something to eat,
> If you find a dead cat you think it's a treat . . .

etc., etc. My associate, Steven Hill, who made the trip to Monaco, told me that the travelling Shed boys sang a 2004 version that replaces Monaco for Liverpool. Good to know that humour is still alive; somewhere, a skein of indelible Chelsea that runs through the fans.

The average house price in Monaco was probably in the region of Frankie's wages for a year at least. Twenty quid for a gaudy cocktail in Jimmy's bar. I had this great mental picture of the late Prince Rainier (not Ranieri with the caterpillar eyebrows; a prince among men) sitting next to Abramovich in the Royal box exchanging puzzled glances as the song rang out. Only Chelsea fans could manage 'Monaco' and 'slum' in the same sentence.

Shortly before half-time on the night of 5 May 2004, Chelsea had one foot in their first-ever European Champions League final – the score 2–0 and the club heading for Gelsenkirchen in Germany where the final was being held. Gronkjaer had curled a shot into the far corner of the net after 22 minutes. Some said it was a cross. Whatever he meant it to do, it put Chelsea back into the game and lifted the crowd. One minute before half-time and Gudjohnsen set up Lampard to drive in the second – Chelsea only had to coast till half-time now and the dream could be fulfilled. They were in a better position than they could have hoped for. But Monaco were famous for rallies. Their clever winger, Rothen, tricked Melchiot on the byline and crossed. Morientes, the best striker in Europe, abseiled in and headed against the bar. The ball flew down, struck the post and was put in by Ibarra. When they played it back it appeared to have gone in off his arm. It was academic, he was so close. Terry, who should have marshalled his defence, was AWOL and the half-fit Cudicini was nowhere on the scene.

Terry was always being compared to Tony Adams but the Arsenal colossus would never have conceded a goal like that. Lampard, dazzling in the first half, was roaming across the pitch struggling to maintain his creative contribution. On the hour, Morientes sealed it. Rothen set it up, working a one–two with Bernardi to shred the Chelsea defence. Terry was cream-crackered, facing the wrong way and yards behind Morientes as he went through to score with a fearsome drive. His error in the Euro 2004 quarter-final was just as sloppy and cost England dear.

The League was extraordinary. Arsenal went the whole season unbeaten, an achievement that will probably never be equalled. Were they that good or was it a question of the League being substandard? Chelsea finished clear of a fading Manchester United and an uninspired Liverpool scraped into the fourth place Chelsea had deprived them of the season before. Chelsea's new fortune had effectively closed off an avenue to ambitious-but-faceless sides like Villa. Ranieri made Chelsea into a version of the George Graham Arsenal team of the early '90s. He made them so hard to beat and gave them team spirit. They failed to score as many goals as they should.

BE CAREFUL OF WHAT YOU WISH FOR

Money couldn't buy you friends but you get a better class of enemy.

Spike Milligan, *Puckoon*

ITV's *Big Match* theme tune, circa 1991, sounds as stale as the bubblegum in those '70s Soccer Star packs but its nascent tones instantly remind me that this is a recording of a Spurs/Chelsea match, second Saturday of the season, bright August, a heaving Park Lane end and no end in sight, baby.

Kevin O'Donohoe, *Cockney Rebel*, 1995

Be careful of what you wish for, so says the Chinese proverb, for you will surely get it. Having achieved the financial security that dogged their past, the club could do what they liked. Buy who they wanted. Kenyon was brought in to run the club at a profit but such was Abramovich's wealth, he could subsidise the club. Imagine if Chelsea Village was torn down and the Shed was rebuilt. A fiver to stand. Old age pensioners, kids and the unemployed could receive special benefits. The only qualification was you had to be Blue. Price rises of up to 31 per cent were reported on season tickets for 2004–05. My vision of Chelsea Football Club was different than most. Money has mangled it over the years.

Abramovich could do so much: make football available to those who were priced out; help MS victim Chris Garland and Weller and Hutch's widows. That's just for starters.

THE SPECIAL ONE

I think I'm a special one.
José Mourinho

Claudio Ranieri was sacked on the May Bank Holiday, 2004. Shunted out from the Guantanamo Bay that Stamford Bridge had become for him. In all, he presided over 199 games, losing just 46 (of Vialli's 143 games, he lost 29). One of Abramovich's apparatchiks did the deed by phone.

Claudio was replaced by the charismatic José Mourinho. A photogenic Portuguese man-of-war fresh from winning the Champions League with the unfancied Porto. Mourinho was a glamorous technical-area impresario, accumulating honours and headlines. With his Persil white shirts and eyebrows like half-moons drawn with a charcoal pencil, the first law of cool was his maxim: don't try to be cool.

I recall the first time I saw a picture of him in front of the West Stand amidst a gaggle of paparazzi – lots of bone structure, brown eyes ablaze with intelligence. I wondered if Stamford Bridge, floating in a sea of oil money, would be big enough to house his ego.

My take on it was that Abramovich always wanted Sven as his coach, but, when that proved difficult, his focus switched. I feel that the players which came in the first splurge – Bridge, Cole, Crespo, Verón and Co. – all looked like his recommendations.

Mourinho was keen to downsize his squad: Hasselbaink, Bogarde, Melchiot and Petit were amongst the early casualties. Verón and Crespo were loaned out to Inter and AC Milan, respectively. The Crespo deal made no sense at all to me – he had a fabulous season in Italy – but the difference between Ranieri and José was that the Italian made guesses and the Portuguese made decisions. Mourinho, in a script that was worthy of *Star Wars*, was to write his own piece of history in the coming months.

SEVENTEEN

THE OUTLAW JOSEY MOURINHO

(HELL FREEZES OVER)

I can buy any man in the world.

Howard Hughes

If the owner is involved in training we would be bottom of the league.

José Mourinho

Everything over the past six months has gone Chelsea's way, and they have been riding a wave of luck of a kind I have never seen in football.

Peter Schmeichel, April 2005

Chelsea won the Premiership at Bolton; it had to be Bolton. Twenty-two years earlier, Clive Walker's goal had saved them from relegation there. My friend Matthew had perished choppering back from Bolton; the irony was too much . . .

A few nights earlier, John Terry won the PFA Player of the Year award; Frank Lampard came second. José Mourinho was the most famous name in the game. Chelsea Football Club were never bigger. We all love a happy ending, but this was getting ridiculous.

Mourinho guided Chelsea remorselessly to the title; they never looked like losing it. It was simply too easy for them. I recall that, I used to sip white wine with John Cobbold, chairman of Ipswich. More often than not, Bobby Robson would be present. Once, he said, 'You must love the game more than the prize, because without the game there is no prize.' Mourinho learnt a lot from Robson when he acted as his interpreter at Barcelona, but I am not sure if he learnt about the game being more important than the prize. He only had one objective in mind for Chelsea: to win and keep on winning. He waged war with anybody that got in his way.

The first game of the 2004–05 campaign gave us the template for the rest of the season: a dour 1–0 victory over Manchester United. Ferguson's side were left trailing behind in Mourinho's slipstream throughout the year as the little unshaven man cut a raffish swathe through everything in his path. Eidur Gudjohnsen, one of the outstanding players that season, headed the only goal. This was after Didier Drogba – one of six debutants that day – had headed on.

Mourinho assembled a team designed to win matches. They were superbly organised, tactically superior to any team in the league and with the most brilliant defence Chelsea ever fielded. The pillar of the side was captain John Terry, who, like Lampard, had improved out of all recognition. In front of Terry, blocking the path to goal, was Claude Makélélé, the greatest defensive midfielder in the world. Alongside the Chelsea captain was Willie Gallas, the fastest defender in the Premier. Flanking him was Ricardo Carvalho, voted the best defender in Euro 2004: a wonderful athlete and clever player. Behind Terry was Petr Cech, who proved that season that he was the best goalkeeper in the world. So good, in fact, that Carlo Cudicini – a great keeper who would have walked into any other side in the land – was restricted to only a handful of appearances.

They always defended with half a dozen men behind the ball. Chelsea's goal was protected tighter than Roman Abramovich's wealth. Mourinho had mastered his effective defensive principles at Porto: at Chelsea he fine-tuned and, eventually, perfected them. Many of his signings – for example, Tiago, Ricardo Carvalho, Jiri Jarosik and Paulo Ferreira – were comparatively unknown when they joined Chelsea. José went for players that suited his system and avoided the egos and problems of megalomaniac superstars who became pseudo-celebrities. Chelsea had restricted themselves to spending a mere £94 million under his command. Mourinho was all about me, me, me. A boxing writer once made the comment, 'Camacho's ambition is to die in his own arms,' about Hector 'Macho' Camacho, the cocky three-time world champ: it was equally applicable to Mourinho.

Chelsea won their next two away games at Birmingham and Crystal

Palace without conceding a goal. Joe Cole, who was to play such a crucial role later in the season, came off the bench to score a late winner at St Andrew's. A few nights later, Didier Drogba and Tiago opened their Chelsea accounts, scoring second-half goals to overcome Iain Dowie's side. In the last game of August, James Beattie, then at Southampton, blasted the Saints ahead at Stamford Bridge with a tremendous drive. It was the first goal conceded by the Blues and set the pattern for the season: to beat Cech you had to produce something extraordinary. Beattie blotted his copybook by conceding an own goal, and Lampard hit the winner from the spot. It was the first of his 19 goals that season; only John Hollins had ever scored more for Chelsea from midfield.

Of the three Premiership games played in September, two were scoreless, and the schizophrenic nature of Mourinho's extraordinary personality started to emerge. As Chelsea dropped their first points of the season at Villa, the outlaw José Mourinho raged at the ref for not giving a penalty when Drogba was tripped by Ulises de la Cruz. Adrian Mutu had missed a chance near the end of the game against Villa. Shortly afterwards, his career imploded as he was sacked for failing a drugs test.

In the game against Spurs, José bitterly accused Tottenham of 'parking a bus in front of the goal', as Chelsea failed to break down their oldest rivals. However, Drogba got Chelsea back on track later that month, when he scored another late winner against Boro at the Riverside. Jimmy Floyd Hasselbaink, now plying his trade for the Smoggies, was well shackled by Terry and Co. that day.

Joe Cole scored the only goal in the first of the titanic clashes with Liverpool, when they visited the Bridge in early October. Little Joe had been a first-half replacement for Drogba but incurred Mourinho's wrath for not attending to his defensive duties: 'After he scored, the game finished for Joe.'

It was a pivotal point of the season. Cole was the only Chelsea player to be publicly criticised by José that year. It was a master stroke, because Cole was transformed overnight from an inconsistent ball player to an all-round, match-winning vital member of the squad.

The next game was their only loss in the Premiership that season: a 0–1 defeat to Manchester City. Nicolas Anelka's penalty was the decider, but once again controversy reigned when TV playbacks indicated that Ferreira's challenge on the Frenchman appeared to be outside the box. Chelsea trailed Arsenal by five points at that stage. Despite the fact they had only let in two goals, doubts were being expressed in the media about their credentials as serious title challengers. Particularly concerning was the absence of flair and true class up front.

THE GODLIKE GENIUS OF ARJEN ROBBEN

In the second half of the following match at home to Blackburn, a player was introduced that was to transform the whole season and raise Chelsea to a higher level. His name was Arjen Robben. If Claudio Raineri had signed the best goalkeeper in Europe in Cech, then Peter Kenyon had guided them to the best winger on the continent. Originally, Robben had looked a certainty to join Manchester United, who had agreed a £12 million fee with PSV Eindhoven. Kenyon, then chief executive at Old Trafford, had lined up a summer move for the player, but, after signing Louis Saha (two goals in all competitions), United wanted to lop £5 million off the fee. PSV were furious and Chelsea stepped in. That's how it works at that level.

Johan Cruyff, the greatest Dutch player of all time said of him, 'Robben is all set to have a fabulous career.' With his nimble dribbling skills, Arjen reminded me a lot of Pat Nevin and Charlie Cooke, but he also had something in his game which even that pair of Scottish maestros lacked: killer pace and a direct approach. Robben looked like a painfully earnest sociology student on his gap year, but he was my Chelsea player of the year due to the fact that his presence in the team lifted their performance by 30 per cent. Gudjohnsen scored his first hat-trick against Blackburn, in a 4–0 rout for Chelsea, but it was Robben that the fans came away from the game raving about.

The Mourinho roadshow then moved to West Bromwich. By half-time, they were leading by a rare Gallas goal. Robben came on in the second half and tore the Albion apart: they scored three times with the Dutchman running amok. Lampard's goal was the pick of the bunch: a superb solo effort.

A stubborn Everton came to the Bridge on 6 November and were beaten by Arjen's first home goal. It was a wonderful effort, starting with a clever flick from Eidur to the Dutchman, who ran from the halfway line before coolly steering in a clinical finish. It was to prove a highly significant result, with Arsenal having finally lost their unbeaten record, after 49 games, the previous month. Chelsea hit the front for the first time, and Wenger's side were never to look as potent again that season.

It was to be a golden autumn for Chelsea: Damien Duff was playing wide with Robben in a 4-3-3 formation, and they terrorised defences, stretching them to breaking point. To come up against a side with two world-class left-wingers was unheard of. I recall Mourinho asking that Chelsea not be judged properly until Robben was in the side. Remarkably, he only played fourteen full Premiership games, plus four substitute appearances, but that was enough to cement Chelsea's challenge and lay the foundations for their title win.

Fulham were then butchered 4–1 at Craven Cottage, Blue Lightning Robben scoring another marvellous solo effort. Fulham's Papa Bouba Diop had equalised a first-half goal from Lampard with an amazing volley. As I said, the only goals Chelsea were conceding were classics.

THE BILLIONAIRES BOYS CLUB

Later in November, Bolton grabbed a 2–2 draw at the Bridge with a fighting performance after trailing to first-half goals from Duff and Tiago. It was a minor hiccup, though, because in the next two games Chelsea handed out four-goal spankings to Charlton and Newcastle. Duff, revelling in his new role, was scoring goals for fun, and even Kezman managed to get on the score sheet, albeit from the penalty spot, against the Geordies.

Then it was the big one away to Arsenal: the game that would severely test the Blues' title aspirations. Thierry Henry gave Arsenal a flying start with one of his specials: a savage volley after 75 seconds. Terry equalised with a trademark header that exposed the frailties in the Highbury defence. Henry, strutting the field like a peacock, was giving him a torrid time, though, and put Arsenal in front with a controversial free kick, bitterly disputed by Mourinho: 'There was nothing right with it. The free kick was unbearable.'

Chelsea fought back, and the trusty Gudjohnsen levelled with a slick header soon after the break. They nearly lost when Henry should have scored from a late chance, but, overall, they were good value for a point. Following on from their Champions League victory over them the previous spring, the ghost of Arsenal seemed to have been laid to rest. A jubilant Chelsea left Highbury with their five-point lead in intact.

Norwich visited the Bridge the week before Christmas and fell victims of another four-goal spree by the Mourinho Mean Machine. Chelsea fans who backed Duff to score the first goal were rewarded when the Irishman opened the scoring yet again. In a real Christmas treat for the fans, Lampard slammed in another of his gorgeous volleys. Once again, however, it was Robben who dominated the game, scoring my favourite Chelsea Premiership goal of the season after a beautifully worked triangle between Lampard, Tiago and himself.

On Boxing Day, Duff scrambled the only goal of a disappointing game against Villa, and then Chelsea faced two hard away games: first against Portsmouth and then Liverpool. Robben scored at Fratton Park in a tense battle, and Joe Cole clinched it with a fine goal in the last minute. Joe was on target again on New Year's Day when he grabbed the winner at Anfield, so often the graveyard of Chelsea hopes. That narrow win was somehow prophetic of the incredible year that Chelsea were to have. It was the first time they had done the league double over Liverpool since 1919. The Blues luck had held when Tiago seemed to handle in the box, but no penalty was given. Even Joe's goal had an element of good fortune, deflecting in off Jamie Carragher. It was a piece of luck that was to come back to haunt them later in the season.

I thought that if Chelsea went into the New Year with a healthy lead then nobody would catch them. This proved to be the case, but the ease with which they won the title surprised even me. Middlesborough were the next to fall as Drogba scored two quick first-half goals to kill the game. Like all great sides, they could cruise for long periods in games when they needed to.

Tottenham were the next challenge. The last time Spurs had beaten Chelsea in the league, Fun Boy 3 were in the chart. In the 2004–05 season, shrewd judges were saying that the sequence could be broken. Spurs had made rapid progress under head coach Martin Jol, and some Chelsea fans were casting envious glances at their England striker Jermaine Defoe – one of the few West Ham stars that had not ended up at the Bridge. With Kezman failing to make any significant impact, it would have made sense to add Defoe to the 'galaxy' of stars at the club. As it turned out, Chelsea won a hard match with a double from Lampard. The first came from a penalty, after a debatable foul by Ledley King on Alexey Smertin. The win put Chelsea a mind-blowing ten points clear at the top, as Arsenal crashed at Bolton.

Mourinho admitted at the end of the season that the Chelsea party, celebrating the winning of the Premiership, started on the coach home from north London. It was now 30 games since Spurs had beaten Chelsea in a league game. Jol believed Robben was as good a player as Holland had produced since Cruyff: 'Chelsea drop off half of the time so they try and punish you on the counter-attack. You can't stop them, because Robben will play on the left and go right. And then you think Duff will go to the left, but then he stays right.'

Portsmouth were dismissed 3–0 the following Saturday, as Chelsea executed a quick double over the Hampshire side. Again, Robben was the executioner-in-chief scoring the second and setting up Drogba for goals either side of his own strike.

At the beginning of February, Robben also gave Chelsea the points at Blackburn, in their most bruising encounter of the season. Blackburn were managed by the firebrand Mark Hughes and were rapidly gaining a reputation as the most physical side in the Premiership. A crunching tackle from South African captain Aaron Mokoena broke Robben's foot and wrecked his glittering season. This happened a few minutes after his great twisting run had ended with yet another stunning goal. Chelsea fans had seen more fly-pasts from him than they would have from the Red Arrows. Arjen made a few cameo appearances in the run-in but was never as effective.

Blackburn threw everything at them that day, but Chelsea's magnificent defence held firm. Cech's world-class penalty save from Paul Dickov ensured that he kept another clean sheet. Throughout the match, Terry fought a running battle with the ex-Manchester City striker Dickov. A Hughie Gallacher for the twenty-first century, Dickov was once described by rock doyen and Sky Blues aficionado Noel Gallagher in these terms: 'He just fouls everybody till he gets booked, then he stops.' It wasn't a pretty sight.

At the end of the match, Mourinho ordered his warriors to toss their shirts to the adoring Chelsea hordes that had made the long way up to the game on a freezing winter's evening. The Roman Empire had been formed by conquering the northern tribes, and earlier in the season Sir Alex Ferguson had doubted Chelsea's ability to collect points up north. The triumphant victory at Blackburn was the perfect answer to all the doubters, and the picture of José in his coat, with his band of brothers stripped to the waist, was one of the strongest images of the season. A motif almost.

The cruel loss of Robben put the breaks on the Chelsea juggernaut. The stats did not lie: before he burst onto the scene, Chelsea's win percentage was 64 per cent; when he played it went up 20 per cent and the goal average per game doubled to 2.2. It took Michelangelo four years to complete the Sistine Chapel, but Chelsea's Dutch master completed his masterpieces in four months. Wenger was of the view that it took a Continental player anything up to six months to integrate to the pace and power of the Premiership, not so with Robben.

By that time, José had taken to wearing his trademark charcoal-grey Armani coat, which was soon to be one of the most famous garments in the land, on a par with Kylie's hot pants. The Man City fans at Stamford Bridge for the next home match questioned the designer authenticity of Mourinho's top coat, chanting that he had purchased it at Matalan.

City sneaked a point at the Bridge to glean an improbable total of four in the season. Along with Arsenal, they were the only side against which Chelsea did not register at least one Premiership victory. David James defied the Chelsea attack with a string of breath-taking saves. Right on time, his Thelonius Monk fingers deflected away a thunderous volley from Lampard: a save that even had Cech stroking his chin.

Another tough away game followed at Goodison Park. The tenacious Toffees, guided by another top young manager in David Moyes, plugged away all season and eventually won a Champions League spot by finishing, a highly credible, fourth.

Beattie, who had scored at the Bridge earlier in the season for Southampton, was now playing for Everton but was dismissed after just eight minutes for a ridiculous head-butt on Gallas. Willie set up Chelsea's winner when, 20 minutes from time, his long-range shot smashed against the bar. Eidur ran in the rebound for his easiest goal of the campaign.

Norwich City were then beaten 1–3 in March to maintain an eight-point gap at the top of the table. Joe Cole had opened the scoring with another cracker. The number one Norwich fan Delia Smith had made the tabloids earlier that season in a match against Man City. Somewhat 'well refreshed', the TV cook had grabbed a microphone at half-time and delivered her now famous 'Let's be having you' plea to the Carrow Road faithful.

The travelling Chelsea boys ridiculed her with the couplet 'We've got Abramovich; You've got a drunken b***h.'

The Canaries were briefly lifted when they did what no other Premier side had done for 1,025 minutes: score against Cech. From the sideline, Mourinho demanded that Chelsea step up a gear, and late goals from Kezman and Carvalho clinched a vital win.

West Brom were the next visitors to the Bridge. As in the first half in the game at the Hawthorns, they put up stubborn resistance. Their strikers did a good job on Makélélé, forcing him out wide and nullifying his influence. Drogba scored the only goal of a dull game, but he missed a stack of chances. Bryan Robson's side later created their own piece of Premiership history by becoming the first side to survive after occupying the bottom spot at Christmas. The spirit they showed that night was to trigger the Baggies' great escape.

Palace, who went down as a result of West Brom's escape, were blitzed 4–1 in Chelsea's next home game. Lampard continued to do what he did all season and scored a great goal. A rare aberration of his then let in Palace for a shock equaliser, but Joe Cole put Chelsea back in front, and Kezman came on late to wrap it up with two scrappy goals. It was a rare bright spot for Kezman. With his desolate scrubland of beard he looked like one of those Phiz engravings that used to decorate Dickens' books, and his distribution was worse than a dyslexic postman. Drogba and Kezman managed a meagre 14 league goals between them all season. Amazing for a side that won the Premiership in record-breaking style.

Southampton, another of the sides sliding to relegation, were the next on the hit list, as Chelsea made it seven straight away wins. Their performances were not as fluid, though, and the rigours of the hard European campaign showed as injuries began to take their toll. Goals were now being conceded on a regular basis, but Mourinho always seemed to have an ace up his tailored sleeve, and in the closing stages of the season Gudjohnsen emerged as one of the dominant forces. José had switched him to a deeper role – similar to that which Gianfranco Zola used to play – and the Iceman chipped in with some vital goals and valuable assists. At St Mary's, he punished Harry Redknapp's side with two neat goals poached against their vinegar-thin defence. Lampard scored with a deflected drive: one of a number of his goals that were deflected that season .

The wheels were slowly coming off as Birmingham came within seven minutes of pulling off a shock win in the next home game, but Drogba came on as a substitute to equalise. It was about as much fun as chewing rubber. Barca chief Frank Rijkaard had criticised Chelsea a few weeks earlier for 'just playing for a result'. Ruud Gullit's boyhood pal's words had an element of truth about them.

The title was now in sight, and Arsenal came to the Bridge, on a chilly spring night, needing a win. They also required a volcanic eruption of Krakatoan proportions to stop Chelsea now. Pires smashed a snapshot against the bar early on before missing a sitter, but that was about it. The game petered out scoreless, and Wenger's men could only watch as the title was torn out of their hands and driven across town in an armoured stretch limo. Ashley Cole, subject of a 'tapping-up' scandal that further exacerbated the relations between the giants, looked the best player on the field.

It was funny how the wheel had turned full circle. Now Chelsea were trying to match the style and goal scoring ability of Wenger's side, whilst their iron-clad defence was as miserly as anything George Graham, or even the Chelsea side of the '30s, could produce. What was the Pet Shop Boys song the North Bank adapted – '1–0 to the Arsenal'? When the epic 2004–05 season was over, Chelsea had a dozen of those scorelines.

Chelsea were limping towards the finishing line when Fulham visited the Bridge for a lunch-time kick-off. Joe Cole put Chelsea ahead with a shot that Lampard would have been proud of, but Fulham equalised and dug in. Robben came off the bench to nutmeg a Fulham defender and set up Lampard for another vital ricocheting goal. It was about the last creative act he produced that season, because a few days later he was injured again playing for Holland in Romania. Eidur wrapped it up with his 100th goal in English football. It was 50 years to the day that Chelsea had won the title against Sheffield Wednesday.

BLUE BOTTLE

Chelsea had to wait another week to clinch their second league championship, with Lampard hitting two brilliant goals at Bolton to take the title. It was fitting that the most complete midfielder in Europe sealed it. The second of his double was a solo run from the halfway line that was good enough to take its place in the hall of fame of great breakaway Chelsea goals. A solo from Clive Walker at Watford in my last full season in charge and a revered Tony Dorigo slalom at Maine Road the year Chelsea went back up to the top division spring to mind. John Spencer also scored a good one in Vienna if I recall correctly.

Frank Lampard was the main man now; he wore the boots. The torch had been passed from Zola to him. It was his time now: an unspoken thing. Terry could have been the player to take on the spiritual leadership of the team, but his previous behaviour off the field suggested otherwise. Any Chelsea fan with half a brain would have found it offensive, yet Mourinho talked of him being worth £50 million. Lampard, meanwhile, is a star that almost every demographic warms to. When his £3.5 million four-storey, white-stucco mansion in the Boltons was burgled it made headline news. Like Zola, he was a legend and nice guy, too: an apparently difficult act to balance if you are a footballer.

The Chelsea fans raised the roof at the Reebok. For the older Chelsea fans, that moment was what it was all about. Winning and losing; being great, being bad. The dream had come true. Few could begrudge the Blues a coronation party 50 years in the making. If the adoring fans had their way, Lampard would still be on the pitch celebrating with them now.

The last few games of the season were anti-climactic. Chelsea were given the trophy after the Charlton game, but first the fans had to sit through 90 minutes of interminable play. In the dying seconds, Lampard stumbled outside the box, and the champs were given a highly debatable penalty. The barrel-bodied Makélélé scored from the rebound after his penalty was saved. It was his first ever goal for Chelsea: a feat he had never achieved in his time at Real Madrid. Makélélé was now one of the gang of four that also included Lampard, Terry and Robben. The pygmy-sized man from Kinshasa led the cultural revolution with his unfussy, horrible-to-play-against style. His goal was greeted with nearly as much applause as when Terry lifted the trophy.

The presentation was as tedious and amateurish as the game. Virtually everyone in the club was introduced, then we had the footballers' wives, girlfriends and kids. I forget how many times they played the Queen record. Surely it should have been Shostakovich. The smell of rotting celery was putrid. The PA failed. The class of '55 were there, too, looking like survivors from the *Titanic*. Abramovich looked down from his eyrie: did a man with billions ever have so much fun? He should have been stroking a white cat.

A few nights later, Manchester United formed a guard of honour to clap Chelsea on to the pitch at Old Trafford. Roy Keane's face was a picture as his eyes narrowed with malevolence. The gulf between the sides was vast and a virtual Chelsea reserve side won 1–3 at a canter. Lampard thought it was their best display of the season, as they played with the swagger of champions. Old Trafford was always a lucky ground for Chelsea. In six clashes between Sir Alex Ferguson and Mourinho, the guy with the spray-on stubble had won four and drawn the others. When Gudjohnsen put Chelsea 1–2 ahead, the Stretford Road end started emptying. By the time the reds did their own half-hearted 'lap of honour', the ground was virtually empty, save for the Chelsea fans chanting the name of Malcolm Glazer: another billionaire who wanted to buy into the extraordinary lunatic culture of English football. That week, the Irish boys, John Magnier and J.P. McManus, sold their shares to him and the biggest football club in the world, utterly solvent, had become saddled with a debt bigger than Abramovich's investment. Arsenal also robbed them of the FA Cup. You just could not make it up.

In the last game of the season, Chelsea drew 1–1 at Newcastle. Lampard scored from the spot, after former Chelsea defender Celestine Babayaro had fouled Gudjohnsen. I like to think Hughie and Matthew were watching from afar.

In 2004, the Boston Red Sox completed the greatest comeback in the history of American sport to beat the New York Yankees and win the American League Pennant and later the World Series. The *Daily News* ran the classic headline 'Hell Freezes Over'. Surely Chelsea winning the Premiership by 12 points warranted the same headline. I can remember when a 2–2 draw at home to Wrexham was a good result.

QUADROPHENA

Chelsea broke more records than Carl Lewis that season. Mourinho had torn up the record book at the same time he dispensed with the rule book. The records were: most points in a Premiership season with 95 (Manchester United notched 92 in a 42-game season in 1993–94: the year they slaughtered us in the Cup Final); most consecutive away wins in the Premiership with 9 in a row; most Premiership wins in a season (29); fewest Premiership goals conceded in a season (15), beating Arsenals total of 17 in the 1998–99 season; and most Premiership clean sheets in a season (25).

The Chelsea all-time records that were smashed would fill up the rest of the book but amongst them were: record number of home games without defeat and all-time best goal difference (plus 57).

For a while, with Robben buzzing, it looked as if they might scoop all four major honours'; it wasn't to be. The Premiership was the holy grail, but they did add another prize to Roman Abramovich's growing collection of footballing Fabergé eggs.

THE CARLING CUP

Chelsea's first match in the Carling Cup was against West Ham. Mateja Kezman (now in Spain) broke his Chelsea duck by scoring the only goal. In a game marred by crowd trouble, Chelsea found it had to break down their old adversaries, then languishing in the Championship and millions of pounds in debt.

What I recall most about that game was the television documentary that was filmed that night about the youthful Abramovich and how he acquired his mysterious fortune. The film crew stopped a young fellow in a leather coat outside the ground and asked him what he thought of the oligarch and his impact on the English game. The fellow replied that Abramovich was 'an a******e, but, then, we are West Ham'. West Ham's return to the big time promised some interesting clashes.

Chelsea travelled to Newcastle in the next round. Substitutes Gudjohnsen and Robben shattered the Geordies with two goals in two minutes. Fulham were next on the agenda. The Blues had trounced them 4–1 in the league a fortnight before, and, when Duff fired them ahead, another goal spree looked on, but Fulham levelled and only succumbed in the last two minutes when Lampard scored.

Manchester United faced Chelsea in the semi-finals, and they fancied their chances of reaching the final in Cardiff after they forced a 0–0 draw at the Bridge in the first leg. Lampard shot Chelsea ahead at Old Trafford in front of a crowd of 67,000. Ryan Giggs chipped in the equaliser, but Duff won the tie with a free kick. It was a gaffe from the United goalkeeper Tim Howard, as he allowed the Irishman's innocuous cross to bounce in and Ferguson experienced his first ever domestic semi-final loss. Goalkeeping was one of the major differences between Chelsea and their nearest rivals. Cudicini had played in the previous Carling Cup matches that season, but Cech made the starting 11 at Old Trafford. Mourinho promised Cudicini he would play in the final at Cardiff, but, due to his unfortunate dismissal at Newcastle, he missed the game. José was keen to keep his Italian goalkeeper happy, and the chance of a medal in the final was a thoughtful gesture, which typified the care and attention he lavished on his squad.

The final at Cardiff was a bizarre match. Cech was beaten within 45 seconds by a crashing shot from an unmarked John Arne Riise. Morientes's unmatched pace left Terry for dead – just as he had done when playing against Chelsea for Monaco in the Champions League the previous season – to set up the chance. It was a lead they were to hold for almost 80 minutes, as Chelsea struggled to gain a foothold in the game. It reminded me of the League Cup final against Stoke in 1972, and for long periods it looked as if Mourinho's first domestic final was to end in tears. After 75 minutes, he gambled again by withdrawing Gallas to put on Kezman. Then, out of the blue, with the game ticking away, one of the great England midfield players thundered in a header from Paulo Ferreira's free kick to equalise for Chelsea. No it wasn't Frankie Lamps; it was an own goal from Steven Gerrard.

Liverpool's favourite son had come within a whisker of joining Chelsea the previous summer. At the last moment, he had decided to stay put and rumours abounded that pressure from the fans had made him remain on Merseyside. He was still constantly being linked with a move to Chelsea, though.

Liverpool had struggled in the Premiership that season, and their progress to Cardiff had been somewhat difficult, to say the least. Burnley had also dumped them out of the FA Cup as they struggled to adjust to life under new boss Rafael Benítez. Ex-Valencia boss Benítez was from the same stable as Mourinho: less flamboyant but canny and highly organised. Like José, he believed in the collective more than the individual.

Mourinho once again showed his outlaw side when he greeted the own goal with his now famous 'shhhhhh' gesture. The image of him putting his finger to his lips still lingers. The controversial moment was perhaps prompted by the fact that Mourinho had received stick from the rabid Scouse fans – who for some inexplicable reason were camped behind the Chelsea dugout – throughout the whole game.

I think that was the time he made the jump from the back page of the papers to the front. After that incident, he was on the front page of the tabloids more often than Abi Titmuss. José and his enormous ego were banished to the stands for the remainder of the game as a result of this altercation. The party line was that it was for his own safety. In the old days, the Scallies would have been over the wall, and all you would have found left of him was a torn Armani coat.

The Liverpool fans had made great play of the difference in cultures between the two clubs. Chelsea had only won the title once at that time. One of the criticisms levelled was that Chelsea had no history (haven't they read this book?): 'Respect is earned, not bought' the Scouse battle flag proclaimed. Mourinho was like a red flag to a bull. He was an apostle for heart-on-the-sleeve football.

The game went to extra time, with Mourinho watching the action from a monitor somewhere in the bowels of the Millennium Stadium. Witnesses said he spent most of the time swearing in his mother tongue.

The Scousers sang their own battle cry: 'Fields of Anfield Road', their take on the Irish folk song 'Fields of Athen Rye', also popular with Celtic fans. You could sense the emotion sweeping down to the pitch. Lampard, the gladiator, clapped his hands above his head and drove the Blue army on. Abramovich could buy and sell everyone in the ground, but he could only watch powerless and transfixed. It was a winter's day, and the roof was on the stadium: the same stadium where Chelsea had performed so badly against Arsenal in their last cup final. The roof nearly blew off early in the second half of extra time when Drogba fired them in front after Glen Johnson's long throw had finally breached the Liverpool defence. It was the oldest Chelsea trick of them all: a repeat of a famous goal scored in another cup final 35 years before. Now there could only be one winner, and they were wearing Royal Blue. Kezman scrambled in the third immediately afterwards, after Dudek had somehow blocked Gudjohnsen's vicious drive unleashed from close in. It was only the second time that season that both strikers were to find the back of net in the same game. Antonio Nuñez – the makeweight in the Owen transfer to Real Madrid – pulled one back in the ensuing madness, but it was not enough.

It was Mourinho's first Chelsea silverware, and Abramovich had secured a trophy in his second season. It was a vital breakthrough and Chelsea's third straight victory over Liverpool that season. To me, it meant so much. Not so long ago, Liverpool had conquered Europe and won everything; Chelsea were just lightweights. Now it was all different. Or so it seemed.

FA CUP

Chelsea's hopes of landing the FA Cup perished in the snow of Newcastle in the fifth round, and the quest for all four major trophies ended: no more *Quadrophenia*. It was similar to the way in which Napoleon's dreams of world domination died in the frozen wastes of Russia in 1812 after his fatal march on Moscow. Mourinho reminded me a lot of Napoleon. Both emperors with worlds to conquer; both incomparable braggarts.

I always thought that of the quad, the FA Cup was lowest on the list of Mourinho's priorities. Chelsea had been unimpressive in the two previous rounds when they overcame Scunthorpe and Birmingham. The Coca Cola League Two side even had the audacity to take an early lead and hold it for 20 minutes. Their 6,000 travelling fans chorused 'Can we play you every week?' Mourinho took it in good spirit, and the Scunthorpe goal scorer Paul Hayes commented later how welcome they had been made to feel by him: 'People call him ruthless and rude, but he took us into their dressing-room and told us to talk with every one: get shirts and autographs. He made it a great day for us.'

Newcastle was a tough draw, and teams of stewards joined the ground staff to clear snow from the pitch, before the game. Patrick Kluivert, the executioner of Vialli's team in Barcelona in the Champions League in the 2000–01 season, scored an early goal to turn the game upside down. It was a goal Hughie Gallacher could have scored, Kluivert thumping home Laurent Robert's cross. That was how it stayed till the break when Mourinho flamboyantly gambled by sending on Duff, Lampard and Gudjohnsen. It was a calculated risk to win a game he felt was slipping away. His substitutions had worked on the same ground in the game before Christmas. However, it seemed a reckless gesture with an icy pitch and ferocious tackles being put in by the Geordie side. Things got worse for the Blues when Wayne Bridge broke his leg in a challenge from Shearer. Gallas and Duff (for a while the most dominant player on the park) then took bad knocks and spent most of the half as passengers. The visitors ended the game with nine men after Cudicini was sent off in injury time for a professional foul on Shola Ameobi.

ABRAMOVICH'S ARMY OF COSSACKS MARCH INTO EUROPE

> José Mourinho is the enemy of football.
>
> **UEFA referees' chief Volker Roth**

> To win the Champions League you need a little bit of luck but not in the Premiership.
>
> **José Mourinho**

For the second year running, Chelsea reached the semi-finals of the Champions League, and, for a while, it looked as if Mourinho, despite fighting on four fronts, was going to pull off the unique feat of winning back-to-back European Cups with different clubs. Personally, I think the alpha male in him hungered for the Champions League even more than the Premiership. He kept referring to the trophy as his cup, and when he lost possession of it at Anfield he looked a forlorn figure. Even collecting the Premiership trophy a few days later did nothing to raise his spirits. Losing to Liverpool drained all the testosterone out of him. The Champions League is the big one now; the Premiership win was fish fingers to the Champion League's Beluga caviar, and I only hope that Chelsea's quest for it will not take as long as the wait for the Premiership.

They won their group convincingly, finishing ahead of Porto, CSKA Moscow (who were sponsored by Abramovich's company Sibneft and went onto win the UEFA Cup) and Paris St Germain. To say that the majority of these games were as dull as ditch water would be grossly unfair to ditch water. The best display was against CSKA in Moscow, where Robben scored his first senior goal for the club.

The Barcelona matches – the first of the sudden-death games – were the high spot of the season for me. Particularly the home game, which was one of the greatest played in the history of Chelsea. Throughout the campaign, Mourinho had relied on Lampard and Terry as his main weaponry against the European sides. Mourinho claimed they were 'psychologically the leaders' admitting, though, that Makélélé was the organisational leader of the team. The tactics were typically English: long balls and a tall front man spearheading the attack. Terry scored three times with his head in the group matches, plundering goals from set pieces. It was hardly revolutionary or creative. As English as Marmite and virtually the same tactics employed by Dave Sexton four decades before.

The Barca game was billed as the showdown between the strongest defence and the most potent attack in Europe. In both matches, Barcelona outplayed Chelsea and had the lion's share of possession: 70 per cent in Spain and nearly the same in London. Duff – who, beforehand, Mourinho had said was not fit enough to play, fooling everyone – set up the vital away goal when his fierce cross was deflected by Juliano Belletti into his own goal. A minute later, Drogba missed a sitter after a wonderful pass from Makélélé split the defence. Both players were the victims of sickening monkey chants from the Spanish fans. I was distressed by this and was sad that, in some respects, little had changed since Paul Canoville had been treated in the same shameful manner more than 20 years previously.

It was not Drogba's night. Frustrated by his shortage of fitness and Chelsea's lack of fluency, he was booked by referee Anders Fisk early in the proceedings for persistent fouling.

At half-time, Chelsea officials were allegedly involved in a tunnel bust-up with Barcelona staff after José Mourinho objected to Barca coach Frank Rijkaard talking to referee Anders Frisk. The fallout from the row was to have severe consequences for Chelsea and Mourinho in particular.

In the 56th minute, Fisk sent off Drogba for a second booking after he followed through on Victor Valdes, the Barca goalkeeper. Reduced to ten men, Chelsea's strategy of containment could not stand the pressure, and the Catalonian side poured in behind the Chelsea lines. Terry looked flustered, and even the immaculate Carvalho was shaken. Substitute Maxi López equalised with a great strike, and then the pacy Samuel Eto'o grabbed the creamiest of winners. Only Cech kept them in it at the finish as Barca swarmed over them. After the game, Mourinho staged a walkout, refusing to speak to the press. Anders Frisk quit football in the wake of the spat, after death threats were aimed at him and his family from Chelsea fans. Mourinho had also lodged an official complaint about the mysterious incident, which was to backfire badly.

After the brouhaha, the undisputed best ref in the world, Pierluigi Collina, was appointed as Fisk's replacement for the return leg at Stamford Bridge. Before kick-off, the Carling Cup was paraded, and they played 'Blue is the Colour'. The atmosphere reminded me of the night the team who recorded that song destroyed Bruges.

Chelsea raced into a 3–0 lead with a burst of irresistible football not seen since Osgood and Hudson were in their prime. Gudjohnsen's clever feet enabled him to slot in the first, Lampard made it two with another deflection, then Duff raced through for the third. If Robben had played, I do not know what further havoc would have been caused.

Then it was the turn of a player who is probably even better than Robben – well, at the moment anyway – Ronaldinho. Playing in beige that night, he produced ten minutes of the greatest skills ever seen on that famous old pitch. The first burst of intoxicating, rhythmic football from the Brazilian won him a penalty that he scored with consummate ease. Coolly placing his shot, he beat the best goalkeeper in the world, playing behind the toughest defence. The equaliser (on aggregate) was, in my view, the greatest goal ever scored against Chelsea at home. It was so unbelievably mesmerising that the fans should not have been allowed to drive home or operate heavy machinery for at least 12 hours after seeing it: a body swerve that deceived everyone in the ground, then a chip shot that was the equal of anything Tiger Woods has ever achieved. The Barca winger appeared to have hardly moved when he shot; Cech didn't, most certainly. The crowd were hushed. Duff was so affected by it that I saw something I had never seen before in all my time in the game (actually, it was the second thing, because I had also never seen anything like Ronaldinho's goal before): Duff asked Ronaldinho for his shirt as they trooped off at half-time. What would that be worth at Christies in 2020?

Five goals in the first half and a feast of marvellous football. It was a great night for me, because in their 100th year Chelsea were playing, and beating, the greatest footballing side in the world. They had come a long way since Gus Mears visited a market garden with a dream. Abramovich's roubles had bought it, though. Don't let anybody tell you different: he bought the team, the manager, the Premiership and cleared the monstrous debt.

Barcelona should have won: they dominated the second half without reaching the heights set by Ronaldinho in that breath-taking first-half spell. Chelsea dug in, and, 15 minutes from time, Terry's header from Duff's corner found the net. With the benefit of hindsight, however, Carvalho had impeded Valdes. I was amazed that the goal had been allowed to stand and surprised that a referee of Collina's stature did not spot the infringement. Nonetheless, it was a wonderful night.

In the quarter-finals, Chelsea met the Panzer divisions of the German champions Bayern Munich, who had ended Arsenal's interest in the competition. It was another amazing European night at the Bridge against the side that had won the trophy in 2001. After another sensational game, the Blues ran out worthy 4–2 winners. Mourinho had been given a two-game suspension for his antics in Barcelona. He missed seeing Cole's early shot deflect in off defender Lucio. The Germans equalised early in the second half, but Chelsea napalmed them with a three-goal burst in twenty torrid minutes to tear the tie away from them. Lampard scored twice: his second, and Chelsea's third, was his best goal of the season. It was a replica of the goals Geoff Hurst – another West Ham legend and my old sparring partner – used to score around the time he was winning World Cups. It was a turn and volley of exquisite power and majesty.

Lampard had a strange game, because for long periods he had to play second fiddle to the charismatic Michael Ballack: two-footed and multi-faceted. In the last minute, the lanky figure in black and red was awarded a penalty and scored in circumstances as bewildering as Terry's winner against Barca.

The late goal gave Bayern a faint chance of salvaging the tie in the return leg in Munich, but Lampard's first-half drive was once again deflected in off the luckless Lucio. Oliver Kahn, the legendary German keeper, cursed his misfortune. The second half was a shambles: Pizarro equalised after a strangely hesitant Cech had saved Ballack's header. Then, in the closing minutes, Joe Cole's superb run took him up to the corner flag. Most players would have run the clock down, but little Joe swung over a perfect cross that floated like a helium balloon. Drogba did what he does best: soar and score. It was Hateley-esque but then he is the twenty-first century Big Tony.

There was still time for the Germans to stroll through the remains of the Chelsea rearguard to score twice: 3–2 to Bayern on the night, 6–5 to the Londoners overall.

The Russian battle tank rumbled on. Liverpool were Chelsea's opponents in the semi-finals: they were all that remained between Chelsea and the final on the banks of the Bosphorous in Istanbul. I was full of misgivings. Chelsea were the better side in the Premiership, but the record books, and the fact that we had inordinate amounts of luck against Benítez's side in the three previous meetings that season, weighed on my mind. Particularly worrying was the fact that injuries had piled up, and the squad was now severely emasculated. Mourinho's biggest error was that he had run the squad down, and in the end it was not equipped to deal with the demands of winning the Premiership and the Champions League. He had claimed in one of his 'high-falutin'' pronouncements at the start of the season, that he only needed twenty-two players in his squad: two for each position. But to have two *fit* players available at, say, the end of March, you need a pool of anything up to thirty players. I hear what you say about keeping players happy, rotation, etc., but where Mr Abramovich is involved you have a different set of rules. You have a *billionaire* sitting up there.

FRANKLY MR SHANKLY

The first game was, unfortunately, at the Bridge: unfortunately because it meant that Chelsea had to face the Kop in the return leg. The Chelsea team had no width that night; no locomotion. They were severely weakened without their wingers Robben and Duff and the defenders Wayne Bridge and Paulo Ferreira, the George Clooney lookalike. Lampard, of all people, missed an easy chance in a drab game. Only a miraculous save from Cech denied Milan Baros a match winner.

In the second leg, Chelsea only had to gain a score draw at Anfield to go through. The team selected by Mourinho might have been chosen by Ranieri at his most perverse: Gallas, a right-footed player, at left back; midfielder Geremi at right back; and Joe Cole, another right footer, on the left. Mourinho's plans were in ruins after four minutes when Riise poked the ball through Lampard's legs, Gerrard flicked on and Baros chipped the ball over Cech. Luis García turned the ball goalwards before Gallas cleared. The referee gave a goal. It didn't look over the line to me but, then, neither did Hurst's in the World Cup in 1966.

Chelsea never got back in contention. They ran the game by dint of hard work but lacked penetration. Mourinho sent Robben on, as he did at the Bridge, but he looked timid. Rumours abounded regarding the extent of his injury and a row with Mourinho about his fitness level. The giant defender Robert Huth, with the Neanderthal jaw, came on for the last 15 minutes, and Mourino deployed him as a striker. I expected more from the most expensively assembled team in the world. When Chelsea needed Terry to come up with a Captains performance he was obliterated by Carragher, who put in a performance as brave as Iraq-war hero Johnson Beharry VC. It was Carragher who blocked Gudjohnsen's drive in the fourth minute of injury time that would have put Chelsea through.

The game ended in pandemonium. It reminded me of the '65 semi-final at Villa Park when an unfancied Liverpool beat Terry Venables's side. Mourinho claimed that, 'the best team lost'. The Scousers celebrated a great victory for football, but in truth they finished a staggering 37 points behind Chelsea in the Premiership. To Chelsea, it was just another sub-plot in this story of egos, money and lack of perspective. The 'true' final between the best two teams in Europe had already been played the night Ronaldinho strutted his stuff. However, it was Liverpool who went on to win the trophy in perhaps the most amazing of the 50 European Cup finals so far.

THE FUTURE (THE POVERTY OF ABUNDANCE)

> Some think $1 trillion has been hidden away by Russian businessmen. If they don't return that, our courts are likely to decide they acquired it illegally. Then they couldn't use it anywhere.
>
> Mikhail Gorbachev, former Soviet President, June 2005

Chelsea looked unassailable financially, but the longer the season went on the more the cracks in the Mourinho system showed. José assembles sides for specific purposes; I am not so sure he builds teams for the future. Granted, he took the jewels in the crown with him when he left, but the Porto side that played Chelsea in the Champions League looked a pretty sorry bunch.

All that rampant machismo; all that rancorous capitalism. Abramovich and Mourinho were really mirror images of each other. Already, Mourinho was starting to look bored: the boredom of a man who is cleverer than the people around him, who has to keep his mind fresh with even more challenges. Perhaps, deep down, he knows his life is both thrilling and empty. Observe how he did not celebrate his Champions League win with Porto or seem to enjoy winning the Premiership. With his self-confidence bordering on hubris, I still see pitfalls ahead. It wouldn't be Chelsea if there weren't.

I will leave the last word with Frank Lampard. On the day he went to collect the Footballer of the Year award from the Football Writers' Association he spoke of winning the title: 'The afternoon of the Charlton game [when Chelsea received the Premiership trophy] was special with all the fans. Later, after all the celebrations in the dressing-room, we went across the road to a place which was full of Chelsea supporters. They couldn't believe we were in there with them, but it was great: the happiest time. People were coming up to us and saying it was the best time of their lives. To make people that happy gives you a great feeling of pride.'

INDEX